On Moving and Being Moved

On Moving and Being Moved

Nonverbal Behavior in Clinical Practice

Frances La Barre

THE ANALYTIC PRESS
2001   Hillsdale, NJ   London

The following materials are reprinted here by permission of the publisher:

Basic tension-flow patterns from *The Role of Movement Patterns in Development, Vol. 2*, by J. Kestenberg and K. M. Sossin, pp. 5, 7-8, 11, Dance Notation Bureau Press, 1979.

Published by The Analytic Press, Inc.
101 West Street, Hillsdale, NJ 07642

Set in Palatino 10/12 by EVS Communications, Point Pleasant, NJ
Index by Leonard Rosenbaum, Washington, DC

Library of Congress Cataloging-in-Publication Data

La Barre, Frances.
      On Moving and Being Moved: non-verbal behavior in clinical practice / Frances La Barre.
            p.   cm.
      Includes bibliographical references.
      ISBN 0-88163-316-X
      1. Psychodynamic psychotherapy. 2. Nonverbal communication.
3. Transference (Psychology) I. Title.
      [DNLM: 1. Nonverbal Communication—psychology. 2. Psychoanalytic
Therapy—methods. 3. Psychoanalytic Theory. 4. Transference (Psychology). WM
460.5.C5 L113n 2001]
RC489.P72 L23 2001
616.89'14—dc21

                                                                        00-038089
Printed in the United States of America
10 9 8 7 6 5 4 3 2 1

Dedicated to
my parents, Vera and Richard La Barre

Table of Contents

Acknowledgments

⧗

The idea for this book sprang from my recognition that two professional worlds I have lived in, dance and psychoanalysis, had been
integrated in my work as an analyst, but their connection not yet
articulated. Further, their integration had helped me approach the increasingly diverse field of psychoanalysis itself as full of complementary rather
than contradictory schools of thought. As a result, I am indebted to an
unusually wide range of teachers and colleagues who have helped nurture
this work.

Teachers and helpers in the dance/movement world showed me how
to live the nonverbal more fully: Katya Delakova, June Ekman, Anna
Halprin, Moshe Feldenkrais, Paula Mason, Fanya DelBourgo, and staff
members at the Laban Institute for Movement Studies.

Bridging two worlds, Dr. Judith Kestenberg, Dr. Mark Sossin, and Susan
Loman, D.T.R., taught me how to understand and administer the Kestenberg
Movement Profile. I am very grateful to Mark Sossin and the late Judith
Kestenberg for their permission to reprint the tension-flow illustrations.

My patients have been unwitting, as well as witting, and wonderful
teachers as they pressed me to understand better and held on while I tried
to learn their ways of being and speaking.

Several colleagues read the first version of the book and encouraged
its further development: Dr. Frank Reissman, Dr. Kathryn Rees, Dr. Mildred
Schwartz, Dr. Stuart Marcus, Dr. Phyllis Urman-Klein, Dr. Elizabeth
Minnich, Mrs. Margaret Rustin, Dr. Emmanuel Kaftal, Dr. Donnel Stern,
and Dr. Michael Moskowitz.

I owe a special debt to Dr. Kathryn Rees, and Mrs. Margaret Rustin.
Kay has been an inspiring reader, easing my doubts and raising good questions. Margaret generously guided me in the art of infant observation and

has been helpfully provocative as I progressed from an earlier version of this book.

Also, I owe many thanks to Paul Stepansky, of The Analytic Press, for his interest and enthusiasm. And immense gratitude to John Kerr, my editor, for his understanding and help in finding what I wanted to say at times when I could not. The skills of Meredith Freedman, Eleanor Kobrin, and Joan Riegel at The Analytic Press have been indispensible in the production of this book.

My friend, Sam Chapin, came to my aid on many occasions with his computer expertise.

My family gives me boundless joy and support. Lucy, Olivia, and Simon are always ready with humor, patience, and love. Colin, my most passionate supporter and toughest critic, has read and reread and pushed me forward. This book would not have happened without his energy and his love.

Preface

⤞⤝

*I*n Part I, I introduce a way of seeing and understanding behavior in formed by my study of non- verbal behavior research, both inside and outside the clinical situation. Making use of this understanding, I go on in Part II to review the ways analysts from Freud to the present have used and viewed nonverbal behavior. Though they tended to employ a singular frame and often approached nonverbal behavior as a problem, these psychoanalysts nonetheless found, described, and made use of many aspects of nonverbal behavior. There is a rich heritage of discussion of the relationship of nonverbal behavior to concepts of gratification of drive derivatives, provision of need, engagement, and participation. Thus, an understanding of nonverbal behavioral structure will aid in organizing what have been disconnected perceptions of it.

But there is still more to be gained in juxtaposing the literatures of psychoanalysis and research on nonverbal behavior. When I describe the variety of nonverbal behavior identified by psychoanalysts and by researchers in nonverbal behavior, the problems that have been created by competition among vying schools of thought become clearer. Competing psychoanalytic schools, and schools of nonverbal behavior research as well, have framed polarized views of the human mind and development, replicating the presumed conflicts of nature and nurture or innate structure and group dynamics and learning. In emphasizing the kinds of behaviors that the analysts saw in their patients and in themselves, and placing those behaviors in the context of research on nonverbal behavior, I directly engage misapprehensions that have ruled psychoanalytic theory and practice by allowing the data of psychoanalysis to be comparable more objectively than they have been before. We can more readily see that the different psychoanalytic foci put in relief different parts of the ongoing stream of behavior: for example, specific body positions and facial expressions and how they convey particular attitudes and emotions, repeating interactive behavior sequences or subtle movements that convey internal struggles, or gesture and posture repetitions that symbolize past experience or present anxiety.

To present a full picture of nonverbal behavior, in Part III of this book I review studies from across a wide range of research foci that bring together data from both clinical and other settings. These studies draw from many disciplines: anthropology, dance, research psychology, sociology, psychoanalysts, and psychoanalytic research. I have organized these studies into three schools of nonverbal behavior research to show how different aspects of nonverbal behavior (1) *structure interaction*, being the physical grammar on the basis of which they also (2) *communicate* through behaviors that respond to other verbal and nonverbal behavioral information, which they (3) *convey*, such as emotion, attitude, character structure, symptom patterns, cognitive structural styles, representations, and cultural features. A key point here is that nonverbal expression is a highly structured communicative realm thoroughly pervasive and operating continuously not in an on–off fashion.

In nonverbal research, too, the research schools focus on different kinds of movement. One theorist, for example, notes which muscle groups in the face operate with different kinds of smiles (Ekman and Friesan, 1982); another looks at which positions of body parts create which impression (Mehrabian, 1969); and still another stresses which strings of movement and action sequences are followed by which others in culturally and subculturally (family, church, therapy) determined patterns (Birdwhistell, 1970). How different theoretical positions create and find different data is more obvious within research than it is in psychoanalysis, and so we can use the understanding gleaned from nonverbal research to clarify where *to* look, where we *are* looking, and where else we *might* look.

From this perspective in Part IV, I use my own clinical work to explore what I have found to be useful implications of integrating a broad frame of reference on nonverbal behavior in psychoanalytic practice. Working with nonverbal behavior leads not just to new ways of understanding old problems, but to new ways of seeing and constructing our clinical encounters.

On Moving and Being Moved

PART I

≳≈≲

The Choreography
of Conversation

CHAPTER 1

Language and Nonverbal Behavior

⚹

*I*t was Anna O, the first psychoanalytic patient (Breuer and Freud, 1893–1895), who called her therapy "the talking cure." In so doing, she framed the overarching conception of psychoanalysis that remains to this day despite the fact that then, as now, psychoanalysts have recognized aspects of nonverbal behavior as essential to their work. In fact, talk was only one thread in the fabric of Anna's work with her therapist among many nonverbal strands, which included symbolic bodily symptoms and emotional expressions, dramatic entanglements and enactments. Consider the following excerpts:

> She used to hallucinate in the middle of a conversation, run off, start climbing up a tree, etc. If one caught hold of her she would very quickly take up her interrupted sentence without knowing anything about what happened in the interval [p. 31].
> This [deafness] too exhibited a feature that was always observable when a symptom was being 'talked away': the particular symptom emerged with greater force while she was discussing it [p. 37].
> The patient herself had formed a strong determination that the whole treatment should be finished by the anniversary of the day she was moved to the country. . . . At the beginning of June, accordingly, she entered into the 'talking cure' with the greatest of energy. On the last day, by the help of re-arranging the room so as to resemble her father's sickroom—she reproduced the terrifying hallucination which I have described above and which constituted the root of her whole illness [p. 40].

Anna O's nonverbal behaviors were reported with explicit reference to their interactive, symbolic, emotional, and cognitive significance. At the same time, and perhaps in particular because of the nonverbal context described, we

3

can appreciate the yearning for containment believed to be accomplished through verbalization rather than actualization. In these sequences, nonverbal expression is regarded as informative to some extent but also difficult to follow or to stage.

The more contained, though no less difficult, cases of the Rat Man (Freud, 1909) and Dora (Freud, 1905b) each illustrate again the expressive body movement and action dimensions of the psychoanalytic setting. When Rat Man got up from the couch and paced anxiously (p. 166), Freud (1909) noted his facial expressions, which were sometimes a composite of conflicting emotions (p. 166). Dora, of course, "fiddled" with her "reticule" (p. 76), prompting Freud's (1905b) famous statement: " He that has eyes to see and ears to hear may convince himself that no mortal can keep a secret. If his lips are silent, he chatters with his finger-tips; betrayal oozes out of him at every pore. And thus the task of making conscious the most hidden recesses of the mind is one which it is quite possible to accomplish" (pp. 77–78).

Despite the early recognition that nonverbal behavior was readable, in time it came to be regarded principally in terms of "acting out," revealing the patient's unrecognized effort to avoid awareness and to relieve or be rid of unconscious wishes and fantasies (Freud, 1914). This overinclusiveness seems to have resulted from the identification of all action with impulsive, disruptive, or repetitive behavior. The problem of containment of action contributed to the undervaluing of nonverbal behavior. Analysts often struggle with the practical problem of coping with nonverbal behaviors of overt and subtle dimensions that occur despite efforts to confine communication to speech. For example, patients may demand overt demonstrations of affection, threaten violence, bring food to share with the analyst, want to meet for a session in a coffee shop, and the like. Subtler difficulties that shape the interaction patterns of analyst and patient are sometimes impossible to observe. These problems, along with theoretical conceptions of language and action, have made it difficult to see how nonverbal behavior is unavoidably involved in *everything* we do and say and thus necessary to understand more fully.

It is paradoxical that the theoretical dilemma with respect to nonverbal behavior began at the moment Freud defined mind and thought as derivative of the body and its actions. His conception holds that thought and verbalization are not only shaped by the body's drives toward action, but also achieved at the expense of drives' full satisfaction. Thus framed, struggle within the mind for and against the body and its action is inescapable. As theory evolved and later theorists took issue with parts of Freud's model, theoretical problems with the body and mental life continued in various forms. There were, of course, revisions over time that expressly sought to move away from the body and toward social conceptions as the central factor organizing mental life. Even in these, action remained polarized with language. All this in the face of the fact that "acting out" is inevitable in any treatment. And so the work of treatment in the pursuit of the patient's revealing thought through speech continued to be ambivalently attentive to action, believed to be the blatant and subtle repetitions that constitute the transference in the interaction between analyst and patient. Since action is inherent in the psychoanalytic situation, dialogue about the place of nonverbal behavior in psychoanalytic theory and technique has been continuous and full of dispute.

In reading the literature of this dialogue, it becomes clear that different layers of nonverbal behavior have been singled out as significant by various schools of thought or by individual psychoanalysts. Hence analysts are familiar with the following kinds of nonverbal expressions: psychosomatic and emotional expression (e.g., Breuer and Freud, 1893–1895; Freud, 1905a; Ferenczi, 1931, 1933; Deutsch, 1933; Alexander, 1950); attitudes or states of body–mind recognized in gestural and postural repertoire or range of muscle tension changes (arrogance, humility, wellness, illness, preoccupation, engagement) (Deutsch, 1947; Reich, 1949; Sullivan, 1954b); such actions as leaving the room, getting up from the chair or couch, taking a tissue, scratching the head, which have been recognized as sometimes aimed at an interactive or symbolic end as well as having a more obvious goal within the sequence (Bion, 1970; Scheflen, 1973); gestural and postural behaviors that are seen as expressions of fantasies (and phantasies), thoughts, or representations of prior interactions (Klein, 1926, 1955; Deutsch, 1947, Bion, 1970).

Furthermore, the conventional distinction between nonverbal behavior and speech is overly simplistic. Clearly, speech content can be constructed as an act as well as a communication about its content. This happens when what is to be expressed is not conveyed through speech content alone. For example, when someone shouts "Fire!" the intent is to cause alarm and flight, not just to explain that there is a fire. The alarm is carried in the way the word is said— through its loudness, intensity, and abruptness. In the clinical setting, when a patient speaks of gory fantasies, it may be not only because they are important to understand in themselves, but also because the patient wants to provoke feelings in the analyst, perhaps by using fluctuating tones of voice to accompany graphic details. And an analyst may convey warmth or arrogance in tone of voice or body position even though aiming only to construct the content of speech as an interpretation. In such vocal and bodily behavior we recognize an enacted countertransferential experience.

Thus the logic of action has been recognized despite the tendency to keep nonverbal behavior in the shadow of language and mind, which are seen as more evolved, more easily contained, and ultimately more valuable than nonverbal factors. This bias, both of theory and of practice, is based on the ongoing but erroneous assumption that language and mind are fundamentally separate from and superior to nonverbal behavior—body movement and body experience, action, enactment. It is particularly opportune now to correct this sometimes overt, sometimes subtle bias since the psychoanalytic community is currently engaged with renewed energy in questions about action, or enactment (Gill, 1983, 1988; Levenson, 1983; Ogden, 1986; Ehrenberg, 1992; McLaughlin, 1992; Gedo, 1994; Lindon, 1994; Busch, 1995; Knoblauch, 1997; Bacal, 1998; Ellman and Moskowitz, 1998).

Now, as before, there are two kinds of approaches to the exploration of nonverbal behavior in psychoanalysis. First, many analysts may grasp the significance of a piece of nonverbal behavior but approach it on a case-by-case basis as a "special occasion" within their work. They have a strong intuitive connection to aspects of nonverbal behavior but no theoretical frame in which to see how their observations fit next to others'. Second, some analysts focus explicitly on nonverbal behavior and can clearly identify behavioral referents that they look for generally. But there is a limitation here: they see behavior through the biases of their theoretical framework and so restrict what can be seen of behavior that falls outside it. They have not connected their work with the large body of literature that is expressly about nonverbal behavior and that would expand their perspectives.

What is needed, therefore, is a comprehensive integration of research on nonverbal behavior as an axis for reengaging basic psychoanalytic premises about action. In my view, this research is fundamental because it alerts us to the intricate nonverbal details of every relationship, including that of psychoanalyst and patient and it enriches the analyst's perception and understanding of *the expression of emotion and attitude* (see, e.g., Mehrabian, 1969; Mehrabian and Williams, 1969; Ekman, Friesan, and Tomkins, 1971; Mehrabian, 1972; Eibl-Eibesfeldt, 1974; Ekman and Oster, 1979; Ekman, Friesan, and Ancoli, 1980; Ekman, 1985), of *symbolic behavior* (Scheflen, 1965; Freedman et al., 1972; Freedman, 1977; Mahl, 1977), of *interactive behavior patterns and rhythms* (Kestenberg, 1965, 1975b; Scheflen, 1964, 1973; Birdwhistell, 1970; Condon and Ogston, 1971; Stern 1977, 1982b, 1985; Condon, 1982), and of *individual differences* in behavior (Laban and Lawrence, 1947; Laban, 1950; Lamb, 1965; Kestenberg and Sossin, 1979). But the ramifications go beyond the practical and technical. Familiarity with a wide range of nonverbal dimensions of human behavior and interaction sheds light on such theoretical issues as how transference and countertransference arise, how we come to understand each other, how "self" develops within relatedness to others, and how drive-related conceptions of psychosexual development may be expanded, understood behaviorally, and integrated within an interpersonal frame. A grasp of the full range of nonverbal behavior makes it starkly clear that we are never "just talking," that we are always influencing each other through subtle and obvious aspects of nonverbal behavior as well as through what we express in words and language.

CHAPTER 2

Talking and Acting

⚹

When I talk with friends and colleagues about my interest in nonverbal behavior, many have their own anecdotes to share. One said, "Oh, you mean for instance when someone sits on the floor in the middle of the room? I worked with someone who did that—he said the chair was too far away and the couch was too close." Another colleague mentioned that a woman he worked with often reversed her position on the couch because she wanted to see her analyst. A friend told me of a patient who used to bring the wastebasket into the middle of the room and at particular moments in the dialogue would "slam dunk" the tissues. Still another spoke of her experience of a male patient who constantly seemed to pressure her for physical contact by leaning very far forward in his seat.

These encounters involved many different aspects of nonverbal interaction. But also, identified as oddly outside normal practice, they point out the difficulty of seeing behavior whole: talking and acting occurring together all the time. Nonverbal behavior is still often defined as quite separate from verbal interaction, in the background, and occurring in unusual outbursts that break away from the flow of conversation. My purpose here is to challenge this convention and to show how these separably identifiable moments are pulled out of what is really an ongoing, uninterrupted stream of nonverbal behavior factors.

Greta, speaking about her personal history, moves frequently side-to-side in her seat, with smooth and evenly flowing glances to the right and then to the left, in rhythmic phrasings well timed with her speech. She is ranging across ideas, exploring the horizon in thought and movement. When she comes to an event that caused her some pain, she holds still, then pulls back in her seat, looks down. She comes forward and upward with her torso and head as she relates how she tried to resolve a problem and sinks back and down as she describes her experience of frustration. She circles her hand as she gropes for

a word or makes gestures reminiscent of the objects or dynamics she is describing. At one point, she strokes the pillow next to her lightly and slowly as
she speaks about how important her daughter is to her and what a solace after
her own childhood with a rageful mother.

All her movements and facial expressions are, up to this point, expectable. They add to my understanding, and they fall well within culturally prescribed, easy-flowing body language. It is easy to imagine the pillow she strokes
to be symbolic of her daughter and perhaps of longings toward me. I have
followed and synchronized my small shifts of position and attitude with her
rhythms, shifting gears smoothly from one phase to the next. For instance, I
shift my position as she completes a shift with her body and thought. I am
moved to tenderness and longing as I react to seeing her stroking the pillow.
Her movements and rhythms are a part of her communication, as they parallel
and amplify her speech content and rhythm.

But abruptly this ease of expression and understanding changes. She is
now less fluent in her speech—she is halting; she starts and stops. Her speech
has faltered, yes, but there is more. I am drawn to look closely at her face. It is
now split. One side of it is drooping, its expression shifting between sadness
and limp neutrality. The other side looks angry. I remark on her stopping and
ask what happened to block her. She does not answer my question but retraces
her steps. Moving back in her seat, she resumes her side-to-side glancing, now
with more tension in her movements, and goes back to a preceding event in her
history. Then she again comes forward with her body and her thoughts but
again falters and drops back.

She has gone from speaking and behaving fluently to halting, conveying
elements of herself to me that she is not aware of and withholding aspects of
her experience from me and from herself. I call attention to her shift and ask
again about her experience as she shifted. She notices with me now that she is
having some difficulty. Reflecting to myself on her split face, I ask her about
her split experience: I wonder aloud if she feels two ways about something at
this point; also, I say, she appears to be cutting up her thoughts, along with her
feelings. She responds that she understands what I am saying, that it connects
with something in her experience and makes sense. She had not realized that
she was angry at herself for feeling sad and could not accept it. Her behavior repeats the way her mother always treated her and also shows her own
attack on her sad, longing feelings. She sighs and weeps, and a new phase of
communication begins.

There is a seamlessness between these verbal and kinesic dimensions of
Greta's and my communication which is as important as anything that she and
I say. She shows me as she tells me, and she shows me when and how she
cannot tell me. These are not actions that leap out at me, but they are neverthe-

less informative and interactively influential behaviors. This kind of movement behavior occurs all the time, though we do not generally remark on it.

Other ways of looking at the ongoing actions that occur along with speech make use of a different level and kind of nonverbal influence. In the following example, repeated sequences of behaviors in speech and action have a meaning that, as I discovered, was not as obvious as it first seemed. The meaning of the acted components of the sequence were revealed later to contradict the self-presentation of their initial appearance.

Marilyn, in negotiating for a reduced fee, cites debts that her husband incurred before their marriage broke up. I voice some doubts that, as she has told me before, her financial situation in fact requires the reduction, but I leave it open for exploration. Marilyn has developed the habit of taking several tissues from my tissue box before she leaves each session. It has taken a few sessions for me to notice that this has become a pattern. I now find myself feeling a bit resentful about her taking them (not how I usually feel about tissues) and experience her newly as greedy, perhaps even as performing a minor theft. I inquire about what she makes of her behavior with the tissues. She says, "I don't know"—she thinks she might need the tissues on the way to work, or perhaps they are a special remembrance of me and the session. I notice to myself that I am not touched, only annoyed.

As I continue to inquire about her behavior, she shows confusion and hesitates in speaking. She runs through a list of feelings that we have met before in other contexts and that for a time seem to fit: she needs some connection to me when she leaves; she feels very needy and the tissues are something to hold on to, she is avoiding the sadness and pain of separation. But those answers are ultimately not convincing to either of us. She realizes reluctantly that she just feels that she needs them, and it seemed to her that I don't. After all, she thinks, they are just there, being offered, so why not "take advantage" of them? Her feelings actually center on greediness and her habitual confusing of need and desire, which she keeps hidden behind a conviction that she is a needy victim or child and her assumption that I will fall into line as a provider. Now we begin to think differently about her "need" for a fee reduction, as well as many other of her difficulties, newly constructed. We can ask how this pattern evolved, whether it stems from anxieties connected to considering another's needs or from habits set up with either withholding or inappropriately giving parents.

Here we have turned her tissue-taking into an example of her way of acting and thinking about what is mine and what is hers. Her actions stem from an attitude that was hidden by a lot of verbalized possible ways of understanding it but that missed something basic in it—that she greedily wanted what was mine just because it was there. We had to experience her attitude in her behavior fully before it could be verbalized. The tissue-taking was a nonverbal statement, whose particular meaning could be grasped only in the context of what was going on between us at that time.

Another patient, Steven, is habitually five minutes late. His repeated set of movements on entering my office shows how another kind of movement analysis reveals vast information about a person's character and his response to the situation of beginning psychotherapy. At first, when Steven enters the room, his hand and head gestures and his steps are small and precise, quick and dabbing. He gazes downward. He turns sharply to close the door behind him, with additional "punch" in his movements. He again turns abruptly to make his way across the room. But, as he does so, he returns to his delicate, dabbing steps, and, as if stepping gingerly on stones to cross a stream, he takes as few steps as possible. When he gets to his chair, he repeats his abrupt, almost militaristic turning and, with a breath's hesitation, sits smoothly. Then, in contrast, he begins to luxuriate in the flow of his movements. Once sitting, he slowly twists in his seat. He creates an undulating, spiraling action by bringing his left hip forward of the right and, simultaneously placing his head back into the chair, he turns his face, first to the left, then slowly sweeps his chin up to center and down to the right. He repeats this sequence several times and in so doing raises his body up on the back of the chair in a corkscrew fashion. In contrast to the abrupt and sharp movements of his arrival, his movements as he settles into the chair are flowing in gradually fluctuating tension and release.

As I watch Steven's behavior, I am aware that I am unusually fidgety. I feel self-conscious about how I am sitting, about my posture. Am I straight, or should I be? Why do I care at this moment? I think about how my experience may be related to Steven's particular way of entering the session. He shifts between light, "dabbing," and strong, "punching" elements in his entrance. He seems to have some hesitation about each of these weight elements. He is also quick or slow in his movements, and he comes late but then gives the appearance of hurrying. Perhaps the opposing time elements in his behavior are a further expression of his present uncertainty or ambivalence. Or are they more basic to his character? In his seat he shows luxuriating twisting, which contrasts with his militaristic, bound, direct, and abrupt entrance behavior. Again, he creates extremes of alternation between poles of qualities of movement related to flow, direction, weight and time. My anxiety about my posture begins to make sense as connected to his rapid oscillations between polar opposites in movement. It takes more than the usual time for me to become rhythmically in tune with him because of his abrupt and frequent shifts between poles.

I think about his behavior: how it might reflect uncertainty about being here or about presenting himself. But alternatively, or in addition, this behavior could be part of his reluctance to do what is required of him. He gives the appearance of complying but simultaneously has expressed his defiance or reluctance. One part, his walking as if on stones to cross a stream, leads me to the thought that he is "afraid of getting his feet wet." This notion seems in keeping with feelings that anyone might reasonably experience at the start of an analysis.

The rest is more specific to Steven. His twisting in his seat prompts me to wonder if he is twisting out of imagined excessive complications in relationships, which his minimalism in greeting and engagement also avoid. This behavior seems also to embody and convey a fantasy or wish in which, and which, he holds back and lets go. Perhaps the wish is to be born and comes from a feeling that he is not yet fully "out" of the "birth canal," a metaphor on several levels. He is not yet ready or able to interact with another person, and he experiences relationships as enormously constricting. I am the midwife and also the mother in reciprocal relation to him, the baby. His behavior may be also a reflection of an "anal" experience, fluctuating between an anal-sadistic stinginess and an anal-libidinal indulgence. He alternately wants to yield his thoughts and to hold them back, to enter relatedness and to hold back. At this stage of our work, his behavior most likely contains a question about whether his encounter with me will be a birth or a waste, to be expelled.

In presenting Greta, Marilyn, and Steven, I have described three distinct kinds of movement and nonverbal behavior that are always present—in varying loadings and with shifting significance—in any segment of action. These examples incorporate three distinct ways of looking at nonverbal behavior developed by researchers in the field that I have designated *the intinsic-meaning position, the cultural position,* and the *school of practical analysis.*

With Greta, I am focused on details of emotional expression, body–self-cohesion, symbolic gestures. This is a view that connects best with the intrinsic-meaning school (see chapter 8). The behavior that becomes significant with Marilyn is a string of actions in relation to an object in my room (the tissues), which can be interpreted only in context as relating to her hidden experience of others as there to serve her, and to her anxiety at being required to be aware of another's needs. Noting her tissue-taking relates best to the nonverbal approach of the cultural school (see chapter 9). Steven's movements are analyzed at the level of how he performs them, and which kinds of qualities of movement. This kind of analysis draws from the views of the school of practical analysis (see chapter 10). So, when we get down to the fine details of behavior that are the focus of different theoretical points of view, it is clear that these schools of thought are bringing forward different kinds of movement and action. Hence, they are best seen as complementary, not contradictory.

These three levels of movement and action inevitably shape our responses and our thoughts as they emerge in countertransference experiences or intuitions. But our responses are often known only in a general or global way—in feelings of comfort and discomfort, annoyance, pleasure. All too often they are not available to us in the fine detail we are more used to in words. For, unless we have developed useful and subtle categories for seeing nonverbal behavior, we generally just react, without being able to transform our experiences directly into clinical data.

Psychoanalysts of different schools of thought who have paid direct attention to the nonverbal realm (see, e.g., Bollas, 1983; Lichtenberg, 1983; Little, 1985; Pine, 1985; Ogden, 1986; Ehrenberg, 1992; Steiner, 1995; Bacal, 1998; Ellman and Moskowitz, 1998), intuitively choose different data, too; data, not surprisingly, that corresponds to their theoretical leanings. In reading these authors, it is clear they draw selectively from the nonverbal according to the focus of their particular analytic perspectives, and they also elicit from their patients certain kinds of behavior through designing a particular structure for nonverbal as well as verbal interaction. Important from the point of view of understanding the operation of nonverbal behavior is that analysts, like nonverbal researchers, focuses on different *kinds* of behaviors. This concentration in itself is not a problem, nor is it escapable. But, given that we encounter all kinds of people and problems in our work, it makes sense to have as broad a range of understanding of nonverbal behavior as possible. The effect of working in this way, as I show in Part IV, is to broaden clinical perception.

In working clinically from nonverbal behavior observation to theory and back to nonverbal theory, I have identified three different psychoanalytic ways of seeing nonverbal behavior. These are grounded in and evolve from (1) the Freudian emphasis on certain kinds of interactive and postural/ gestural body behavior as symbolic of inner, structural conflict and traumatic past experience; (2) the interpersonal and relational emphasis on present and past interactive behavior inside and outside the consulting room as relevant to the patient's methods of handling interpersonal security needs; and (3) British Object Relations emphasis on seeing current interactive behavior and actions toward the self, subtle and overt, as symbolic of anxiety stemming from innate inner conflict within the patient's object world. Each of the three positions focuses on different kinds of behavior, and so none of the three positions in itself is sufficient to all cases or all times (see Part II). We need to be able to recognize, through a wider understanding of the operation of nonverbal behavior, the moments of shift required of us. Indeed, while it might be tempting to think that the three types of psychoanalytic understanding of nonverbal behavior have a one-to-one correspondence with the three types of nonanalytic nonverbal research, they do not—and it is this lack of correspondence, in fact, that provides an opportunity for broadening our understanding and reorienting our perception.

Thus, research on nonverbal behavior can enrich psychoanalysis by enhancing our abilities to separate observation and interpretation, and so to become more flexible in making use of observations that do not necessarily conform to our dominant theoretical position. Of course, the complete achievement of this aim is theoretically impossible since perception is always guided by implicit or explicit theories that determine what we regard as significant in what a patient says and does. But theories of observation, distinguished from our theories of the mind and development, can move us toward a broader view that enhances our work. When we work from such an enriched set of observational structures, we can see and do more. And also, from the opposite direction, we can better categorize and follow intuitive experiences gleaned from our dominant theories and more globally experienced countertransference "state" through our knowledge of how nonverbal behavior generally operates. It is thus possible to locate more precisely which behaviors are contributing to the interactive experience of the particular psychoanalytic situation. Working from actual behavior can lead to a fuller repertoire and range of possible procedures and ways of understanding. In the process, such an approach can help undo exaggerated and unnecessarily limiting conceptions of practice built on a belief that one must choose between polarities rather than live in the tension they represent.

CHAPTER 3

Attunement

S creaming angrily, Barbara bursts into my office. Taking large strides, she brushes by me, throws her arms upward at a steep diagonal, and lets them fall to slap her sides as she shouts and paces the room. She continues for several minutes, and then, still shouting intermittently, she settles on the edge of a chair. Nancy, in sharp contrast, enters with careful and precise steps. She speaks quietly as she sets her bag neatly by her chair, pauses, and pulls her close fitting skirt under her. She sits with her arms held tightly against her body, her knees pulled together. All her movements occur within a narrow space around her body, and they are precise, always as if she is carefully arranging a curl. Leon walks as if his feet were pressing through a substance that resists and then yields to his step. His body is contained in a narrow space as he steps toward the chair, but then he sprawls in it, his arms opened wide over the chair arms, legs spread, feet turned on edge, ankles on the floor. And Bob walks in quickly but awkwardly, clutching and still reading papers he's been looking over in the waiting room, while he barely keeps hold of his open briefcase. He sits at the edge of the couch, speaks for a minute or two about the work he is immersed in as he puts the briefcase away, and then lounges on the couch or lies down.

These four entrances are distinctly different from each other. They are "first impressions," which set me thinking. But before that they are ways of behaving to which I react: they "move me," physically push or pull me, shaping and modulating my behavior. In a circular way, I go on, reacting to and shaping the other person's next move. For, although at one level conversation is turn-taking in a verbal back-and-forth, there is also a continuous relatedness of movement contributing to the feelings and words that arise. I think of conversation, from this perspective, as a dance/theater piece, with words and music. The choreography is partly improvised—the result of creative and unplanned changes initiated by the interactants—and to some extent a set play, since many elements are repeated the same way each time.

In a theater piece, we view rhythmically, spatially, and dynamically related interactions of bodies and voices. And even when, on occasion, the play is a series of monologues or dialogues, there are still many dynamic elements beyond the content of the spoken words that contribute to the meaning and to our responses. Just so, in conversation, even in the specially constructed psychoanalytic conversation, we are moving together with another, initiating sound and motion, and responding to what we see, feel, and hear, all at once. Physical interactive patterns are quickly established that have an effect on what we think and feel. This occurs even if an analyst is being careful to maintain a restricted range of behavior in order to avoid an ordinary conversational manner.

In this nonverbal process, the conversants may become highly attuned to one another, even synchronized in movement, or, clashing in their movements, they may not connect. The act of speech itself is motoric, and speech is felt as well as heard. Speech patterns—rhythms of tone and intensity change, phrase lengths, and accents—are the audible part of the whole continuum of behaviors that create meetings and partings. The activity of speaking is inherent in the creation of meaning. Also integral to speech, symbolic gestures precede or go along with the verbal representation of ideas. Other kinds of gestures are necessary to the coherence of speech, because they foster the speaker's ability to retrieve words and construct meaningful sentences. Culture and context dictate many gestures that occur, the occasions on which they occur, and the significance they carry. How such gestures are performed, separate from their meaning, is individually constructed and seen in the dynamics of gesture and posture.

As a participant in the analytic work, I initiate contact as well as follow my patients with my movements and words; and, because each person I work with is different, I move and speak somewhat differently with each of them. For example, when Barbara rants, I generally lean up and forward a little in my chair, and I speak louder and faster to her than is my norm. I feel agitated, a bit anxious, in tune with her agitation. As she paces, I speak, gesture, and make small movements in rhythm with her rhythmic phrases of sharp rises in intensity and bursts of loudness. But I am not angry and so my own rhythm is just a bit slower than hers, and I am less intense. But my difference is not so great that I am distinctly out of step with her.

Nancy generates a different process in me. As with Barbara, I feel a little anxious but for a different reason. I am aware of Nancy's anger even though she is at pains to keep it hidden. I find myself uncomfortable as we talk, for in my effort to be in "synch" with her, I tend to hold my breath and become rigid in my upper body. When I start to shift my breathing back to my own rhythm, Nancy begins to cry and speak vehemently, for in her connection to me she has also relaxed her breathing. As I breathe more easily, we both move around in our seats. She reaches for a tissue and comes back to engage me now a little less constrained in her movements.

Leon does not yet have room for engaged interaction. He limits himself to succinct answers to my questions and takes no initiative in leading the conversation verbally or motorically, nor does he have any visible physical reaction to any of my movements. I feel mounting frustration and discomfort as he answers questions with no elaboration. I sit up and forward as I ask him questions about his life and his experience; he moves to hold his head up with his right hand and keeps his eyes closed. I have no hope of a collaboration leading to understanding unless we can somehow shift this posture and attitude, which so thoroughly close me out. The problem is not just that he is not speaking enough. Equally important is his walling himself off from any physical connection to me. Leon's steps on entering suggest an experience that elements outside himself control him. His manner of standing, body narrow and stiff, then sprawling, calls up in me the idea that he feels he has been pushed into the chair. I create these images as hypotheses to work from in asking questions and making suggestions for thought.

My interaction with Bob is easier for both of us. I am accustomed to his nonverbal "preamble" in which he keeps away behind the papers he brings, still immersed in his work. He gradually shifts toward an easy, interactive flow as the session moves along. I feel quite comfortable with Bob. The synchronized flow of movement and words becomes so easy at this phase of our work that, as we talk, there are times when the slightest shift in my position will be followed by his resumption of speaking, or we may each begin a movement shift with or without speaking at the same moment. This ease of interaction without words will later immerse us in problems different from those Leon presents initially.

Connection and Disconnection

The varied dances of conversation that make for attunement and misattunement involve the following layers of nonverbal behavior: (1) the beat, (2) phrases of rising and falling intensity changes, (3) phrases of bodily shape changes, (4) distinct posture and gesture shapings, (5) changing, maintained, or recurrent body attitudes or positions, (6) movements specifically related to physical objects and other people, and (7) sequences of interaction lasting minutes, hours, or weeks and containing all of these layers. Such sequences are transactions that include nonverbally expressed emotion, patterns of engagement and disengagement, of attention and inattention, and expectations, all often outside awareness. "Music" is provided by the tonal changes and rhythms of the voice, which also operate in time with the beat common to speech and body movements.

The beat to which the bodies and voices of all participants synchronize when conversation becomes attuned is based on species-wide primary brain rhythms. These are pacers that integrate all body movement, including speech (Byers, 1976, 1982; Chapple, 1976). Human beings are thus geared to synchronize and desynchronize movements to facilitate and direct conversation. We synchronize to move together to a shared beat when we sing, dance, or work together, and we desynchronize to interrupt and change flow.

Behavioral manifestations of human beings' common brain rhythm pacer can be seen cross-culturally. In anthropological studies of three films of people from different cultural groups—one, Netsilik Eskimo; a second, the bush people of the Kalahari Desert in Africa; and the third the Maring of New Guinea—body movement changes of all kinds occurred at either five- or ten-frame intervals (Byers, 1976). For example, in the film of the Netsilik Eskimo, although there are minimal movements in observers of a person skinning a seal, all the incidental movement—shifts in weight, idle movement of sticks, turns of the head, hands touching the face—occur along a shared beat. This rhythmic structure was also seen in a film of an American family dinner in which a high degree of synchrony of movements occurred (Condon, 1976). On this occasion movements of all kinds occurred in clumps. For example, one person might lift a bowl, another reach for something, and a third shift in a chair, all simultaneously. Or, as one person was talking, that person and others were moving different body parts synchronously with the rhythm of the speech. Synchronizing happens regularly in clinical conversations with some patients—we shift positions simultaneously, or one of us shifts position just as the other begins to speak. One may observe this behavior, too, in dinner or group discussions, on talk shows, and in groups on the street.

The beat is just one dimension of attunement. Other aspects of movement may facilitate or make attunement more difficult. For one thing, particular gestural phrases or shifts in intensities of movement or speech can be difficult to get past or get "into" because of differences in behavioral features carrying cultural, familial (subcultural), or temperamental and other innate physical characteristics. Gestural/postural phrases and patterns of intensity change can share the beat but differ in kind, coming from culturally different body language repertoires (Birdwhistell, 1970; Eibl-Eibesfeldt, 1971, 1974, 1975). Differences such as standing closer or farther away, using more

or fewer hand, head and arm gestures along with speech, employing different kinds of gestures, looking with more or less direct and frequent gaze—
these nonverbal behaviors may be inviting or off-putting because to enter
conversation is to join in a dance or a game of jump rope. You feel the pull
to join, to respond physically. You watch the rhythm of the dance or of the
rope's turning and get the rhythm before you jump in. But if the dance
gestures or the jump rope chant is unfamiliar, you may back away or stumble.
Likewise, conversational movement that feels strange, and so not easy to
move with, hinders our getting to the common beat.

Persons speaking with an accent are not only shaping sounds differently, they are also using distinctly different patterns of intensity and shape
changes, vocal tonal shifts, and gestures and postures as they speak
(Birdwhistell, 1970). For example, we generally feel that English body language is more "reserved" than our more free-flowing American movement
style. In an English person we might notice more moderate levels of intensity but more frequent small, abrupt increases in intensity. English moments of abrupt rise or fall of intensity do not occur in the same places in a
phrase as American ones do. There may be more frontward and upward
directional movement in English gestural language than in the American
version, which might have more breadth and side-to-side movement in
gesture. Thus, an American in an English setting might well seem to be
"too much," or impolite, even if in her own American culture she is considered reserved by comparison with others. In America, an English person's
comparative reserve might be thought angry, defensive, or withdrawn. Yet,
despite differences, it happens that when two distinct groups of people live
together, over time their attributes of movement tend to become more similar to each other, as Efron's (1941) famous study of the distinct gestural
languages of Italian and Jewish immigrants to the Lower East Side of New
York City demonstrated. But, initially, these kinds of differences can interfere
with good communication.

Interactive shifting in and out of synchrony in conversation happens
most of the time outside awareness. In ordinary interaction, we do not
consciously lead or follow in synchronizing. Typically participants are not
aware of direction coming from any one of them. The process is mutually
regulated much of the time, or leadership may oscillate back and forth or
be dominated by one. Indeed, the degree to which one leads or follows,
ignores, or overaccommodates to the other person is quite significant in
how the interaction will go and in how it will be experienced by each person. Such dynamics arise out of the specific movement characteristics of
the individuals who come together. Most often there is a subtle exchange
of leadership and following as direction flows back and forth without
decision or conscious action.

I have found that following the nonverbal process closely brings into view extensive useful detail that we do not usually notice. For example, Barbara does not seem to be paying any attention to me in her ranting. Initially her behavior is demanding and fully commands my attention, making me follow. Indeed, she would probably become more angry were I to suggest that she sit down or calm down, or if I remained neutrally "unmoved" by her. I follow her lead and unchallengingly echo her intensity level in my voice and body tension. But not quite all the way. Without my thinking about it, my intensity in tone of voice comes down slightly at the end of each phrase that I have joined, and I slow the pace a little. And, although she was the original initiator, she gradually responds to slightly lowering intensity and decelerating pace until at last she sits down.

In contrast, Leon does not follow or lead at all. He presents a frozen stance, a set body posture that does not shift in response to me and does not engage me, but frustrates all my attempts to connect. And while Nancy at first seems closed and in control of the flow, she shows more "openness" to interactive movement than either Barbara or Leon. At first, I find myself mirroring her held chest, but I cannot sustain a mirroring that inhibits my breathing. So, although I have shifted into her body posture, I revert back to my own breathing pattern with a deep breath and a sigh. Then I find that she has followed me and loosened up. As she begins to speak again, there is a flow of more mutually regulated leading and following that I can feel and watch in the rhythms and patterns of intensity changes.

Similarly Bob controls the pattern of our interaction, at first, keeping me at a distance by relating only to the objects he brings in with him—reading papers pulled from his briefcase, he is continuing his work. Then he shifts from this private relation to those objects and leads me into a space with him by showing something to me, drawing me into his space, and talking about what he is thinking. Soon he is more comfortable, no longer at the edge of his chair, but sitting back or lying down. We become attuned rhythmically through our vocal exchange and what we can see and hear of each other's movements. It is an easy give-and-take, with leadership exchanging in a way that does not require my attention as we enter his new stance through which he will engage his difficulties in another arena.

While it may be obvious that synchrony is important in communication and a basis for the generation of meaning, it is perhaps not so obvious that its interruption and changes of rhythm are meaningful: they are shifts that get attention, create change, or initiate something new (Stern, 1982b). Thus, I can sense when Bob and I, for example, have gotten in and out of synchrony, as we move along together or work to get our mutual bearings. When we are in synchrony, I am in a state of easy attentiveness, in which my thoughts are influenced by the subtle shifts and breaks in his vocal and physical rhythms and intensity changes. I tend to ask a question when I sense a break in the flow that is not phased in with the flow of his speech. Thus, I "associate" not just to his words, but also to this more subliminally experienced level of interaction. He takes in my thoughts expressed vocally, rhythmically, and physically and reacts to the physically expressed shifts in my attention and connection. He may comment directly on our shift or, more usually, react to it without awareness. Then I may or may not pick up on the shift in him and wonder what has happened that we have not noticed. Also, I or he may interrupt the flow when he shifts his stance or position, signalling the start of a new "chapter."

Conversation that is really "engaged" can occur spontaneously and also by choice. People purposefully engage and disengage, though they are not always aware of how they do it. Evidence of what is happening in such situations can be seen in filmed interactions. In a film of the Maring of New Guinea, two groups are arguing about the killing of a dog that belongs to members of one of the groups. Many people speak, and about half the people observed move in rhythmic relation to the speech of one of each of the two opposing speakers (Byers, 1976). Thus the group's movement indicates their agreement with one speaker and disconnection from the other.

These shifts in and out of synchrony occur in the considerable movement that goes along with speech we do not usually notice. Yet we visually and kinesthetically receive the visible aspect of the beat that affects our behavior and our understanding. There are significant variations of movement in individuals, but, in all cases, movements of different parts of the body correspond to different units of speech (Kendon, 1972). The larger the speech unit, the more body parts are involved in speech-preparatory movements and in the movements occurring during speech. Larger movement waves fit over larger segments of speech, such as words or phrases; and smaller movement waves, contained within the large one, fit over smaller segments of words, syllables and subsyllabic tone changes. Evidence, again from filmed interactions, shows that the boundaries of movement waves of listeners coincide with boundaries of movement waves of speakers. Also listeners may move hands or eyes, even blink their eyes, in a synchronous rhythm with the speakers (Kendon, 1972).

Speech patterns themselves then can be the central *movement* element in an interaction. We are all probably familiar with the experience of being put to sleep by a patient. We think about why this might be happening in relation to the patient's and our own motives. But we do not necessarily think about how it happens. Often the patient is using a lulling rhythm of gradually and only slightly rising and falling intensity changes that rock us to sleep. The lulling tones, rhythms, and gestures may be specifically motivated, perhaps by the desire to avoid contact or intensity. But they may also be linked to temperament and thus express the patient's innate difficulty in engaging others.

So we are drawn into or shut out of connection and understanding through movement and sound. It is extremely disturbing to speak with someone who cannot or will not participate in such movement flow, for instance when Leon created a complete barrier to connection by shutting his eyes and by not moving at all in an initiating or responsive way to me. Before any other work could go on, it was crucial for me to attend first to the blocks to communication that he was creating. But often blocks are subtle, harder to discern. Yet one will feel that something is "off."

Such blocks to communication, subtle or obvious, may occur in a frozen "body attitude." Body attitude refers to the shape of the whole body, its alignment in space, including how body parts are positioned in relation to one another, as well as favored positions of the whole body (Kestenberg, 1965; Lamb, 1965). We all have a fairly stable body attitude—a shape the body favors and returns to readily. For example, some people typically stand with the head behind or forward of the chest. Some have slightly concave- or convex-shaped chests. Some stand very erect; others drop the weight of the upper body to the right, left, forward or backward of the pelvis. These are often innate patterns that do not shift or, despite shifting with training, leave traces in repose.

Body attitude may dictate and limit the range of a person's expression or be able to change for different interactive situations, expressions, or specific tasks before returning to the favored position. (Scheflen, 1963, 1964; Mehrabian, 1969). Within the scope permitted by the stable body attitude, changes occur as the whole body flows from one emotion or other psychological state to another. Each position is particular in its organization: for example, "lamenting" is conveyed by head on chest or eyes looking up to ceiling, arms pulled tightly across chest or opened outward or upward; "questioning," body tilted to one side, head turned slightly to one side, gaze to the side opposite to the turn, eyebrows raised; "presenting," body straight in the vertical, arms held slightly bent at the sides, gesturing with words; "challenging," body erect, chest forward, arms tensed.[1] Nancy's body attitude, for example, is strong vertically, emphasized by tightness in her arms as she holds them at her sides. Her expressive range is fairly broad, but she favors "presenting" and "confronting," which are very close to her body attitude at rest. She sinks backward into a concave chest position but does not come forward equally, unless she rises strongly. Her held-

---

[1]The descriptions of various positions are inspired by Scheflen (1963, 1964, 1965) and Lamb (1965).

back chest suggests that she holds back from a challenging stance that she might otherwise be drawn to.

In addition to responding to the emotional state conveyed in a body attitude, we monitor and react to body attitude and tone of voice for the way they express varying degrees of interpersonal positiveness, responsivity, and status or dominance (Mehrabian, 1969, 1972). We subliminally draw this information from specific salient behaviors: the lean of the torso, arrangement of arms and head, degree of relaxation or tension of the whole body, and the immediacy and pace of speech and tonal qualities of voice. Leon's body attitude moved toward dominance in its suggestion of nonchalance—the relaxation and spread of his limbs. But it did not quite get there, and instead he appeared passive and victimized because his feet were not planted firmly but were flopped and bent at the ankles.

When body attitudes are frozen, feeling "connected" in conversation is impossible; we are adrift when we cannot affect the other. As we have seen, the phrasings of two or more people in conversation are related in precise rhythmical terms and follow closely the shifts and cues in the movements of the conversation partner (Dittman, 1972; Duncan, 1972). Breaks in the synchrony occur to create "chapters" but cause no rupture in the communication, as with Bob and me. Body attitude readjusts; speech phrasings change. Beyond being the basis for understanding, such mutual shifting in and out of interpersonal synchrony seems to be associated with good feelings, which support the interactive connection and allow the process of making sense to flow easily.

When interpersonal dissynchrony is extreme, it is generally felt as uncomfortable and can direct attention to the meaning of the dissynchrony itself (Chapple, 1970, 1976; Byers, 1976, 1982). For example, I followed Greta, whom I described in the last chapter, quite well until she lost her own easy flow and her self-synchrony within her own movements. Her body became desynchronized with itself when her facial expression split and her speech faltered. Her body attitude was disorganized. Consequently, I became unable to synchronize with her. But the break in the interactive flow led me to search for the meaning of the disruption rather than allow it to disengage us. Such searching is, of course, my role. In other circumstances, had this been a conversation between acquaintances, she might have shifted out of the area of discussion that created the split in order to regain her integration, and we would have gone on with something new, allowing her to continue to avoid her difficulty within this area of herself.

The generally good feeling associated with synchrony does not obviate the possibility that synchrony can be held on to for too long, maintaining an interactive set beyond its usefulness. For fear of separateness and difference, people may overly attune to each other. We can be lulled into good, "together" feelings and yet miss important information or the need to differentiate. Or synchrony and dynamic attunement can be seductive and hide an aggressive, hostile intent, as when someone feigns friendship through attunement to gain an advantage for destructive aims. In that case, dissynchrony operates to break the set and allow for change.

So we lead, follow, interrupt, and shape dynamic shifts along the beat, creating rhythmical and repeating phrases of intensity change from high to low, in both audible tonal changes and visible muscular tension changes (Birdwhistell, 1970; Byers, 1976; Kestenberg and Sossin, 1979). In addition to being the line along which we engage or disengage, intensity waves contribute to meaning through the way they express aspects of an individual's personality or self. Individual expression lies in how movements of all kinds are performed. For example, Barbara's and Nancy's contrasting manners express anger in physically opposite ways, which show their different attitudes toward their world and toward me and my potential participation in their experience. My own manner conveys and constitutes aspects of myself, as well as my attitudes and expectations of others. The differences in me that each person I work with stimulates are the basis for my understanding them.

CHAPTER 4

Temperament, Interaction, and Self

⋊⋉

Three middle-aged people were talking to each other on my street corner. One woman moved langorously and spoke intermittently. A second woman spoke to the first rapidly, her speech and movement abrupt, reaching high intensity. The third person, a man, stood between the two women, but a little closer to the second woman, who was doing most of the talking. I could see that he and she were both looking directly at the first woman, whose gaze was down except when she raised her head slowly with a slight increase in strength as she responded briefly. The main speaker repeatedly thrust her head forward toward the listening woman and lifted her hands to the sides of her head, with a punch in the air as she did so. The man echoed her by standing up straighter and shifting his weight from one leg to the other as she gestured in the air. His gaze moved from the speaker to the listener and back to the speaker. As she was spoken to, the listening woman at first looked down, then briefly turned her face straight up, before tilting her head back down. When she brought her face down again, she twisted her body left, leaving her right shoulder forward toward the other woman. In a pause in the speaking woman's action, the listening woman stretched up somewhat and nodded "yes," but then resumed her twisted posture downward to the left.

Observing this particular group interaction, I could see a lot of what was happening emotionally and dynamically *between* the three individuals at that moment. From a distance, not hearing what was being said, I had the impression that the two teamed-up speakers were trying to persuade the second woman of something. If I could have filmed the action in close range, I would have included in my observation their eye blinks, eyebrow raises, movements of the mouth, and use of fingers; and I might have seen more synchronization as well as dissynchrony in the conversants. I could see some details of the listening woman's facial expressions—her lips pushed forward but held flat as she nodded "yes," suggesting that she meant "no." She gave some evidence of assenting, but without entirely engaging with the other two. Her half-hearted agreement was apparent in the way she maintained her lower level of intensity of movement and sound—she did not really "get into" what they were saying to her. Also, she made gestures toward them, but her posture retained her averted stance, her right shoulder turned with some strength *at* the others as if to ward them off.

If I were to take up another level of analysis, I could discern whether these were individuals of a single ethnic group, Anglo- or Latin-American, for example, both equally likely on my street corner. I would look to compare the frequency of direct gaze and touch and at how close they stood together—Latin-American body language, on average, using more frequent, direct gaze, closeness, and touch than is used in Anglo-American body language (Argyle, 1988). I would also check for distinctive gestural and postural repertoires that are particular to each group.

But still another level of analysis is necessary to find the *individual* within the context of the particular group dynamic or cultural repertoire. To do this, one must consider the individuals' characteristic movement repertoires, which form the basis for their respective behavioral practices, and also their options for other kinds of relating. At this level of analysis, one must search out whether the three participants—the persuaders and the unpersuaded—are playing out (1) a transient dynamic about an immediate issue, which would reveal only their reactions to the current issue; (2) a group dynamic that occurs *specifically* when these three individuals get together, which would inform you about their particular relationships to each other; or (3) a more stable dynamic that one or all recreate in many or all their relationships, revealing more about the individuals in the group.

Differentiations of this kind involve the way temperaments create individual variations in *how* gestures are performed. I could see that the movements of the persuading woman were very intense, abrupt, and frequent in moving toward and away from the other woman. The woman to whom she spoke was much more gradual in her changes of intensity, and she never reached the level of intensity shown by the persuader. Were these ways of behaving part of the set of behaviors relating to persuasion alone, or were they reflections of core aspects of each individual's temperament? To find out, one would have to ask further questions. Does the persuader ever show the capacity to reduce her intensity to match better the second woman's mood of the moment or temperamental style? Does the man have the ability to be more of a mediator? If so, rather than only echo the first woman's intensity and frequency, he might have *translated* it into the first woman's more comfortable body range by repeating, more gradually and less intensely, what the first woman was saying. Or is he temperamentally more like the persuader and unable, as well as unaware of the need, to mirror the woman they are trying to persuade? Is the woman they are trying to persuade persistently unable or unwilling to adapt to others by changing her level of intensity; and, is she in fact, inducing higher levels of intensity in the other two in their efforts to move her? These are the kinds of questions that an analyst might pursue about each patient.

To answer these questions about individual behavior options in body movement terms, we need to look not just at *which* emotions or attitudes are expressed but at *how* they are expressed. The smile is a good example here. Smiling is an species-wide action that is innately wired and intrinsically meaningful. It occurs and signals pleasure in many human cultures (Eibl-Eibesfeldt, 1971, 1974, 1975; Ekman, Friesan, and Ancoli, 1980; Ekman and Friesan, 1982, O'Sullivan et al., 1985). Yet, after babyhood, the meaning of any particular smile cannot be taken for granted because smiling is also formalized and trained as part of etiquette. So, although we still smile genuinely and spontaneously for pleasure, much of the time we are smiling or not smiling as part of what is expected socially by our family or local culture. Indeed, in different places in America, people smile with different frequencies, but these differences cannot be taken as a sign of degrees of happiness in these locations (Birdwhistell, 1970).

Where is the individual, then, if the meaning of a particular smile (1) is very much context determined and (2) derives also from the smile's innate, primary meaning? The individual is revealed in the *way* he or she smiles. For example, one person's smile, whether dictated by etiquette or occurring spontaneously, may burst out suddenly and broadly, while another's develops slowly, remains small, and perhaps mixes with a variety of other emotions. Still another's smiling might vary across a few dimensions to match different circumstances and aims. The manner of a smile when one is authentically pleased or when one is smiling because of etiquette expresses that individual's personality. The *how* of individual movement and significant differences among people can be discriminated more closely by differentiating their patterns of (1) movement *tension-flow*, and (2) *posture-gesture merging*.

Tension-flow (Kestenberg et al., 1975; Kestenberg, 1975b; Kestenberg and Sossin, 1979) indicates the continuous flow of tension and release (binding and freeing) in the muscles of the body. Tension refers to the degree of energy, vigor, or force in an exertion. In movement, intensity is increased by using more tension in the muscles. This can happen in two ways (see Figure 1): (1) if a strong impulse occurs at the beginning of a movement, the movement goes into high-intensity free flow; or (2) if the movement impulse is opposed by antagonist muscles, as when one is lifting a heavy

1)   2)

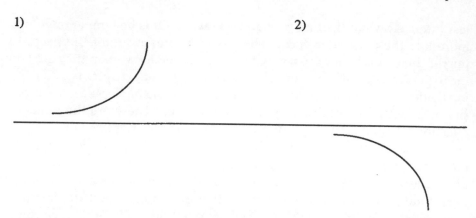

Figure 1: Left, a representation tension-flow from low to high intensity in free flow. Right, tension-flow from low intensity to high intensity in bound flow.

weight or when a muscle is tensed isotonically to show how big it can be, the movement will go to high-intensity bound flow. Figure 1 illustrates how this difference may be depicted.

Tension-flow rhythm patterns are specifically suited to certain activities, but also occur independently as individual expressions, like signatures, that differentiate one person from another. Tension-flow rhythms are subject to some conscious alteration and unconscious accommodation through life, but a basic patterning remains constant, reflecting certain unchanging dimensions. These personal movement characteristics are not so much outgrown as they are augmented through interactions with the environment and with other people. They form the basis for interactive and personality patterns (Kestenberg and Sossin, 1979).

Definable patterns of tension-flow are visible and are experienced in the subjective flow of feelings of comfort and discomfort. They influence the kinds of activities and people that are sought after or avoided and the ways a person is experienced by others of varying temperaments. From infancy onward, patterns of tension-flow function as a guide in seeking or avoiding activities and people that are attuned or mismatched with this flow. For example, you may know a person whose tension-flow is of low intensity, gradual, and fluctuating—someone you might think of in connection with ballet dancing or painting, but not easily with weight lifting, or heavy construction. The latter activities require evenly sustained high intensity, achieved abruptly. The ballet dancer would have to encounter some very strong external motivating force in order to begin serious weight lifting. Likewise it might take some doing to get the weight-lifter to take up ballet. Even then, successful performance might be in question for both.

Tension-flow rhythms are defined as combinations of simpler rhythm units that are essential both to certain kinds of tasks and to elemental bodily functions. Distinctive rhythms are associated with the following actions: (1) sucking, biting, (2) straining, twisting, (3) running, stopping, (4) undulating, swaying, and (5) jumping, leaping. These rhythms are fundamental to overall physical functioning. For example, straining, a rhythm characterized by an abrupt rise in intensity of muscle tension and evenness of tension, before an abrupt descent in intensity, is used in defecating and also in lifting heavy objects, in holding and releasing one's breath, and in opposing another person or force. Each of these rhythms can also be grouped according to the libidinal phases and zones to which they correspond. Thus, (1) sucking and biting are *oral phase* activities; (2) straining and twisting, *anal phase;* (3) running and stopping, *urethral phase;* (4) undulating, swaying, *inner genital (uterine or scrotal) phase;* and (5) jumping and leaping, *outer genital (clitoral or phallic) phase.* There is also indicated a "libidinal" or "sadistic" version of each phase's movement pattern connoting the lesser or greater amount of effort involved, or, in more subjective terms, the more indulging or contending quality in the movement.

Kestenberg (1975a; Kestenberg and Sossin, 1979) developed an integrated approach to individual temperament, development, and cultural influence based on these groupings (which I detail further in chapter 10). Thinking about the relationship between qualities of movements, zones of the body, and phases of development is useful in grasping an individual's temperament, developmental history, and current or prevailing preoccupations and aims. Certain movement attributes appear stronger than others, depending on constitutional factors. Familial interaction patterns may also downplay or heighten individual trends, but the core temperamental pattern remains nevertheless. Also, in relation to cultural trends, particular tension-flow rhythms become associated with gender constructs: "inner genital" swaying is associated in both sexes with culturally defined "feminine" identifications (awareness of the inside, tenderness, wishes for babies, etc.), and "phallic" leaping in both sexes is associated with "masculine" identifications (awareness of the outside, assertiveness, urges to penetrate, etc.). The association with gender constructs takes place as developmental trends occurring in both boys and girls are shaped by interactions based on cultural definitions of female and male.

Figure 2 illustrates the various rhythm patterns. Tracing the rhythms with a pencil, and feeling their "timing" as you do so, will be helpful in picking up the feeling of the rhythms. The upward movement is to free flow and downward to bound flow. The greater the amplitude in either direction, the higher the intensity. "Neutral" intensity is at the center line, neither free nor bound, but flaccid.

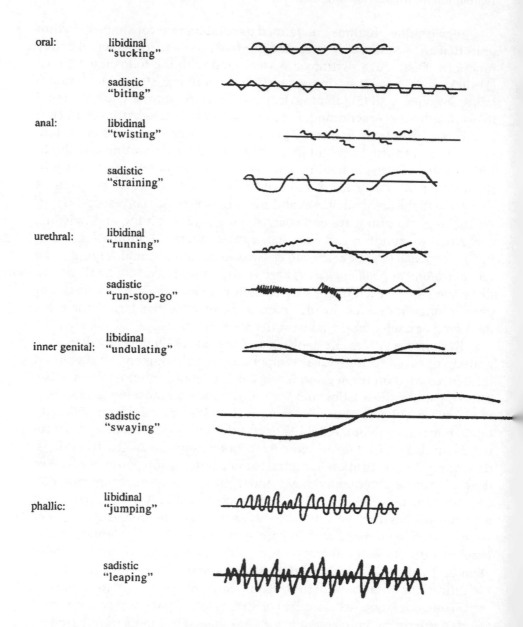

Figure 2: Basic tension-flow patterns (Source: Kestenberg and Sossin, 1979, pp. 7–8. Reproduced by permission).

Figure 3: Phallic, anal, oral, and inner genital/feminine rhythms mixing with and following upon one another (Kestenberg and Sossin, 1979, p. 5. Reproduced by permission).

Figure 3 illustrates a tension-flow rhythm pattern showing phallic, anal, oral, and inner genital rhythms mixing with and following upon one another. The person with such rhythms is a bit jumpy, excitable, exciting, wth lots of abrupt movement and likely similar characteristics in vocal tonal change.

Figure 4 demonstrates how typical recordings of two individuals' patterns can be compared and contrasted.

One can learn from Figure 4 that person A uses low intensity, gradual changes of intensity containing some smaller intensity fluctuation; whereas person B uses high intensity, with mostly abrupt changes and less fluctuating flow. Several lengthy recordings of tension-flow would be needed to ascertain their overall tension-flow patterns.

People use these rhythms in various activities for which they are necessary, and they also more generally use them in speech and breathing patterns, in cognitive functioning and in regulating their interactions with other people and the environment. Thus, a person who is born with a physically greater propensity for straining rhythms will be more likely to carry these rhythms beyond the body functions and other activities that specifically require them. Their straining rhythm shows up in a long attention span that involves holding attention evenly (still body and gaze) for long stretches, and also waiting or holding on as well as resisting. People whose behavior lacks the longer tension-flow patterns of holding tight (abrupt increase of tension held evenly, abrupt decrease of tension held evenly) or swaying (gradual increase and decrease of tension), but emphasize the shorter phrases of sucking (low amplitude, frequent gradual increases and decreases of tension) or leaping (high amplitude, abrupt and frequent increases and decreases of tension), have shorter attention spans or some-

Person A: Person B:

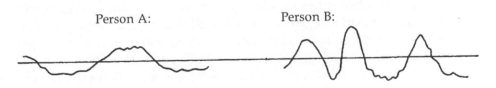

Figure 4: Two different individuals' tension-flow patterns.

times have difficulty with attention. Tension-flow patterns are usually mixed in behavior (the arm and hand move quickly in short phrases of tension-flow, while the rest of the body is "containing" shorter units with longer units of swaying or holding tight). Of course, at times the whole body is organized in one repeating phrase, as in leaping or running or moving a heavy object.

Just as it shapes preferred activities, overall or predominant tension-flow shapes personality. A person who uses mostly even flow is likely to be unruffled and even tempered, possibly sluggish or stubborn; whereas another person's flow adjustment creates more pliancy, adaptability, twisting, restlessness, or shyness. High intensity characterizes those who are easy to anger or frustrate; low intensity is associated with those who are low keyed, depressed or calm, and not easily frustrated (Kestenberg and Sossin, 1979). These are not metaphoric connections, but metaphor builds on such connections. These links occur in the actual unities between physical and mental functioning, that is, between what is physically and mentally done, subjectively felt, and interactively experienced.

The feature of tension-flow rhythms most important to analysts is the involvement of these rhythms in motoric/kinesic and emotional attunement (Kestenberg, 1965). Two people with extremely different tension-flow patterns may find good communication—getting in synch—quite difficult at times. One person of very low intensity and another of very high intensity might find each other threatening simply because, without any thought about it, they are so rhythmically dissimilar that they do not feel comfortable with each other. Their tension-flow combination creates a pull toward a center that does not feel right to either of them, or it creates a tendency toward oscillation between extremes with little meeting. If they are not prejudiced against their opposite temperaments (either by bad experience or by a lack of experience and fear of the unknown), and they each have some capacity to move outside their average range, it is quite possible for them to move into mutual attunement or oscillation at moderated gradations of intensity. But, as is often the case, unpleasant experiences, or lack of experience, interferes.

Yet opposites can attract as well. One person can find interaction with a very different other either calming or stimulating. Again, this response may depend on experience, attitudes toward difference, and additional temperamental characteristics. You may have noticed that with certain people you become more lively. I have two friends, quite opposite in temperament, who both affect me in this way. With one, whose tension-flow patterns are of a much higher intensity and abruptness than mine, I move into a higher intensity range than is my norm in order to meet her. With the other, who is much lower in intensity, more gradual and even in her fluctuations, I also increase my intensity and frequency of movement to bring her up to a level of intensity and change that is closer to my own. Otherwise I would be in danger of falling asleep, not because the content of our conversation is boring, but because her rhythmic changes in speech and body are so gradual and lulling.

Mothers often know about their children's temperaments from how they move about in utero. Tension-flow patterns are in place before birth. Parents in many cases attune to their infants without special attention to the process. This kind of attunement is essential for parents to achieve with their infants even when there is a temperamental clash, because good-enough matching is decisive in determining whether the timing, quantity and intensity of their interventions will be received well by their babies. If this matching is achieved, then later, less close attunement can help to augment the child's basic repertoire, leading the child to add additional tension-flow attributes to his or her repertoire by attuning to others.

Play is often made up of a combination of matched and surprising, clashing movements and rhythms—for instance, games of peek-a-boo, tickling, "I'm gonna getcha," which are timed and intensified to delight (Stern, 1982b). But even play must be geared to meet well enough a baby's temperamental range. A very quiet baby with gradually fluctuating tension-flow is tickled and surprised with far less energy than a very intense, abruptly changing, high-energy baby.

Depending on an individual caregiver's own temperamental range, it may be easy, difficult, or in between to attune to a particular infant's temperamental attributes. Without good early attunement, the occurrence of clashing can be traumatic, and destructive to an infant's self-development. We can see that interactions go better when a caregiver can move in synchrony with an infant's own rhythms, for his or her interventions flow smoothly and receive a welcoming response. We surmise that these interventions feel better to the baby than less attuned ones do. Also, we can imagine that an adult well matched to a baby is experienced by the baby as belonging with—as an extension of—the self rather than an outsider who cannot be assimilated. Without this attunement, baby and adult partner are uncomfortable with one another, a state of affairs that challenges and can destroy attachment, and the capacity to love.

The dynamics between infants and mothers show the process clearly. If you were to join me at one of the "New Mother–New Baby" classes I teach, you might be struck first by the behavioral similarities of the infants there who range in age from two weeks to four months. They all curl, stretch their bodies, and fling their limbs. They gaze about or sleep, and their hands open and shut as they cry or suck. But as you looked longer, you might also begin to notice some differences between them. One moves much more frequently than another. Looking closer, you can see that another's jerky, abrupt movements contrast with her neighbor's smoother, more even movements. One four-week-old lolls his head to one side when he is lifted, while another can already hold her head up by herself. All the babies cry lustily, but even within that loud register, you can hear intensity and timing differences in the babies' vocalizing. One cries in long stretches, taking in big gulps of air in between; another, less intense, in short bursts, a little less loudly, taking smaller breaths each time.

As you watch the mothers, you might notice how different the mother–baby pairs are despite their similar activities. The mothers, like the babies, differ in the intensity, timing, and directedness of their movements. You can begin to distinguish those who are comfortable with their babies from those who are not yet at ease. Each mother and baby pair has its own holding shape. One mother cradles her baby at her right breast by bringing her left shoulder well forward, to tuck her left arm under the baby and left hand under the baby's head, while she holds the right breast in her right hand. Another holds her baby at her breast with the same arm as breast and leaves the other arm free to attend to other things—speech-related actions or reaching for things. Each very different shaping reflects both mother's and baby's body needs and attitudes. Where mother has found what baby needs and what she needs, both are comfortable. But frequently one or both may not be well met.

Some mothers quickly discover effective ways to soothe their babies, while others struggle to do that. Mothers eagerly report how much the babies vary in the amounts of sleep they want and when they want it and in how well they suck and how much. Less obviously, mothers show, but do not so readily say, how much and what kind of physical contact each baby wants. Babies all need "tenderness," but some respond well to energetic rocking or firm swaddling, whereas others want a lighter, less firm hold and more gradual motion. Mothers are busier with active babies who need help to make the frequent stimulating visual and muscular changes they desire, whereas other mothers, dealing with less motorically active infants, need to adjust their babies' positions less frequently. Some mothers initiate interaction with their infants who respond or turn away; other mothers, who interact only when the baby calls, leave some, less active babies alone for long stretches.

Differences in the ways parents and babies match or clash are critical in shaping the relationship and, thus, the baby's growing personality, sense of self, and openness to experience and learning. Too much clash can create a traumatic sense of feelings being unmet, of being unloved, and even of hatred toward the other. This is as true for the parent as for the child. Parents may suffer from hurt feelings with an infant who is very unlike them and who demands a kind of engagement that they find difficult or impossible to perform. But too close a match can also create problems for parent and child by limiting new learning. When these dimensions of experience can be seen during consultation, parents are helped to accommodate to the specific temperamental needs of their children and to understand better the kinds of problems they are encountering.

In addition to tension-flow rhythms, individuals' patterns of "posture gesture mergers" (PGMs) appear to be inborn aspects of temperament and do not vary after physical maturity except in small ways (Lamb, 1965; Lamb and Watson, 1979). A posture-gesture merger is perceptible as the enlargement of a gesture, a movement using one part of the body, into an engagement of the whole body. For example, when someone moves to shake hands, not just with the hand, but by stepping forward with the whole body and changing the whole posture as well, this is a posture-gesture merger. Individual differences show in the use of specific movement dimensions of shaping and effort, which give an individual flavor to the culturally prescribed handshake pattern. Within the prescribed set, some people step sideways into the handshake; others bob up and down as they reach with the hand. Such integrated movements involve the adjustment of the whole body in action (Lamb, 1965; Lamb and Watson, 1979). The particular use of space, that is, how a PGM is performed, suggests aspects of the person's overall character or personality, that is, of mind as well as body.

We can see overall character in PGMs because the preferred dimensions of PGMs are carried into and shape all activities. In my office, they are visible in the ways people come in and sit down. While my patients all enter through the same door and lie on the same couch or sit in the same chair, each demonstrates an individual PGM repertoire on entering. One, for instance, reaches across herself, twisting in the chair to put down a coffee cup or bag on the side opposite to the hand in which it is carried; another stops and straightens before she sits and places her bag on the same side that she uses to carry it; a third moves very quickly to the seat so that the walking in and the getting into the seat, are one phrase, and then leans forward while talking. These kinds of differences can be codified and linked with three affective/cognitive attitudes of "exploration/attention," "intention/presentation," and "decision-making/operation" (Lamb, 1965). The relative proportions of movement in the horizontal (side to side), vertical (up and down) and sagittal (front to back) dimensions, associated with emphasis on space, weight, and time, respectively, indicate the strength of the corresponding three attitudes for each individual (see Table 1). These physical emphases and the attitudes they correspond with are also describable as three phases of action taking: exploration, forming an intention, and the execution of the intention.

DIRECTION	Horizontal	Vertical	Sagittal
ATTITUDE	Exploration/ Communication	Intention/ Presentation	Decision Making/ Execution of Action
MOVEMENT	Spread/Enclose	Rise/Descend	Accelerate/Decelerate
DIMENSIONAL EMPHASIS	Space	Weight	Time

Table 1: Correspondences between direction, attitude, movement, and dimensional emphasis.

(1) The exploratory phase, in which horizontal movement, spreading and enclosing, a taking-in of space, and an emphasis on focus, indirect or direct, are most important (the person who reaches across the body to put down a held object);

(2) The phase of forming intention, in which verticality, an emphasis on rising and descending, and the weight elements, increasing and decreasing pressure are most noticeable (the person who stands and straightens before sitting and carefully puts down a bag on the same side on which it is held);

(3) The execution of action, in which the sagittal (forward and backward) dimension of movement is most stressed, with an emphasis on timing, accelerating and decelerating (the one who dashes in, sits and leans forward).

Ideally, everyone would be able to think and move equally in all three dimensions. But few people show a thoroughly balanced amount of movement of each kind in PGMs, so that most have talents and deficits in one or another area of action taking. Some are better explorers/communicators, others better at intention/ presentation, still others better at decision making/operation. For example, one person I worked with was a strong decision maker/operator (sagittal or forward–backward movement, emphasizing the time dimension, i.e, accelerating and decelerating). She was not inclined to explore; thus her actions tended to be impulsive, not well thought out. Later, in a better adaptation, she became able to include some exploration, although it remained subordinate to operation. At this point she could explore with an eye to her goal, that is, strategically finding out only what she needed to know to accomplish her goal. In contrast, another person, who was stronger in exploring/communicating, would explore without any connection to a goal. He would easily get lost in aimless wondering and wandering. Our work in part involved helping him see this aspect of himself. Better using a propensity for exploration, a person can enjoy the process and be able to come up with several alternative plans for action or alternative explanations for the same question but still get on to action when required.

These different behavioral styles of integrating posture and gesture appear to be innate and to exert global effects on one's movements and attitudes toward participation in action. The behaviors arising from basic temperamental differences are not themselves intentional; rather, they have far-reaching effects on organizing both conscious and unconscious behavior, including *the shaping of intention itself*. Later in this book I explore the basis for this assertion in detail.

Interactions involving these dimensions are quite apparent in physical movement but most often are out of awareness. One can see such physical differences and how they shape interaction in street life everyday. I observed a good example on my walk to work. I was behind three boys on their way to a nearby high school. They walked along in the same rhythm, but there the similarities in their movements ended, despite their seemingly happy engagement in lively conversation as they walked along. The boy in the middle was, not surprisingly, "the center" of the relationship of the three. He was the one whose movement was the most balanced in three dimensions (use of the vertical, horizontal, and sagittal, parallelling his balanced pressure, focus, and timing). Also he was the only one of the three who was clearly strong in movement in the vertical, the dimension associated with weight/pressure, intention/presentation. He stood very erect, held his shoulders broadly, and strode straight ahead, but turned sideways to each of the other two boys as they spoke. The boy on his right had significantly more emphasis in the horizontal (side-to-side) dimension than in the vertical or sagittal. His path wavered from right to left, showing an emphasis on focus. He talked a lot, using both hands gesturally as he walked along. He carried his bags on his shoulders at his sides, exaggerating his width and his emphasis on the horizontal plane, instead of having one backpack in the center of his back the way the other two did. The third boy, on the left, emphasized the sagittal direction. He kept running ahead and falling behind the other two, scurrying to catch up, and overshooting the mark, clearly showing an emphasis on time. He was loose jointed, his posture was curving, his chest concave. Given these temperamental leanings, I thought that the boys probably functioned well as a team—the boy on the right as the explorer/communicator, the boy on the left as the operator/doer, and the boy in the center able to do some of the other two, but adding, more strongly, the third dimension, the formation and presentation of intention, which in this triad would tend to be his emphasis.

Often, a symbiosis of such individuals in action produces a team, in which one person takes on exploration, another makes and presents plans, while another brings the results into action. But, just as often, clashes and problems of coordination can occur. In a couple who sought my help, this level of behavior was involved. Each had a different style of PGM and a correspondingly different emphasis in action. Underneath the variable content of their arguments was the constant question about which was more important, exploration or doing. Their differing abilities in these areas were uncoordinated. She would ask a question about the day's events, in a hurry to get to a decision about what was going to happen; he would not answer but would raise what seemed to her to be irrelevant side issues. An argument would ensue, neither person able to see the importance of the other's concerns. They did not see how they each fit into action sequencing and how they might coordinate better.

Too much matching also occurs and can lead to inaction. In a different couple, the partners were both explorers and could get little accomplished, because each had difficulty moving through forming an intention to making a decision. They were both successful medical researchers who teamed up at work with other people who raised money to support their research, and made decisions about what to research. But at home, life was a mess, because they had only each other to rely on. They felt like failures in running a household and in helping their children to do what they had to or get anywhere on time. In addition to working with the psychodynamics that operated to block their attention to their problems, it was also crucial to take stock of their movement dynamics. They had to find ways to compensate for strong disinclinations to make decisions and take action.

Similar dynamics can have a strong effect on the interaction of analyst and patient. Patterns are inevitably established between the two that are the result of, and that express, the individuals' preferences and their histories—what experiences and understandings have led them to their current behavioral repertoires. In work with individual patients, the connections between movement attributes and attitudes are fundamental to the therapeutic relationship and are especially important to address in difficult or stalled analyses. If the patient's basic sense of self seems unreflected in the analyst, it may be because of temperamental differences that need to be examined. On the other hand, too close a match may lead to the analyst's and the patient's inability to see what else needs to happen.

These characteristics are bedrock in personalities, not learned or only defensive behavior. Rather, such tendencies are the source of difficulties and defenses, as well as of talents. Often a person's life problems have developed because parents were unable to see and work with the gifts and limits of their child's temperamental leanings. Such problems do not therefore dissolve through psychodynamic interpretation alone. But they do often enter the analytic relationship, allowing the analyst to understand and work with the patient's basic approach quite directly if the analyst recognizes this dimension at work.

PART II

❧

Psychoanalytic Theory
The Setting of the Unseen Scene

CHAPTER 5

The Body

The problem of action and other nonverbal behavior in psychoanalysis was initially related to the mind–body problem as it was construed in drive theory. The body was understood multidimensionally by Freud (1905a, 1915b, 1920, 1923) as a material reality, as the source of mental life, as a medium for symbolic representation of mental life, and as the object of its own drive for satisfaction (autoplastic activity and narcissism). Freud's position was paradoxical. While he took a materialist position on the mind–body problem—that mind is ultimately body—he also retained the Greek and Cartesian conception about the separateness of mind and body. The concept of drive was designed as a bridge between the worlds of mind and of body: drive refers both to an aspect of the process of somatic excitation and to somatic excitation's representative in the psyche. This psychic representation has four parts: a quantitative intensity factor (pressure), a qualitative defining factor (coming from the somatic source), an aim and an object that are quite variable and contingent (Freud, 1905a). Freud's concepts of drive and instinct, the pleasure principle, the reality principle, and the compulsion to repeat underlie the way in which action was construed and posed as a technical problem for the analyst. The idea that mental activity, especially thoughtful verbalization, can take place only when action is inhibited (the rule of abstinence) comes from Freud's extension of these distinctions and definitions in a theory of thought as a derivative of bodily experience, especially sexual.

Freud's (1905a) delineation of the concept of drive emerged at first in his description of the development of sexuality. Freud disputed the commonly held view that sexuality was confined to a specific aim and operation of the genitals alone. He defined "sexual" aims as manifold, and as "located" in many organs and functions (i.e., within component instincts

41

and psychosexual stages: oral, anal, phallic, and genital). Sexuality thus became a general experience of pleasure seeking, with an ultimately genital goal. Aims derived from all phases were seen as subordinate to the genital phase of sexual development by virtue of their preceding and contributing to its emergence. But Freud's conception also included observations of component instincts' dominance over the genital in some cases. Thus he postulated that the integration of component instincts and their subordination to the genital zone might or might not occur, depending on constitution and reactions to social factors. This way of thinking provided a way to understand many body symptoms and actions as diversions from the body's ultimately sexual genital aim or as fixations to component instinct aims. The corollary was that such understanding would free the instinctual energy at its source in order to redirect it away from symptomatic expression or incomplete development into better or more mature channels. In addition, the central place of the Oedipus complex (Freud, 1923) as an unavoidable developmental problem is tied to Freud's conception of the innate primacy of the sexual aims and their necessary psychic and behavioral elaboration.

The place of the pleasure principle in the rationale for inhibiting action and other nonverbal behavior becomes clear in relation to Freud's juxtaposition of it with the reality principle. Together they explain how the aim of drive satisfaction takes detours and suffers postponement because of reactions to the dangers and conditions encountered in reality (Freud, 1915b, 1923). The reality principle emerges after the pleasure principle and is revealed in the development of the conscious mental functions of memory, judgment, and attention and also in the replacement of immediate motor discharge or action with thinking, trial action, and reality testing. The reality principle does not completely displace the pleasure principle, which retains its centrality in the unconscious primary process, where connections between the bodily sources of drive and its more direct and polymorphous perverse aims and objects can be elaborated. Here again, the goal of analysis, drawn along these theoretical guidelines, was to promote the channeling of such processes into speech, because if the process were expressed nonverbally, the motivation for understanding their sources and redirecting their aims would be reduced along with the pressure of the drive for satisfaction.

And, finally, Freud (1920) added the "repetition compulsion," which he elaborated as the tendency in mental life "beyond the pleasure principle" to repeat that which could not be remembered (Freud, 1914). He explained this as the tendency of the repressed drives to continue to strive for discharge. In addition, trying to explain repetitive symptoms that were clearly not aimed at the reduction of unpleasurable tension or at pleasure

(e.g., "traumatic" neurosis, dreams obviously not wish-fulfilling), he ultimately moved back to the body and postulated the death instinct, or drive
inherent in all organic life to return to an earlier state of disorganization.
He imagined it to work in a quiet way, usually overshadowed by the clam-
orous life instincts. Mental life was then conceived as a struggle between
opposing tendencies—the life and death instincts—and as a detour from the
purely organically determined, immediate action-response cycle of
reproduction and dissolution.

In giving primacy to the body, as the basis for mental life, Freud (1905a,
1915b, 1920, 1923) placed the body at the center of analysis and made the
struggle with and against bodily expression and action an inescapable feature of his theory and practice. The struggle in treatment was to reduce the
patient's disguised drive expressions—symptoms and repetitive patterns of
behavior—to their elemental drive terms and not to foster yet other substi-
tutive satisfactions, which would divert from achieving their true understanding through verbalization (Freud, 1912b) The analyst was to ensure
this understanding by refusing to satisfy a patient's demands for interaction or other gratification or to fulfill the roles the patient tended to impose.

But, at the same time, the patient's tendency to find substitute satisfaction creates the transference, which Freud (1912a, 1914, 1915a) recognized both as another resistance to reporting or remembering and as the
vehicle through which the analyst and the patient could begin to understand the patient's repetitions. This view involved fundamentally the decision to treat the patient's feelings for the analyst not as real and present but
as derivative of a previous time and more primary bodily experience. The
analyst must remain at a distance from the drama, offering understanding
through interpretation away from the immediacy of involvement. The rationale for the distance was not the need to respect social structures and
cultural taboos against bodily contact but, rather, was that it was necessary
to the development of thought and its dominance (Freud, 1912a).

The patient was to told to refrain from taking action of any kind, within
the analysis and even in daily life, in order to allow the underlying, physiologically derived, but psychologically experienced "drives" to emerge into
consciousness. The treatment was seen as a struggle inside the patient,
played out in the transference, reflecting past experience and an inherent
conflict between instinctual life, intellect, and cultural restrictions of instinctual gratification—that is, between seeking to act, inhibition, and understanding (Freud, 1912b, 1914, 1915b). The inevitability of encountering
the patient's compulsion to repeat instead of remember fits into this context as well (Freud, 1914). Wishes for direct involvement with the analyst
were understood only in this light.

Among Freudian theorists there were disputes over aspects of these points. For example, Alexander (cited in Fenichel, 1945) thought that the "acting out" character was more amenable to cure than were those with "symptom neuroses," traditionally treated by psychoanalysis. He believed that because an acting out patient does not go into an "autoplastic regression," but maintains contact with the world through action, such a person would not have to learn to reengage the world after the analysis was over but would develop new behaviors throughout the process. Fenichel (1945) disputed this view and reasserted the traditional Freudian belief in the antipathy between action and thinking, external and internal, by stressing that a patient must change "alloplastic behavior into autoplastic behavior" in order to be cured. That is, Fenichel believed that any cure must involve first change on the inside, in thought through insight, rather than through a possible interplay between internal and external aspects of change, thought and action. There was no clinical testing of whether or not internal change first was possible in all cases or of the idea that change through action might expand Freud's original conception of body–mind.

This party line opposing action and thought notwithstanding, Freud allowed a practical caveat. He believed that concessions to the patient's wishes toward the analyst and the analyst's active participation were occasionally necessary. Concessions were not to be extreme lest the patient be "spoiled," feel too well, and as a result withdraw from engaging the difficulties in life (Freud, 1915a). Yet Freud fed, loaned money, and gave advice to patients at times (Gay, 1988). These concessions were seen by Freud as expedients, not as steps inherent in the "cure." They were tactics to be used when necessary to hold on to the patient until action could be replaced by understanding through verbal interpretation, the truly curative technique that linked the present derivative expressions of desire to their primary sources.

In the process of struggling with dilemmas that arose within this particular choreography, analysts proposed alternative ideas about how to cope with patients' nonverbal behaviors and how to think about thought in relation to action and the body. These theorists disputed the psychoanalytic distinctions between action and talk, tactic and technique, and the mind and the body. Distinctions created by Freud that permitted perception of one layer of salience were discovered to be barriers later to the perception or formulation of other kinds of experience that could not be accommodated within them.

Three explorers of the body–mind connection after Freud (1905a, 1915b, 1920, 1923), Deutsch (1933, 1947), Reich (1949), and Alexander (1950, 1963), are distinctive in their leaps from the details of body–mind behavior to social concerns, across the chasm of Freud's closed-system approach to body–mind. Freud had emphasized the endogenous factors over socially induced factors in normal and neurotic development. These three changed this emphasis without abandoning Freud's original formulations. Reich (1949) summarized most clearly that characterology entails the study of the effects of "economic situation," food, housing, clothing, work, and "social superstructure," moral codes, laws and institutions, on the "instincts" (p. xxii). In making this connection, each of the three had a grasp of quite different aspects of the body and its expressive or resistant role in communication.

Deutsch (1933) and Alexander (1950, 1963) both pursued Freud's (Breuer and Freud, 1893–1895; Freud, 1915b) earliest distinction between the hysterical conversion reaction and the actual physical components of various emotional and psychological states. Hysterical conversion involves a physical symptom (such as paralysis or a tic) as a representation of a specific psychological conflict that is expressed in symbolic body language and disappears when the psychic core is made conscious in speech. The second group of symptoms, the physical components of emotional and psychological states, Freud believed, were not treatable through psychoanalysis, for these were thought to be physical manifestations of emotional states, and without psychological meaning that could interpret them away. For example, altered heart activity, blood pressure, muscle twitches, alterations of appetite, and the like were thought of as essentials of, or equivalent to, an anxiety attack, signaling the body's natural reaction to fear and stress. The physical symptoms were thought to exist alongside the anxiety, or to constitute it, and not to represent a repressed conflict. Deutsch and Alexander were not satisfied with this distinction which aimed to establish what psychoanalysis could treat.

Deutsch (1933) considered both kinds of symptoms—those symbolic of a psychic conflict and those which were components of emotional and psychological states—to be categorizable as hysterical conversions proper. That is, he grouped conversions and physical components together by a presumed unified function understood in drive-theoretical terms as means of discharging and preventing "accumulations of psychic energy," which occur when action is inhibited. Deutsch's view assumes that action is an ongoing psychic and physical necessity—and envisions action as a product, as it were, of life. "Accumulations of psychic energy," he thought, were factors in both functional and organic disorders, in neurotic and healthy patients alike throughout life. He also argued from an unspecified hypothesis that they were both expressions of personalities with unconscious readiness to experience certain affects that, in turn, create changes in physical functioning (even in the tissues). These changes in physical function are caused by an outpouring of hormones influencing vegetative neural functions and organ functions. Deutsch included in the "language of the organic" such processes as blushing, nervous headache, or sweating. These processes allow the "discharge of pent-up libido," of affect debris—burdensome, he thought, to the unconscious and to the body. In this respect, he adhered to Freud's libido theory that body/sexual energy fueled the mind and created "pressure" toward expression. A well-functioning mind–body, then, produced and "let out" its action products, as well as its thought products. But some individuals, due to constitutional factors, might overstress certain organs.

Deutsch (1933) also postulated that "somatic compliance," the designation of organ or system to be afflicted, might arise from constitution or organic injury earlier in life, which could affect the formation of the body ego and body image through development. But also assessing patients' life situations and emotional conditions, he carefully traced the onset of chronic symptoms back to earlier periods. Current symptoms could be indicative of a conflictual time earlier in life and constitute a fixation to a set of interactive and emotional features. He found also that the choice of organ might arise from unconscious identification with a "significant other" suffering from a complaint in the same organ system. Thus, Deutsch emphasized the representational and socially influenced aspect of all body manifestations, and he recommended that their connections to their social/psychological context be interpreted and the social conditions altered. For although it was important to express the affect or conflicts in the symptom, repetitiveness was wearing—and symptoms point to stress.

Although Deutsch allowed for constitutional factors in conversion hysteria, he was more definitive than Freud in attributing causation to societal forces that demanded that people suppress too much the expression of elemental drives and wishes, necessitating these physiological reaction patterns for the maintenance of health.[1] He believed that, while it might be true that the physical components of rage were not reducible through in-

---

[1]We may be tempted to dismiss this direction in thinking because of its link to Freud's widely discarded libido economy and because such cases have all but disappeared from our experience. Yet I have recently spoken with patients in clinical intake interviews whose symptoms bear striking resemblance to these descriptions. One was a young man suffering from multiple physical symptoms that his doctors despaired of curing: stomach pains, headaches, and bronchial symptoms. His father had been shot and killed two years before I saw him, and one year before the onset of his symptoms. He had spent the year between his father's death and his symptom formation in a haze, just trying to finish school and unable to grieve. The man regarded his physical symptoms as quite distinct from the problems he had in relation to his father's death. He did not accept his physician's diagnosis of "conversion" symptoms. And, indeed, the picture was unclear, for some of his stomach symptoms did seem to have an organic basis, though other symptoms did

terpretation, the cause of the rage could be treated by treating conditions, and the rage allowed expression. Thus, he argued that action was biologically necessary and not to be replaced by thought.

Like Deutsch, Alexander emphasized the ongoing necessity for action and implicitly questioned Freud's assertion of the need for inhibition of action. But, unlike Deutsch, Alexander (1950) held to Freud's (1895) original distinction between conversion hysteria and organic psychosomatic disorders, which he termed "vegetative" neuroses. According to Alexander, a vegetative neurosis is not an attempt to express or discharge an emotion (or quantity of psychic energy), but it is the physiological response of the vegetative organs to constant or to periodically returning emotional states. Elevation of blood pressure in rages does not relieve the rage, or express the rage but it is a component of the experience that prepares the body for fight. Thus, repetitive rage may create a vegetative neurosis of high blood pressure. Or while the increase of gastric secretion under the influence of emotional longing is not the expression of or relief from the emotion, it prepares the body for feeding and nurturance. Thus, ulcers caused by excess secretion are vegetative, not conversion, neuroses. These are *preparations for sequences of motoric, interpersonal, and physiological activity* that do not occur. Alexander maintained the significance of chronic preparedness for action as a straightforward, nonpsychological, organic link between experience and symptom with no necessity for a symbolic or meaning-related connection. The interpretation—the meaning—is the discovery of what caused the rage or the longing. Alexander, basing this idea on patterns of the autonomic nervous system, emphasized the cyclicality of bodily effect on mental life, as well as the effect of psychology on body problems.

Thus, Alexander (1950) thought that the coexistence of psychosomatic and psychogenic factors must be assumed, and that there were intrinsic, biological links, distinct from representational ties, in the body—mind processes that explained the kinds of symptom that occur. But, like Deutsch (1933), he differed from Freud (1895) in stressing that many symptoms were treatable by correcting the social problems and situations that had given rise to them. His perspective on the social derived from his understanding of the body's innate connections to action/interaction. He listed social factors that he thought heavily affected bodily systems: the quality of

---

not. In a second case a woman came for treatment of her hysterical leg paralysis. She was quite indifferent to her symptom and showed very little distress. Her history revealed her father's violent death by shooting when she was three years old. His death was not referred to in the family, and he was replaced immediately by a stepfather whom she loved—and life went on without grief or understanding. But the patient as a teenager gradually stopped going out and then could no longer walk.

infant care (breast feeding, weaning, toilet training), traumatic emotional accidents in infancy and childhood, the emotional climate of the family and the personalities of significant others in the family, and later emotional experiences in intimate interpersonal relations. These were seen in their effects on an individual's *arousal and expression ratio*: how relationships might stimulate the body toward an action sequence that involves physical and physiological processes and then also suppress the completion of action, leaving the body and the situation unchanged.

Alexander's work on psychosomatics carried with it the expectation that "cure" of the adverse social/interactive conditions would cure the physical conditions that are linked to them in a recurrent gestalt. Unfortunately, the reversibility of psychosomatic disorders through interpretation is not always possible. First of all, physical ailments do not all have a connection to interactive factors or a psychological cause. Moreover, although a symptom might be triggered psychosocially, once it has been triggered it is not always curable through understanding or through changes in the personality or interactive structures. Instead, the physical symptom and personality tendencies seem to be part of a whole that is vulnerable to stressors in both physical and psychological domains because of a unity of body–mind factors. That is, for example, the asthmatic individual may be highly sensitive both to physical allergens and to emotional slights. Nevertheless, Alexander aroused awareness of the mind–body gestalt, important to psychoanalysts in helping patients come to understand their social contexts and take more control over psychosomatic syndromes.

Alexander (1950) delineated many syndromes and pointed out their psychological aspects. He thought of physical disorders as parallel to emotional expression. For example, he found that asthma attacks were frequently connected to suppressed cries for the mother:

> [M]ost asthma patients spontaneously report that it is difficult for them to cry. Moreover, attacks of asthma have been repeatedly observed to terminate when the patient could give vent to his feeling by crying . . . immediate improvement occur[s] in a number of cases after the patient has confessed something for which he felt guilty and expected rejection. . . . Confession establishes the dependent attachment to the therapist which was disturbed by the patient's guilt feelings and expectations of being rejected. Speaking (confessing) is a more articulate use of the expiratory act by which the adult achieves the same result as the child does by crying [p. 138].

Here Alexander has wrapped together the patient's inhibited expression, the transference, and need for a dependent connection to the therapist. The asthma is a symbolic as well as a direct physical result of the (denied) inhibition and dependency.

Alexander consistently found heart-related disorders to be linked with anxiety and rage through the connection of heart action to these states of emotion and arousal:

> The interaction of organic and emotional factors is in some cases most intricate. . . . Chronic free-floating anxiety and repressed hostile impulses are the important emotional factors in such disturbances. Hostility stimulates anxiety, which, in the typical manner of neurotic vicious circles, increases the hostility. Such a neurotic nucleus . . . is perhaps more common in intimidated, inhibited personalities. Occasionally they can be observed in individuals suffering from a circumscribed type of phobic anxiety who otherwise appear quite active and aggressive [p. 142].

In that extract Alexander showed the kind of health problem that results from the body's preparation and readiness for fight–flight action sequences that stress certain organs. The body's embeddedness in the social context is assumed.

Deutsch (1947) elaborated a second line of development in his thinking about the body. Expanding on Freud's observations, he was dealing with the body, not in its organic dimension, but as the medium for the expression of symbolized aims. Deutsch recorded his patients' changes of position and posture while they were on the couch and called this study "posturology." For example, he told of a woman who, lying on the couch, would describe feelings of coldness and numbness of her hands or itching and tickling in her legs. These transient sensations not derived from organic symptoms, accompanied memories of being reprimanded by her mother or of performing for her father (p. 200). On another occasion, using representational movement, rather than physiological experiences, she put her hands on her chest (a "don't touch" kind of gesture) as she recalled finding a condom as a child. When she thought of her younger brother, she withdrew her arms from under her head and remembered her mother scolding her for spanking her brother. She lay on her right side, after asking her analyst permission to do so; and, remaining in this position for months of analysis, recalled fantasies and memories of her brother and father. Deutsch called these "involuntary" positions (p. 201), that is, postures assumed without consciousness of their representational link. Another woman he noted spent three years in analysis in the same position, with very little variation: she would start with both hands resting on her abdomen, then move her left arm upward so that the left hand could rest on her forehead. The patient's intermittent initiatives to turn to the right by crossing the left leg over the right were never completed. Deutsch found that these postures accompanied the thought of defying her mother and her yearning to turn to her father (p. 201). These behaviors are representational, not primary reactions, but part of a symbolizing repertoire, in which the body is the medium of expression of thoughts or feelings.

Deutsch gave theoretical account of these significant kinds of changes of posture as "the integrated response of [the] motor apparatus to unconscious psychological complexes" (p. 209), representations of "the primitive actions and attitudes of infants. . . or. . . the release of primitive instinctual drives, with the relinquishment of defenses" (p. 210). Also, he restated Freud's (1905b, 1914) understanding that, in states of instinctual conflict, repressed emotions or defenses are expressed in body behavior. But Deutsch went beyond Freud in stating that motor behavior becomes less restrained as analysis progresses rather than less necessary as Freud's original conception had suggested. Deutsch found that involuntary movements in analysis did not seem to be "acting out" because they were not a flight from insight but accompanied the insight. These observations and nascent theoretical challenges were neglected in subsequent analytic work until the work of Mahl (1968, 1977). which established more systematically the positive connection, rather than the classical assumption of antagonism, between acting and verbalizing. (We will return to this subject in Part III.)

Like Alexander and Deutsch, Reich (1949) emphasized the social milieu as implicated in creating the need for a fourth kind of nonverbal behavior. Unlike the expressive movements emphasized by Alexander and Deutsch, the movement Reich noted, "psychophysical armouring," is the defensive use of one unchanging body attitude. He pointed out that the exaggerated politeness of one person was as much motivated by anxiety as the brutal behavior of another. The difference, he thought, was to be found in variations of environmental influences leading to the choice of opposite defenses. At first Reich simply refocused the analyst's attention in a new direction, emphasizing the patient's body structure and manner instead of the verbal content of communication. He noted the frequent observation that people were "hard and soft, proud and humble, cold and warm, etc." and explained that these were different forms of "armouring of the ego" against external and internal dangers (p. 14).

Reich's shift of focus did not at first change his use of verbal interpretation as the mode of intervention. He redirected the content of interpretations, emphasizing instead of the content of speech, the interactive effects of a patient's body attitude, that is how the body is held and the manner of speech.[2] He began his formulations because of frustration at patients' in-

---

[2]Reichian therapy is distinguished by the idea that directly changing the body's armoring will itself lead to change in psychosocial functioning.

ability to follow the fundamental rule to free associate (p. 8). He believed that salutary change lay in the direction of questioning the reasons for the patient's *manner* and *method*, which prevented open engagement with the analyst. He noted the patients' "haughtiness" or "confused" manner, for example, as body-based phenomena that were motivated by the need to control simultaneously social relations and body–mind state. He contrasted his analysis of these features to the view, held prior to his work, that such problems could be dealt with through nonneutral tactics of persuasion, teaching the analytic method and reassuring the patient of its ultimate usefulness. Instead he termed these patients' ways of behaving "character resistances," which he thought were as much determined by early experiences as were physical symptoms or fantasies.

Reich provided insight into the multifaceted behaviors employed by his "resistant" patients to defend against change and against the analyst's inquiry and presumed authority. For example, he described a young male patient's use of an ironic "smile" as a resistance that emerged almost intractably when Reich confronted the patient's previous aggressive actions (provocative talk, remaining on the couch after the end of the hour, making "threatening" gestures toward the analyst's head). The smile was eventually traced to a screen memory of its first use against the patient's mother when she caught him "playing horse" with his penis exposed. Reich understood the smile as, first, an attempt at conciliation; then, a way to hide from fear; and finally, a denial of the young man's humiliation (pp. 67–72).

Like Alexander and Deutsch, Reich regarded action as an ongoing necessity. He was interested in the way social conditioning restricted full drive development. And following drive theory, he believed that the form of expression carried at a muscular level led to biological reactions that were the basis of psychic manifestations and ideations. Furthermore, Reich thought that becoming conscious of the *meaning* of symptoms would bring only partial relief. Most important was the achievement of definitive somatic fulfillment in the form of mature genital sexual gratification (p. 14), which was inhibited by frozen character structures. In this way, he emphasized action over insight.

Reich showed how body postures could be defensive, opposing change while Deutsch and Alexander showed the indirectly communicative aspects of posture and illness. All three, despite differences in the details of what they saw, maintained a strong critique of "society" for creating the need for the defenses and covert or diverted expression through illness. "Society" for Deutsch and Alexander meant social interpersonal relations; and for Reich, the social conventions that inhibit interpersonal relations.

Without challenging drive theory, they each moved toward a view of the body as a realm of experience and expression, receiving and structuring in an ongoing fashion, rather than as a repository of givens, "drives" statically conceived or historic experience merely stored in the body–mind, to be relayed later to "mental" processing. Neither Reich, Deutsch, nor Alexander saw any contradiction between ideas about the body as a primary source of motivation and behavioral production and conceptions of social influences on motivation and behavior. They asserted that there is a direct link, however it may become tenuously held or abandoned, between the body and socialization.[3]

Also committed to theories of the social origin of motivation and behavior, Sullivan developed a theory more radically distinct from Freudian theory than the three discussed. He eschewed entirely concepts of body–mind with their to him objectionable implications about inner and outer worlds. He renamed the distinctions between inner and outer experience "private and public modes," according to his intention to "operationalize psychiatry," that is, to use conceptualizations based on what was observable rather than hypothesized (Sullivan, 1953, p. 19). Instead of linking the body with socialization, Sullivan (1953, 1954a) put social interaction and learning at the center of human development and declined to discuss mind–body philosophical issues. He distinguished needs for satisfaction, which he regarded as biological and body derived, from needs for security, which he conceived as psychological and interactively determined. Sullivan (1953) cited the long dependency of human beings and the lability of inborn potential as evidence that the idea of "human instincts in anything like the proper rigid meaning of maturing patterns of behavior is . . . preposterous" (pp. 20, 21).

In making this radical distinction, Sullivan introduced a view of human experience that is different from prior versions. He placed at the center of focus behaviors that occur *only between two people* rather than inside one. Recall that Alexander, Deutsch, and Reich viewed socialization from a point of view inside body–mind; that is, they sought to explain an effect in a person of a cause outside. The details of behavior that Sullivan underscored show a view of an additional layer of interactive involvement, which is not a replacement for their views but adds to it. Sullivan's radical concept of mind–body—both what it allowed him to see and what it did not allow—differentiates an entirely different arena of social influence.

Sullivan (1954a) conveyed his distinction between social and biological through two concepts, which he traced developmentally as he attempted

---

[3]This kind of approach continues in the French psychosomaticiens. For example, Grunberger, Fain, Marty, Braunschweig, David, de M'Uzan, and to a lesser extent McDougall and Green, are cited by Oliner (1988) as giving to psychosomatic phenomena primary importance in their work.

to bring the social aspect of infant life forward of the physiological aspect. On one side is the rhythmic, biologically determined alternation between euphoria and tension, and, on the other, anxiety, in Sullivan's view arising completely from the social world. Anxiety comes from the meaning the "mothering one" gives to her experience of her infant, a meaning that depends on social conditions, taboos, and aims (for example, the mother's anxious replication of the social condemnation of masturbation or a person's anxiety about social competition). He designated tensions that periodically lower the state of euphoria of the infant as "zonal needs" relating to the infant's biological existence. These are addressed through the "mothering one's" activity. In his move away from the body and any implication of drive, Sullivan thought the experience of such needs might be generalized and located within the infant's social world as a "need for tenderness," reciprocated by the arousal of a tension in the mother relieved by her giving tenderness. In this approach, the specific physiological and physical needs are much less important psychologically than is the need for "tenderness," and the manner of relating takes precedence over the actual physical need. Thus, Sullivan saw the infant's physical needs not just as contained within, but subordinated to, the social environment. This subordination is justified, in Sullivan's (1954a) thinking, by the complicating and to him, purely social fact that "the tension of anxiety, when present in the mothering one, induces anxiety in the infant" through the interpersonal process of "empathy" (p. 41).

The tensions of anxiety, as opposed to those of physiological need, pertain to the interpersonal environment, whose connections to the physical and physiological domain is incidental. The relief of anxiety results not in physical satisfaction, but in "security," a psychological state pertaining to the interpersonal world, not the body or the inner world. The tension of anxiety is not relievable through the action of the infant or through direct ministrations to the infant's physical zonal needs by the anxious parent. It is not associated with particular bodily sensations but is located in the *mental* state of the parent and transferred through the empathy involved in interaction. Sullivan (1954) postulated that, to escape what would be an escalating pattern of infant distress and increasing maternal anxiety, the infant goes into a state of "somnolent detachment" (p. 57), a precursor of dissociation, removing herself or himself from the loop of cycling anxiety.

In Sullivan's radical departure from Freudian body theory, he observed behavior from a different angle. Sullivan (1954b) made detailed observations of interpersonal body attitude behavior, which he thought reflected attempts to avoid anxiety by controlling behavior connected to expectations of threats to security. He pointed out how people control their own perceptions and conversations with others through distractedness or alertness, vagueness or attentiveness, understanding cooperativeness or unwillingness to be led, or deliberate obtuseness (pp. 108–110). He noted as well the kinds of attitudes that were conveyed nonverbally toward the interviewer: "reserved, guarded, suspicious, hostile, or contemptuous . . . supercilious, superior, conciliatory, deferential, or apologetically inferior" (p. 112). These attitudes reflected past experience and reactions to it. He made special note of how important it is to watch for changes in attitude as an interview proceeds, as a way of being guided toward useful approaches to reducing the patient's anxiety.

Sullivan's theoretical pragmatism led him away from a search for first biological causes, and toward observing the patient's "characteristic *patterns* of living," (italics added) in which he saw the effects of past experience with others. Past experiences had taught patients to expect certain kinds of reactions from themselves and others and to find that it was better not to know very clearly about certain aspects of themselves and others. Sullivan observed, for example, how someone might have the same repeating thought each day and never notice that this was happening or its significance. He showed how another patient avoided comprehending his anger toward his parents by not connecting his feelings to their prohibiting normal social contact with peers. Sullivan was most interested in empowering his patients with a better understanding of what they wanted of others and of the simplest way to go about their interpersonal transactions. He regarded acceptance in the social group rather than drive satisfaction as the primary goal and stumbling block.

Thus, sharpened distinctions between social and biological factors basic to Sullivan's observations helped him to see the details in patterns of behavior occurring between people that were not seen by others. But all such distinctions must make sacrifices to clarity. Most important in this instance is the question of whether or not in all cases such sharp distinctions need or can be made between physical and social needs or between body and mind. These distinctions are difficult to maintain across the board, since, for example, ministering to an infant's bodily needs for satisfaction invariably becomes interactive, so that the need for biological "satisfaction" is always also "a security need." Taking necessary distance from Freud's search for biological "first causes" of mental phenomena, Sullivan did not consider the connection of his own field of study—socially organized interactive phenomena—to body process. But it is in and around the satisfaction of zonal bodily needs that the caregiver's feelings are significant at first. And while anxiety may often have a social (between two persons) rather than a physiological (inside one person) origin, it is nevertheless experienced physically and physiologically (inside one), communicated (between two), and coped with at first psychologically and physically (inside one) as well as socially (between two).

The significance of this more complicated idea of interaction and the body is overlooked because of Sullivan's useful distance from classical theory's neglect of social interaction. Sullivan's distance and classical theory's neglect of his views led to the creation of an unnecessary sense of practical incompatibility. Two problems inherent in the body–mind arena were unaddressed both by Sullivan's unwavering focus on the social realm and in Freud's reduction of the mental to the physical: (1) the physical/physiological is too sharply divided from the social; and (2) the physical and the physiological are not at all differentiated. That is, physical, body interaction patterns occuring with or without anxiety or awareness are repeatedly sought after and shaped in the habitual interaction between child and parent. These patterns may be separate from, as well as integrated with, physiological needs for food, warmth, bodily grooming, and support. These distinctions and relationships are expressed to some degree by Alexander and Deutsch, and later by Winnicott.

Klein, also regarded for many years as renegade, took a theoretical position just the opposite to those of Sullivan and of Deutsch, Alexander, and Reich. She began with an unaltered version of Freud's (1905a, 1915b, 1920, 1923) conceptions of drive (especially as elaborated by Abraham, 1924). Her discoveries actually shifted her center of focus significantly even though she maintained her orthodoxy. Even though Klein believed she was thinking strictly about drives, she was finding the edge of drive theory that implies physiology's innate connection to others—in the object of the drive. Also, Klein did not retain the idea that action should be inhibited in order for thought and understanding to emerge. Her lack of concern about inhibiting action in favor of talking was due to the age of her patients, many of whom were so young they could barely speak. She interpreted their action and play in terms of a language of the body, which she assumed to be innate and universal. The body language drew from Freud's original conception but became her own. In breaking the tie of inaction and thought, she also broke the until then unvarying connection of thought back to physically anchored drives. Instead, she moved into the less clearly physical terrain of love and hate, which she asserted are innate and instinctual, though they are also intrinsically interpersonal.

Klein delineated a way of seeing in nonverbal behavior feelings, thoughts, attitudes toward "inner objects." She postulated unconscious "phantasies" which were composed of drive experience and the lively images of the object of the drive. Klein found that she could identify a child's anxiety about her or his inner objects by watching the child's play and reactions to Klein's interpretations of the play. More often than not, she saw in child's play straightforward drive expression or drive expression disguised symbolically—not repetitions of experienced behavior and inter- action, as Sullivan, Alexander, Deutsch, and Reich might. For example, in the analysis of Peter, she interpreted his "bumping" together two horse- drawn carriages while he mentioned the birth of his new baby brother, as symbolic of his own personal image of parental intercourse and the aggres- sion he imagined associated with it (Klein, 1955). Klein brought words to the child's symbolic play, which was the child's only means of expressing anxiety of unknown origins. She watched for the shifts in anxiety as she interpreted the child's play, and she saw in the visible reduction in anxiety a confirmation of the utility of her interpretations.[4]

Klein gave increased weight to Freud's conception of the body's shap- ing mind through the power of the drives, especially his postulated "death instinct" (Freud, 1920). Her shift of emphasis opened new territory. She developed a theory that the perceptible derivative of the death instinct was the envious attack on life-giving objects and experience that she saw in her patients' behavior, and in infants' primitive experience. The Kleinian body– mind comprises powerful opposing passions—extreme and primitive struggles with life and death, feelings of love, hate, greed, and envy for objects and for the powers they are thought to possess (Klein, 1957). Klein interpreted the death instinct, or innate aggression as she understood it, to be the basis for destructive aggressive impulses inherent in all human be- ings that, although turned outward in various ways, nevertheless indirectly harm the individual by depleting life experience and arousing intense anxi- ety. Thus, she inexplicitly moved away from Freud's sexual theory by plac- ing love and hate, life and death in the center while leaving sexual aims in a secondary role.

Although she de-emphasized the importance of actual interactive ex- perience, paradoxically, Klein's drama moved into a social arena through her emphasis on the child's self-determination in struggling with depen- dency, the biological need for others. She seems to have seen psychopa- thology as arising from a failure to accept the vulnerability created by this inescapable biological dependency. Envy is the result: attacks on life-giv- ing objects that have the power to frustrate, abandon, or deny help on which life depends. In her experience, envy was a primary experience of ordinary

---

[4]In this respect, her work seems similar to Sullivan's: despite beginning from opposite theoretical poles, they meet in their close observation of behavior, and their grasp of the interpersonal significance of the appearance of anxiety. But the different weight they each give to the importance of inner–outer, biological–social genesis of difficulty leads to strikingly different interpretive content.

infants, in varying strengths depending on constitutional factors, one being the innate capacity for love. She paid attention not just to the blissful
"oneness" experiences of infancy, but also to the helpless and terrorized
feelings of the infant driven by hunger and the need for nurturance.

Ideally, Klein (1946) thought, envy is overcome during development
and transforms into more healthy forms of aggression in the service of life,
jealousy, and competition. Much of this movement depends on the shift
from the "paranoid-schizoid position"—the experience of terrorizing need
that threatens to destroy the self or consume or destroy the life-giving object or anything seen as frustrating—to the "depressive position," a steady
awareness of the need to preserve the loved and needed aspect of the object
even during a frustrating experience.

Although Klein did not think of her theories as social or interpersonal—
and indeed, reading her leaves one with the feeling that the child's experience is entirely generated from the inside—her conceptions are fully about
the individual's struggle with interpersonal connection. The infant mind is
sometimes pressed by tormenting drives to imagine an external world that
it seeks—one that perfectly matches its experience and needs. She thought
that environmental influences did not create the child's experience but
might ameliorate the child's intense aggression through appropriate care.
Environmental influences could also foster development toward the depressive position or, through poor care, reinforce the paranoid-schizoid
position.

A position between Sullivan's and Klein's on the biological/body–so-
cial/psychological continuum was taken by Fairbairn (1940, 1941, 1943,
1951). The differences between them rest on their differing positions on
first causes: Fairbairn (1941, 1951) redefined first cause as object seeking.
Sullivan (1954a) strategically begged the question, insisting on observation
of what actually happens between people, rather than theorizing based on
an unobservable first cause or on a hypothesized "inner world." Klein (1946)
placed first the overwhelming experience of drive, which places self or object
in jeopardy. Fairbairn (1941) shifted focus to the social arena without entirely dispensing with the drives, but without giving them—especially the
death instinct—the weight that Klein had. The child's need for the mother
was not to be reduced to or thought of as derivative of the biological body
needs, but as existing in its own right, with the drives serving as modes of
attaining the object. In this view, drives become "libidinal attitudes. . .which
turn out to be merely techniques for regulating the object-relationships of
the ego" (p. 31).

> [T]he function of libidinal pleasure is essentially to provide a sign-post
> to the object . . . [rather than the reverse in which an] object is regarded

as a sign-post to libidinal pleasure; and the cart is thus placed before the horse . . . *the whole course of libidinal development depends upon the extent to which objects are incorporated and the nature of the techniques which are employed to deal with incorporated objects* [p. 34].

Thus, Fairbairn viewed body-behavior symptoms and nonverbal acts or character structure as manifestations of techniques for dealing with incorporated objects, which were the result of actual experience, rather than inventions of a mind driven by body experience. Fairbairn declared it necessary to deny the primary importance of libidinal or aggressive body-states to undo the reduction of social needs to libidinal needs. Like Sullivan, he said that social needs have their own track and that the psychological development of an individual is not predetermined but receives essential and formative input from others as to what is expressed and how.

Thus Fairbairn's (1941, 1951) theory also reduced the significance and role of the body itself in normal psychological development and in the etiology of pathology. Yet he maintained the Freudian emphasis on the inner psychological world as opposed to actual ongoing social experience and activity, "operations" in Sullivan's lexicon, as the arena for change. Behavior was interpreted by Fairbairn (1941) as manifesting "techniques . . . employed to deal with incorporated objects," (p. 34) rather than as Sullivan (1954a) suggested, "parataxic distortions" of real experience (pp. 28, 29) built on problematic or limiting relationships in the past.

Winnicott (1949b, 1954, 1956, 1958, 1960a, 1963a) took another route, joining together an emphasis on innate constitutional factors and one that gave more importance to environmental influence, including nonverbal interaction in analysis, a significance it had not been given except by Alexander. But Winnicott's position, while it connected with others, was also distinct—as shown by its centering on yet other behaviors.

In Winnicott's (1949b) view the "psyche . . . [is] the imaginative elaboration of somatic parts, feelings and functions, that is, of physical aliveness" (p. 244). Winnicott saw the need of some patients to regress in their relationship with their analysts to what Winnicott and his patients regarded as an extremely "early" level of functioning. He thought that regression created the opportunity for the new nonverbal and kinesthetic experience that was necessary for the patient to repair a pathological, too early differentiation of mind and body. The new element was Winnicott's keen sensitivity to the analyst's and the patient's *physical impact* on each other. He included even words as a part of their physical relatedness, something he grasped intuitively without specifying their rhythmic and tonal attributes.

His thinking was based on the idea that infants are born in a state of psyche–soma oneness, in which the good-enough environment is a physical/social one that ideally tends nearly perfectly to all the infant's needs, both "instinctual" and "primitive ego needs" (Winnicott, 1949b). From Winnicott's perspective, only in the course of time can experience be categorized as separately physical, emotional, psychological, or social, since, at first, all these dimensions are encompassed experientially and expressively within the physical and physiological. He intuitively understood that what adults might regard as a purely social motivation—that is the need for social interaction distinct from intense physical and physiological needs-states such as hunger, and cold—is experienced by an infant first physically, kinesthetically in gaze, touch, sound, and movement. Also, though some social needs may seem to have little to do with what we identify as somatic needs for sustenance, they nevertheless belong to the physical/kinetic sphere in their expression and experience, and they regulate arousal, emotion, and various other "states" that are physical, physiological and psychological (Stern, 1985).[5]

Winnicott (1949b) made use of Klein's understanding of phantasy—of the connection of drive and imagined object. He said that the infant imagines the breast and needs the real breast to meet adequately the inner experience of the phantasized breast. The specificity is important: hunger, strictly speaking, may be met by food, but the full experience of being held and understood emotionally is specified by the infant's physical makeup (what we would now call temperament) and phantasy. Problems arise not just internally, as Klein's work suggested, nor just externally between the actual parent and child, as Sullivan's position suggested, but in the transitional space between imagination and reality. The infant does have in a sense a good experience "in mind" that interacts with what is met in experience. Psychic development occurs as Winnicott's infant gradually becomes able to compensate for the ordinary, good-enough mother's deficiencies in attunement to these specific social/bodily needs through mental activity (phantasy/thinking). The infant gradually takes responsibility for and control of interaction with the physical/social world and closes the gap between what is wanted and how it is wanted, and what is present and available. That is, through mental and physical activity, the infant can gradually endure ordinary failures in attunement. What is wanted and what can happen are differentiated as the infant realizes that mental activity does not by itself bring the desired object—action is often needed. In addition, the object that arrives is often different from the one imagined. When the demand on the infant to compensate for maternal failure to match the imag-

[5]The work of Spitz (1965) on hospitalism underscores that social needs are biological as well.

ined need is too extreme, and too early, there occurs a loss of connection between rather than a differentiation of psyche and soma.

According to Winnicott (1949b), in psychopathology, despite the early disruption and loss of connection between psyche and soma, traumatic events are kept "catalogued" (p. 247) (presumably in somatic memory) so as to be accessible later to reevocation and remembrance and then elaboration in language. They are not psychically elaborated or altered except when a good connection of body–mind and mother is maintained in an ongoing and good-enough relationship, so that new actions erase the old. Winnicott stressed that the details of these "cataloguings"—too early to be connected to speech—could be accessed only through reliving in "acting out." Thus would be generated a new actual experience with the analyst, presumably in a return to the mode of kinesthetic experiencing in which the psyche is relieved of the overwork that is damaging to psyche–soma integration. Such integration Winnicott (1949b, 1960a) thought was captured in the experience of the "true self."

Winnicott's "true self" refers to the infant's guiding focus in the transactional processes between what feels right or wrong in her or his experience and an environment over which the infant has only limited control. The true self presupposes an infant born with distinctive inclinations and needs that require particular and distinctive responses: feeding, holding, grooming, even when well-intentioned and performed in a kindly way, do not necessarily satisfy. The individual, specific ways of handling that are required are determined by individual needs, which Winnicott indicated the good-enough mother can intuit. The limits of the infant's capacity to adapt to an ill-fitting environment (beyond the gestural methods that signal pleasure and displeasure and by which the infant tries to modulate interaction [Stern, 1985]) rest upon the baby's ability to imagine and to manipulate his or her mental engagement; manipulation through large motor action is not a choice at this early age. Thus, the overstressed infant overuses the psyche, which must separate an aspect of the body–mind that is connected to what is needed from another aspect, which continues to participate in interaction (the false self).

In this way, Winnicott united Klein's (1926) instinct-based "phantasy" (see also Isaacs, 1948) with an interactive model. The infant needs to have a good-enough match between what he or she can "phantasize" as wanted, on the basis of innate temperamental/body–mind characteristics and the ministrations of the caretaker. When good-enough adaptation of the mothering one does not occur over a sustained period, the infant disastrously loses trust in the parent, in the self's perceptual mental apparatus, or in both. This loss of trust occurs because, if the infant opts not to die by rejecting the crucial, but wrongly applied, physiological ministrations, she or he must make a choice: to attack perception itself, to change the phantasy of what is needed, or to disconnect internally from the phantasy altogether. In these ways, the infant lessens the painful experience of wanting a particular way of handling or of wanting at all. The capacity to want, or to identify what is wanted, remains, but it is relegated to the painful catalogue of somatic memory of suffering the wrong kind of care. And, according to Winnicott (1949b), this memory can be retrieved only through a painful reliving, an enactment in regression to an early state of mind, whose usefulness depends on the understanding of the analyst often conveyed without words.

Summary

In this brief review of key figures in psychoanalytic history, I have identified four distinct positions in relation to the concept of the body and mind: (1) the body as the originating source and symbolic manifestation of psychological life; (2) the impact of the social world on the body-mind so conceived; (3) the body de-emphasized as a factor in mental life in favor of the impact of the social experience of the individual; and (4) Freud's concept of the body–mind, including drive, altered to directly incorporate social needs or experience. The first, the Freudian position, was held and developed further by Deutsch, Reich, Alexander, and Klein. But Deutsch, Alexander, and Reich moved through Freudian drive theory, without basically challenging it, to the second position, the concern about the social causes of psychological illness. The third, developed by Sullivan, placed social development in the center and discarded body-based theories of mental development. Klein, who maintained Freudian metapsychology, and Fairbairn, who changed but retained it, subtly shifted from the original drive concept to emphasize love and hate of objects, phantasized or internalized experientially. They hold the fourth position, along with Winnicott, who added to rather than revised theory in retaining the internal focus of Freud and Klein while equally stressing the actual care the infant receives.

These are distinguishable positions that recognize and engage *different kinds of behavior*: (1) body symptoms mimicking illnesses and body postures that represent psychic and interactive conflict; body postures that control interaction and represent ideas, conflicts, and events; activities that obstruct the possibility of fuller recognition of experience; (2) physical and emotional symptoms that reflect inadequate care or poorly balanced social relations that cut off expression; (3) patterns of interaction based on a desire to maintain interpersonal security; and (4) behaviors that directly or indirectly express primitive anxieties about the inner world of objects, and include mental actions directed at one's phantasized mental contents.

Technically, the second position alone makes no demands for change in the activity of analyst or patient from that of the first position—interpretation remains the major activity of the analyst, and verbalization that of the patient (Deutsch, Reich) The third position stresses either new content areas to be interpreted (Fairbairn) or the importance of the analyst's and the patient's active engagement in changing life situations (Alexander, Reich, Sullivan). The fourth position (Klein, Winnicott) makes strong demands for technical change and places greater emphasis on the role of the actions—beyond interpretation—of analyst with the patient.

CHAPTER 6

Interaction
The Patient's Action

≫≪

*A*s noted in the previous chapter, psychoanalysts' views about action were initially tied to conceptions of the body's role (through the intermediary role of the id and drives) in both creating and interfering with thought. Through intuitive affinities linking the idea of body with action, it was implied that action is in conflict with thought and understanding as a function of mind. Despite the philosophical relegation of action and the body beyond the pale, psychoanalysts still had to contend with both the inevitable action without thought and frequent demands for direct interaction made by the patient. Later views challenged the original conception of the role of the body and action in thought. But the challenges did not remove the difficulty of contending with action, and there are consequently a number of approaches to action. At first within the challenging conceptions, the actions of the patient and analyst were separated. In more recent conceptions, the simultaneity and reciprocity of the two participants' positions have been recognized.

Patient Action

Theorists' points of view about patient action address which behaviors to allow or encourage, or they observe what the patient strives to do—defensively and constructively—with the analyst. Freud's (1913, 1914) view of patient action and understanding was consonant with the philosophical views of his day and may also have been given more weight because of the early, seemingly simple success in clearing away bodily symptoms through talking and interpretation. This success led to a fairly simple idea of patient–analyst interaction. First, the patient was to make no changes in external circumstances during an analysis. In addition, the patient was to take only a passive position in relation to his or her thought processes, and observe them as though they were passing scenery on a train ride. This position rested on the idea that the work of analysis involved seeing and, at most, reordering what was already "inside" the patient, that is, that nothing new needed to be added and that changes to be made in the social context could occur only after this reordering was accomplished. The train went in only one direction, inside to outside. Actual experience for Freud was always the unfolding or expression of what was inside—as bodily symptoms and patterns in the "materialization" of the inner world. And the inner world would be reordered by allowing it to come to be spoken about.

Early dissenters found that this method worked with some, but not all, people—they saw how patients' overt and large-scale action of different kinds was often useful to analysis rather than merely unavoidable. Later revisionist theorists dwelt on the usefulness of working with, not against, other subtle perceptual and communicative processes that involve action.

In Deutsch (1947), Alexander (1930, 1950; Alexander and French, 1946), and Reich (1949) the thread of the importance of the body described in the previous chapter was carried into their attitudes toward patients' actions. They each recognized the physiological importance of action and singled out different aspects of the active, motivated nature of patients' body-based symptoms, postures, and characteristic body attitudes.

Deutsch (1947) extended Freud's thinking on the symbology of the patient's unconscious activity in body postures and movement during analytic sessions. He noted for example, that:

> [P]ostural configurations included holding her hands under her neck when fearful of being punished for masturbation; her right hand was lifted and her left hand held protectively over her head when she was angry with men. Her left hand was usually raised when she was in a rage against her mother. Both arms were lifted when she felt hostile with both parents. Both arms were outstretched backward when longing for approval [p. 201].

The patient's nonverbal activity here was understood to parallel growing awareness. At the same time, other nonverbal behavior might be expressive of internal conflict, which was to be interpreted as such and brought into conscious awareness through its transformation into language. Deutsch's understanding of this kind of behavior on the couch was linked to the drive-based idea of abreaction, the energic release of repressed libido.

This kind of observation and understanding was extended by Reich (1949), who examined the sustained nonverbal behavior resulting in a character structure or body–mind attitude that had interactive-defensive as well as self-regulatory functions:

> The patient is good looking, of medium height; his facial expression is reserved, serious, somewhat arrogant. What is striking is his measured, refined gait. It takes him quite some time to get from the door to the couch; plainly, he avoids—or covers up—any haste or excitation. His speech is measured, quiet and refined; occasionally, he interrupts this with an emphasized, abrupt "Yes," at the same time stretching both arms in front of him, and afterwards stroking his hand over his forehead. He lies on the couch in a composed manner, with his legs crossed. His dignified composure hardly ever changes at all, even with the discussion of narcissistically painful subjects. . . . One day tears came and his voice began to choke; nevertheless, the manner in which he put the handkerchief to his eyes was composed and dignified [pp. 180–181].

For Reich, analysis demanded reference not only to the text of internal conflict, but also to the patient's present nonverbal behavior, here the creation of a sustained, rigid action pattern and body attitude that did not permit engagement in the work of analysis, or change through learning. Reich stressed that action would come before thought and that the patient's behavior had to change in order for any new thinking to occur. Theoretically committed to libido theory, he emphasized the connections of mind, embodiment and interaction. Indeed, he said, "the disconnection of the impulses from the total personality results in an impairment of the total activity" (p. 151), which results later in an impaired ability to work and an inability to achieve genital satisfaction.

Alexander's (1930, 1963; Alexander and French, 1946) view of patient action was quite distinct from Reich's or Deutsch's. He did not take note of the kind of rigid body attitudes that Reich described. Nor did he focus on changing or static posture and gesture as had Deutsch. Alexander stressed patients' tendencies to recreate unhelpful patterns of interaction and consequent needs to be engaged in actual, new interactive patterns, not just verbal interpretation. For example, one man sought explicitly to have the analyst impose rules the way his father had. The analyst did not comply, thus changing the interactive pattern of what each might do or say with one another (Alexander and French, 1946, pp. 55–56). Nothing is said here about muscular or psychosomatic involvement or "resistance." His patients seemed to accept readily the new rules of play offered to them by their analyst. Alexander's patient was straightforwardly responsive to the analyst's new offerings, and, though sometimes challenging, he was not rigidly so.

Although Reich and Alexander agreed that patients' problems were the result of early frustration of impulse imposed socially, *each presented different kinds of patient activity*. The muscular behavior Reich described was not changeable through corrective emotional experience simply understood or presented; it was a chronic body restriction that could allow only one kind of interaction and thus prohibited new experience. Until its defensive, restricting role was made clear, learning was not possible. But Alexander and French (1946) described the patients' interactive rules of play that are a different kind of nonverbal engagement not involving a *frozen* body attitude. Rather these behaviors were based on expected responses of others and could change when the expected responses changed.

Deutsch, as I noted in chapter 5, stressed unconscious, representational actions which might be repeated for some period of time as part of the analytic process. These behaviors were seen as symbolic of aspects of relationships being discussed in treatment. They are not "stances" or "body attitudes" either passingly or chronically sustained. Rather, they are gestures that may occur whatever body attitude or rules of play are in place. Recall, for example, the patient who put her hands on her chest in a "don't touch" kind of gesture. Such a gesture can occur whether a person maintains a chronic rigidity or not; it is a separate kind of movement process.

Thus, Reich, Alexander, and Deutsch presented three kinds of patients' nonverbal behaviors: (1) an active, chronic, and rigid restriction of the body's range of movement resulting in the manifestation of a person's character structure as a frozen body attitude; (2) an interactive, shifting body-attitude along with rules of play with the analyst (who, in these versions, takes a particular, prescribed, reciprocal body attitude aimed at "understanding," or "challenging," or "providing"); and (3) shifting, symbolic movements and postures that augment what is said. All three theorists depicted different configurations of body posture, body attitude, muscular tension, control of breathing and motion, and organic involvement as representations of conflict and as ways of acting—to express what was forbidden and to maintain self-control and control over others. The activity defined in this conception involves the body as the object acted on; the body is at once the medium of expression and a source of the need for action.

Ferenczi (1919, 1925, 1926) and Alexander and French (1946) offered another view of patients' nonverbal action, in contrast to the classical stress on inaction. They discovered the learning- and memory-enhancing dimensions of patients' action. Alexander and French (1946) thought that not all of a patient's problems might enter into the transference and those that did not could be accessed if the patient's activities in outside relationships were examined and encouraged:

> Like the adage, "Nothing succeeds like success," there can be no
> more powerful therapeutic factor than the performance of activities
> which were formerly neurotically impaired or inhibited. . . . The chief
> therapeutic value of the transference situation lies in the fact that it
> allows the patient to experience this success in rehearsal, a rehearsal
> which must then be followed by actual performance [p. 40].

He includes a plea to discriminate between those occasions when teaching
and informing might be essential or enough and those times when a more
involved transference analysis might be required.

Ferenczi's (1931, 1933) position on action incorporated the transference situation. His reasoning underscored the narrative information that
could be retrieved through "acting out." Years later, Ferenczi (1931), wanting to amplify and clarify inner life, fantasy, and past experience, advocated receptivity to the patient's "acting out" experiences of early childhood with the analyst. He described one such patient's activity:

> [A] man in the prime of life resolved after overcoming strong
> resistances, and especially his profound mistrust, to revive in his
> mind incidents from his earliest childhood. Thanks to the light
> analysis had already thrown on his early life, I was aware that in the
> scene revived by him he was identifying me with his grandfather.
> Suddenly, in the midst of what he was saying, he threw his arms
> around my neck and whispered in my ear: "I say, Grandpapa, I am
> afraid I'm going to have a baby!" Thereupon, I had what seems to be
> a happy inspiration. I said nothing to him for the moment about the
> transference, etc., but retorted, in a similar whisper: "Well, what
> makes you think so?" [p. 129].

Here the action is of a very different kind—it is within a play arena, not real
life. And, for Ferenczi, the action facilitates memory and its elaboration by
allowing the patient unrestrained emotional expression. In accord with
Freud, he regarded it as an occasionally necessary tactic but not a factor
theoretically intrinsic to cure. On paper, at least, Ferenczi's cure remains
the verbal interpretation and understanding that came after the patient's
action, understood as symbolic, not the new interaction taking place in the
acted-out fantasy. Still, there is an implicit recognition that for some patients, action itself is a necessary step in "cure."

Alexander and French (1946), on the other hand, saw patients' actions in current life circumstances as necessary for change: learning new
behavior was their theory of cure. Reich agreed with this idea but concentrated on patients who had not remained "open" to experience, rather than
on those for whom crucial experience had more simply not "happened."

Alexander's (1963; Alexander and French, 1946) greater emphasis on deficient interactive factors in etiology parallels his stress on the importance of
the analyst's active provision of a "corrective emotional experience," beyond interpretation. Where he might have looked for resistant character
patterns, he looked instead for the need for new patterns of experience.
He and French (1946) found in patients' behaviors repetitive, nonadaptive
interaction sequences inducing unhelpful role reciprocity in others, but
not muscularly frozen body attitudes:

> The patient tried at once to impose the old father–son pattern on
> the therapeutic situation. His attitude toward his father had been
> one of rebellion mixed with an almost unlimited admiration and
> passive devotion. He made efforts to induce the analyst to impose
> strong rules on him, to dictate his behavior. . . . At the same time,
> there were immediate signs of competition with and rebellion against
> the analyst. . . . His unconscious tendency was to push the therapist
> into the role of the tyrannical father, against whom he could rebel
> and with whom he could compete without any sense of guilt [p. 57].

The behavioral level that Alexander described is different from the one
that Reich had described. Alexander focused on inflexible interactive patterns involving shifting body attitudes, not on one action frozen within the
actor's body. In the absence of a rigidly held bodily position, the action
patterns noted by Alexander are more amenable to change through the
encounter with a different reciprocal role. For the level of action that Reich
found, this was not possible because of unattended restriction at the muscular level, which does not allow the interactive responsivity that requires
change at muscular and rhythmic levels.

Sullivan (1953, 1954b) and later Bion (1962, 1967, 1970) addressed the yet
different ways patients refused or were unable to take in new experience.
Sullivan's concepts of anxiety, selective inattention, and the "self-system" are
the core of his approach to understanding the perceptual level of action in
addition to the muscular level. Sullivan thought that children experiencing
anxiety when a parent felt anxious about or disapproving of some behavior,
learn to avoid the anxiety by avoiding the behavior that goes with it. This is not
a simple, behavioristic view. Sullivan's (1953) "self system" evolved to control
awareness through dissociation, by restricting perception to those areas of experience that protect from anxiety (pp. 19–22). Sullivan (1954a) explained how
the self-system affected the interview situation:

> [Y]ou must realize that whenever you are dealing with a stranger,
> both you and the stranger are very seriously concerned with matters
> of appraisal, of esteem, respect, deference, prestige, and so on, and

that all of these are manifestations of the self-system. . . . This means that all through the development of the interview situation, however prolonged, the interviewee is showing efforts to avoid, minimize, and conceal signs of his anxiety from the interviewer and from "himself"—that is, in a certain locution, keeping himself from *knowing* he is anxious. . . . People conceal their anxiety from themselves and others by the promptness with which they do something about it [pp. 130–131].

Also, Sullivan's (1954b) descriptions of "signs" and "symptoms" of mental disorder may be seen as descriptions of various kinds of patients' actions to avoid the perception of anxiety and what might be stirring it. For example, he wrote, "apathy . . . is a way used to survive defeat without material damage" (p. 174). Sullivan noted that the analyst's efforts to get to something useful will be thwarted because "the effort of the apathetic person is directed toward simply getting done with things" (p. 174). Similarly, states of sadness or depression, elation, ecstatic absorption, overdramatic extravagance, hesitancy or indecisiveness, tenseness, gross anxiety, psychopathic fluency, and fatigue are described in terms of the way they structure a dialogue and, simultaneously, awareness. These constitute for him patterns that come from a normal repertoire of "human adaptive performance" (p. 184) but that may be used in areas for which they are not constructively adaptive. They are nonverbal behavior patterns that limit action and interactive possibility by restricting perception of alternative modes. Other body–mind attitudes and states, in Sullivan's view, can have such an impact: states of alertness (attentive or distracted), intelligence, responsiveness (understanding cooperation or obtuseness or deliberate obstruction). These are patterns of interaction affecting perception in particular.

At still another level, more like that described by Reich (1949), Sullivan (1954b) found these characteristics in interactive body attitudes (i.e., sustained, although not necessarily chronic organizations of body and mind), such as reserved, guarded, suspicious, hostile, contemptuous, supercilious, superior, conciliatory, deferential, or apologetically inferior (pp. 108–112). Sullivan did not "place" these attitudes in the body or link them with drive satisfaction, as did Reich , and he did not discuss how they are expressed behaviorally. Yet, indeed, they are carried and conveyed physically, nonverbally, and they are body attitudes that can be chronically sustained or passingly employed. He stressed their impact on perception and learning and their interactive significance, especially in the way these attitudes pull for "reciprocal emotion" (which touches on the dimension both Alexander and French, 1946, were sensitive to). Thus, patients' actions, for Sullivan, were understood to organize a level of body behavior that controls perception and action with another.

Sullivan stimulated patients' active searching for answers to questions relating to problems, rather than passive receptivity in relation to thought processes. And, because of his commitment to action as teacher, he also encouraged the formation of developmentally important transformative relationships outside the analytic dyad. For example, Sullivan (1954a) was struck by preadolescents' need for a "chum" or "buddy" (p. 372). He thought that if this had been absent in development its establishment during the course of a psychotherapy indicated positive growth. He found that, for a time after such a development, a patient's interest in the work with his analyst might diminish, but that after a while, "a favorably changed patient is again at work with the psychiatrist, tracking down the ramifications of the disability from which he is now recovering" (p. 372).

Chumship is an especially important step in the development of the ability to expand options and to think about one's experience, but not always achievable by people who arrive at preadolescence "strikingly marked with the malevolent transformation of personality" (p. 253). Many who are too defended against their need for tenderness cannot develop such friendships at all. Instead, relationships are marred by hostility and power struggles. Chumship and membership in a preadolescent group is especially important because it provides a late opportunity to undo malevolence, defined by Sullivan as the change of the need for tenderness into direct mischievousness or passive-aggressive attack that has resulted from parental neglect or abuse of the need for tenderness.

If we look more closely at what a chumship entails, it begins to seem very much like the continuing function of a good-enough mother (Winnicott, 1949b, 1956, 1963a; Bion 1962, 1967, 1970), who can absorb and identify with the child's anxious feelings without becoming overwhelmed. Its good effect is accomplished through the intensity of the relationship, the loving interest shown in the other (which is mutual), and the taking on of "each other's successes in the maintenance of prestige, status, and all the things which represent freedom from anxiety" (Sullivan, 1954a, p. 246). Through it, Sullivan said, the "self-system"—the ways in which a person prevents awareness of issues that create incapacitating anxiety—can become modified (p. 247) and loosen up to incorporate better ways of handling difficulties. It can modify a number of problematic adaptations through "useful experience in social assessment and social organization" (p. 257).

Bion's work was similarly grounded in understanding patients' actions in relation to their analysts, particularly actions that interfere directly with perception and understanding. Bion observed actions carried out on mental capacity and organization and not primarily on the body's muscular organization. These involve the use of "projective identification" and the use of the analyst as a "container" for unbearable experiences of the patient. For example, Bion (1967) wrote:

> When the patient strove to rid himself of fears of death which were felt to be too powerful for his personality to contain he split off his fears and put them into me, the idea apparently being that if they were allowed to repose there long enough they would undergo modification by my psyche and could then be safely reintrojected. On the occasion I have in mind the patient had felt . . . that I evacuated them so quickly that the feelings were not modified but had become more painful [p. 103].

Bion held that projective and containment experiences are expressed and experienced nonverbally in body and speech action often long before an analyst can verbalize "about" them. In the material just quoted, he was describing his work with a schizophrenic patient: the patient–analyst interaction at that point was characterized by the patient's desperate and violent "phantasies" of projective identification, which Bion thought were a reaction to his experience of the analyst as hostile and defensive (p. 104). Bion described how the patient indirectly and symbolically showed this hostility in the content of speech, in the actions of speech juxtaposing certain content shifts, and in movements of the body and affect expression. For example, for the first 20 minutes of a session, his patient made three isolated remarks that had "no significance" to Bion. The patient then made a remark about a girl who understood him, followed by a convulsive movement. Bion's intervention followed, at which point the patient commented about a "blue haze," interpreted by Bion to mean a destruction of the patient's good feelings about being understood. Of importance here is that this interaction took place in the arena of the patient's nonverbal and spoken acts attacking the analyst's and his own "mental" (internal) experience.

To explain this kind of phenomenon, Bion (1967) elaborated the importance of projective identification and containment in the mother–infant relationship and its continued necessity in relation to the analyst:

> I felt that the patient had experienced in infancy a mother who dutifully responded to the infant's emotional displays. The dutiful response had in it an element of impatient "I don't know what's the matter with the child." My deduction was that in order to understand what the child wanted the mother should have treated the infant's cry as more than a demand for her presence. From the infant's point of view she should have taken into her, and thus experienced, the fear that the child was dying. . . . An understanding mother is able to experience the feeling of dread, that this baby was striving to deal

with by projective identification, and yet retain a balanced outlook. This baby had had to deal with a mother who could not tolerate experiencing such feelings and reacted either by denying them ingress, or alternatively by becoming a prey to the anxiety which resulted from introjection of the infant's feelings [p. 104].

Plainly, Bion's conception of anxiety and its interactive communication is similar to Sullivan's view. Unlike Sullivan, however, Bion thought the "attacks on linking" could occur because of inborn characteristics, or primary aggression and envy, as well as in retaliation against the unreceptiveness of the mother to the projective identification of the infant. The infant destined to be psychotic, Bion thought, is "overwhelmed with hatred and envy of the mother's ability to retain a comfortable state of mind although experiencing the infant's feelings" (p. 105). That is, in just the reverse of Sullivan's (1954a) description of the *contagion of anxiety*, Bion (1967) described anxiety's *failure to be communicated to* the mother or her inability to accept empathically an extraordinarily intense need for such resonance.

Bion was most closely concerned with the patient's needed activity of projective identification and the analyst's reactions to it, which are observed in the enacted, verbal and nonverbal process between the analyst and the patient. Because Bion's patients were schizophrenic, their language expression was often not what we would usually expect within psychoanalytic discourse. The expressions included strong physical movement reactions along with the expressive stream of words.

Bion's (1967) noting such behavior connects with Klein's earlier work with children whose speech was also less developed than we expect of adult patients. In his effort to understand his patients' communication and their reactions to him, Bion, like Klein, incorporated even quite subtle movement behavior he observed.

Winnicott's position (1954, 1956, 1960a, 1969) that patients' action beyond talk is essential to cure is in agreement with aspects of both Sullivan's and Bion's work, but his view departs from both of theirs in certain ways. Like Sullivan, and unlike Bion, he stressed the importance of what actually happened between parents and children, rather than the impact of innate aggression, as a source of difficulties. And, like Bion's, his idea of what happened incorporated aspects of experience that Sullivan regarded as irrelevant or excessively imaginary: his view derived from concerns about internal object relations and psyche–soma connection. Winnicott emphasized the patient's action in regression within the analysis as curative. He believed that patients' behaving in some ways like infants was crucial in some cases, even for persons who functioned, from an external perspective, quite well as adults.

For example, he described the case of a young, high-functioning woman who reacted to analysis by becoming extremely dependent, at first in a hidden way, despite her appearance of self-reliance before she began. This development occurred shortly before there was to be a lengthy summer break. She had a dream of a tortoise whose shell had softened, and she killed the tortoise to save it from unbearable pain. Winnicott (1963a) found that she was becoming "ill . . . in an obscure way" (p. 249). And he felt it urgent that she be able to "feel a connection between her physical reaction and [his] going away." She enacted a traumatic episode of infancy:

> It was in one language as if I were holding her and then became pre-occupied with some other matter so that she felt *annihilated*. . . . In her healthy self and body, with all her strong urge to live, she has carried all her life the memory of having at some time had a total urge to die; now the physical illness came as a localization in a bodily organ of this total urge to die [p. 250].

The difference both from what Bion had developed and what Sullivan was working with from a different perspective is Winnicott's engagement with the patient's body in an explicit way. For Sullivan, the body was not a central concern. For Bion, the patient's body involvement was a kind of representation, another language. For Winnicott, it took a more central place as physiological body in itself and in its direct connection to mind.

Winnicott went on to say that the patient was able to make use of his interpretation to become physically healthy and to let him go. "The amazing thing is that an interpretation can bring about a change [physical], and one can only assume that understanding in a deep way and interpreting at the right moment is a form of reliable [physical] adaptation" (p. 250). He said that later in the analysis with her, verbal interpretation would not be enough or would not be needed. The curative aspects had to do with Winnicott's understanding of problems stemming from early mishandling of the infant's body–self needs, which integrate social and physical/physiological aspects. Such early deficits, he believed, could not simply be understood and verbally interpreted but must be rectified through interaction with the analyst and involve relinquishing the need to understand and mediate behavior through language.

There are parallels in what Alexander and Winnicott said about patients' action and the theory of cure. Winnicott's (1960c, 1963a) holding and management and Alexander and French's (1946) view of the "corrective emotional experience" both stress the curative element of present interaction, but each developed a mode with a significantly different "feel." The two focused on different developmental eras, kinds of issues, and different layers of nonverbal behavior and action. Alexander stressed current experience between patient and analyst as reparative of inappropriate action patterns stemming from parental behavior patterns that were overindulgent, or overcritical, or restrictive. These problematic patterns derive largely from youth rather than early childhood or infancy.

Winnicott, in contrast, placed emphasis on patients' reenactment of the very earliest period of life and on their own rather than the analyst's activity. But also Winnicott's idea of "action" here emphasized "being" more than "doing." Patients, in Winnicott's view, had to be allowed to reach a state in which thinking and being were not separate. The idea that such a state is reparative rests on an implicit conception of thinking as having occurred at first in a pathological way, as "doing," implying the exercise of preconscious control, to compensate for environmental failure. Thinking can later also become "being," but only when the rupture, instead of differentiation between psyche and soma, is mended through the adaptation provided by the holding environment—the analyst's action.

In summary, technical recommendations in relation to patients' activity vary according to the analyst's view of what the patients needed as understood through their actions: for Freud (1923), to bring the body-based mental experience, unconscious activity in fantasy, acting out, and gestural behavior into language; for Reich (1949), to make conscious and release the rigid muscle activity that inhibits new behavior, learning, and change; for Alexander and French (1946), to learn new interactive rules of play both with the analyst, in relation to an experience that the analyst provides, and through examination of relations outside; for Ferenczi (1919, 1925), to enhance memory of significant events and processes through action within the analysis with the analyst; for Sullivan (1953, 1954a), to "learn through doing" outside analysis, understanding through verbalization within the analysis what and how to change; for Winnicott (1949a, b), to heal a split between psyche and soma through the direct experience of being with the analyst in primitive states of psyche–soma; for Bion (1962), to learn through remobilizing the psychic growth-producing capacity of projective identification in the patient and containment in the analyst.

Each of these theories of cure through patient activity draws on different patient behaviors—none is a synthesis of the others. Though there are some overlapping observations, these theorists focus attention on different kinds of patient activity. Each theorist also developed views about the corresponding appropriate activity of the analyst.

CHAPTER 7

Interaction
The Analyst's Action

≫≍

The theories of body–mind and thought, as well as of interactive need/ deficit I have just described in terms of patient action, also prescribe particular kinds of actions that the analyst should take. Freud's (1912b) original idea was that the patient needed only to allow what was repressed (and already "inside") to become expressed verbally and reorganized in thought. Different behavior was to *follow* from such internal rearrangement. In that case, it made perfect sense that an analyst's action, beyond listening with "evenly hovering attention" and interpretation, would be only an occasionally necessary "concession" to the patient's momentary lapse of faith in the process.

Subsequent theorists have recommended a wider repertoire of analyst activity derived from various theories of body–mind functioning and different views of what patients do, suffer, and need. As we saw in the last chapter, some analysts focus on patients' obstructive behaviors or on patients' inability or unwillingness to free associate. Others notice the absence of necessary, actual interactive experience. Yet others note activity that fosters remembering through enacting experiences that, in some cases, cannot find direct expression in language. Still others attend to the patients' recognition of the analyst as a "real" figure beyond the transference.

Understanding what ails a patient, interpretation of the patient's behavior, and the analyst's response to the patient together constitute a choreography of behavior within the setting. Theory and action go together. For example, if one thinks a patient cannot or will not free associate, a response is called for that differs from the response to a patient who is deficient in an area of interactive experience.

But before going on to describe the analyst's role in various choreographies, we need to frame a distinction that may not be obvious. Often when we speak of an analyst's activity, we have in mind an overarching conception of how analysis cures. That is, we tend to equate analyst activity with the therapeutic action of the analysis. Of course, the therapeutic action of the analysis finally takes place in the patient's responses to it—even if what takes place in the patient's response is derivative of what happens in the interpersonal interaction between patient and therapist. What the analyst does or does not do, in this context, makes its contribution to the therapeutic action of the analysis by creating new action (internal and external) of the patient. Illuminating how the analyst's action may or may not be linked with therapeutic action, however, is not the explicit focus here. What I wish to emphasize is not therapeutic action, though ultimately that is at stake, but more simply the kind of activity, qua activity, that the analyst undertakes. That is, this reading of analyst activity emphasizes the analyst's behavior, including nonverbal behavior, as another dimension of psychoanalysis: a primary level of stagesetting by analysts of varying persuasions as they set up the psychoanalytic encounter.

One point of this discussion is to underscore what everyone may sense but not know in a formal way. There is a repertoire that has been invented over time that includes patients' and analysts' behaviors and that allows room for theme, variation, and improvisation. A wide panoply of possible responses, ranging from prohibition (Freud, 1912b) and injunction (Ferenczi, 1926) all the way to physical holding (Winnicott, 1969), has been discussed in the analytic literature. Discussed, too, are the ways these kinds of actions may be tied to interpretation—or not—according to the model of mind and body an analyst employs. In what follows, then, my aim is to remind the reader of the diversity of approaches, some explicit, others tacit, to nonverbal behavior and what the analyst may or may not elect to do about nonverbal interaction.

On a historical note, many different ideas about how an analyst may or may not act arose in the context of an expansion of, and sometimes a revolt against, Freud's founding assumptions. Since this way of reading the historical record, having been covered in many texts devoted to the issue of therapeutic action, is familiar to many readers, I adopt it here as a convenience. But my point is not to reenter old debates or to arrive at an all-encompassing synthesis, which are the ordinary goals of a historical survey. Rather, I wish to show that there exists a wide-ranging and variegated tradition, which, taken as a whole, offers a broad assortment of useful ways of working. Right along, analysts have been considering the choreography of the patient–analyst interaction, without recognizing it as such.

Ferenczi was innovative technically in his efforts to deal with patients whose behavior did not fit the original model. Without mounting any direct challenge to the Freudian position, Ferenczi's "active technique" (1926) and his "child analysis within adult analysis" (1931) were his solutions to two different problems that he encountered in practice within the Freudian theoretical inside-to-outside frame.

One problem arose from patients who seemed unable to free associate or who abused the fundamental rule through trivializing their speech. The standard procedure was to interpret this behavior, or to educate and persuade the patient to cooperate (the caveats). Ferenczi (1919, 1924, 1926) found instead that asking direct questions and making suggestions, even offering frameworks for fantasizing, helped his resistant patients reach useful information.

He was careful to affirm the Freudian convention that such interventions were to be utilized as tactical maneuvers to get things back on the proper curative track of neutral verbal interpretation (Ferenczi, 1925). He linked the usefulness of this nonneutral behavior to one of Freud's (1915a) own guidelines, "renunciation," in the service of memory and awareness. Freud would tell patients to stop certain activities, understood as "sexual" pleasures, in order to foster fuller consciousness of underlying desires to emerge. But Ferenczi (1924, 1926), without challenging the metatheoretical rationale for this, employed the obverse and found it useful to direct patients to perform an activity purposefully in order to overcome inhibition and, simultaneously, to discover the reasons for the inhibition as the activity is performed. Thus, he was working with the idea of action as an enhancement of understanding and memory. He also directed patients toward or against certain thoughts and fantasies, in order to focus on central concerns that he thought they were avoiding. In summary, Ferenczi employed directive, nonneutral speech action of the analyst to stimulate activities and thoughts in the patient which, contrary to the central Freudian theory, he found could enhance awareness.

Another aspect of Ferenczi's (1931) activity in the nonverbal sphere is found as he encountered patients' spontaneous "acting out" of interactive segments from childhood. He found that, by joining in these spontaneous scenes of childhood, he could help patients gain access to thoughts, memories, and feelings that otherwise would not be accessible.

Ferenczi (1931) sometimes played a role in the enactment of interactions between the patient and a person in the patient's past. For example, acting the spontaneously assigned role of a patient's grandfather, he allowed the patient to sit on his lap (p. 129). Ferenczi's behavior violated taboos against gratification, nonneutrality, acting out, and bodily contact, which were believed to take the energy away from thoughts' movement toward consciousness (Freud, 1912a). But Ferenczi's experience suggested that, in some instances, action and interaction enhanced memory of pathogenic moments and resultant structures; whole-body action is itself a symbolic expression of as yet unthinkable thoughts that these patients did not have ready access to through verbal expression without mediating activity.

In a slightly different direction, emphasizing patients' deficits in experience rather than access to memory, Alexander and French (1946) considered nonneutral and nonverbally mediated interaction with the analyst, whether tactical or not, to be directly responsible for cure—"the corrective emotional experience." Unlike Ferenczi, Alexander and French did not simply follow a patient's spontaneous symbolizing action to indicate what his role might be. They took the lead in relation to their conception of a patient's deficits of experience—the need for something to go in, not just to come out—based on their understanding of the patient's parents' unhelpful attitudes. Their definition of analyst action included nonneutral speech acts, in which the analyst's attitude toward the patient's behavior is consciously designed to make a clear statement in verbal content and nonverbal, paralinguistic behavior that counters the problematic role "assigned" to the analyst by the patient's behavior.

Alexander and French prescribed that the analyst deliberately use physical positions and behaviors that were opposite to the ways the patient's parents had behaved. They believed that the analyst's "corrective" behavior this was necessary to allow the patient to develop appropriately and that such behavior could shorten analysis.[1]

Alexander and French's (1946) paradigm was the "case" of Jean Valjean, the criminal of Victor Hugo's Les Miserables, who was "cured" by the unconditional and unrelenting loving behavior of the bishop whom he had robbed. They quoted Hugo:

> He felt indistinctly that the priest's forgiveness was the most formidable assault by which he had yet been shaken; that his hardening would be permanent if he resisted this clemency; that if he yielded he must renounce that hatred with which the actions of other men had filled his soul during so many years, and which pleased him. . . . One thing which he did not suspect is certain, however, that he was no longer the same man; all was changed in him; and *it was no longer in his power to get rid of the fact that the bishop had spoken to him and taken his hand* [pp. 68–69; italics added].

Valjean's conversion took place within minutes. It depended, however, on Valjean's sudden recognition of his hatred, along with the bishop's kind-

---

[1] Alexander (1963) and Alexander and French (1946) experimented with many tactics to shorten analytic therapy, such as reducing the development of the "transference neurosis" through active dispelling of its manifestations.

ness. Alexander and French seemed to believe that such recognition could occur with regularity. This idea constitutes the core of the difference between their point of view and that of others (for example, Sullivan, 1954a; Klein, 1927a, 1946) who stress that, while many a patient may be a Valjean in relation to inner objects and people in their lives, the patients' behaviors toward them are not as obvious and may take them years to perceive. Nor are their partners in interaction, even their analysts, as perfectly good as the bishop seemed at that moment, further confusing the recognition of their own hatred. The salient aspect of "cure" seems to be the perception of difference and new possibility, which has in Valjean's case overridden the destruction of the good object, or the malevolent transformation.

Alexander did not elaborate on the subtle ways in which the changed behavior of the analyst would be curative. His ideas are based on a very straightforward learning theory. Thus, his point of view has come to seem oversimplistic and also overoptimistic about the possibility of the patient's perceiving the difference. And, he had a straightforward belief in analysts' ability to exercise control over their interactive behavior. Yet, despite the fact that his learning theory is too simple to stand for all, his "principle of flexibility" (Alexander and French, 1946, p. 25) is an important critique of psychoanalytic dogma. He based the idea on his understanding that having only one technique means we select the patient to fit the technique. He made a case for analysts' broadening technical options to include reeducation through new interaction. He showed, by adding a range of proposed options for interaction, that psychoanalytic technical requirements not only are methods to get out of the way of the patient's thought but also stimulate reactions. He wrote of a case that he had supervised in which the female analyst's adhering to the strict guidelines of psychoanalytic treatment was in active opposition to the patient's expectation that she would behave as his overly indulgent and protective mother had. Through this opposition the analyst brought to the patient's attention his sense of inappropriate entitlement (Alexander and French, 1946, p. 321). He justifiably challenged the idea that standard technique is "neutral" and said instead that everything the analyst does is a correct or incorrect emotional experience and that technique should be judged on this basis.

The positions that Alexander and Ferenczi took were seen as too extreme and for many years were cut off from mainstream psychoanalytic theorizing. They did not adequately challenge the theoretical rationales that held the technical options in place. But even Sullivan (1953), working within his very different theoretical perspective, maintained a clear distance from direct engagement with the patient's pulls for connection. His distance operated through his emphasis on examination of relationships outside the analysis.

Sullivan developed his lines of thinking in a way that was sharply distinct from the lines developed in the Freudian track, so there was not much cross-fertilization. Although Sullivan (1953, 1954a) firmly believed that learning was central to cure, there is no explicit theoretical tie between his views and Alexander and French's (1946) or Ferenczi's (1919, 1926). Sullivan independently developed rationales for distinctive analyst activities—some of which paralleled and some which challenged Ferenczi and Alexander. First of all, there was no explicit place in his treatment for reliving or redoing experience, but only for learning new and better modes of action and interaction, seen as integrated nonverbally and verbally. Yet, by extrapolation, Sullivan's theory of the interpersonal nature of anxiety allows that the patient's interactive experience of the analyst's nonverbally expressed lack of anxiety—alternatively of the analyst's appropriately placed anxiety—is curative in Alexander's sense, that is, "corrective." Good management of anxiety, and Sullivan's (1954b) caveat about patients'needs for an "impossibly secure" (p. 87) relationship with the analyst are in fact parts of a corrective experience but are not seen as such. For Sullivan, they remained in the realm of tactical expedients, more or less as such actions once had tactical value for Freud and Ferenczi within a different theory of the "curative."

Nevertheless, Sullivan (1954b) elaborated in rich detail his awareness and use of nonverbal elements of the type that structured interactions in his communications with patients. In his use of action Sullivan intended, like Ferenczi (1919, 1926), in his more verbally mediated "active technique" to direct the dialogue to useful material. Sullivan (1954b) did not hesitate, for example, to interrupt patients or indicate, through grunts, noises, or shifts of posture, vague disapproval of a trend in a patient's behavior.

> In the *accentuated* or *accented transition* you do not use one of these polite ways of moving yourself and the patient hand in hand from one topic to another, but you rustle your feathers. . . . In my case I usually begin to growl, rather like a ball bearing with some sand in it, just to indicate that something is about to happen. I want to drop what is going on, emphatically; not in such a way that it is forgotten forever, but with such emphasis as to disturb the set, as the old experimental psychologists might call it. I want that which has been discussed not to influence that which is now to be discussed. Suppose the person has just been showing me what an unutterably lovely soul he has. I will then sort of growl a bit as a preliminary to saying something like, "With what sort of person do you find yourself really hateful?" [p. 45].

Sullivan stressed that this directive process was necessary to get past a patient's unrelenting verbal obfuscation, and to reach useful information.

He worked in this way to manage patients' anxiety, the task he regarded as the analyst's central function. He managed that anxiety, rather than only interpreted it, his goal being the discovery of new ways of behaving, *not* necessarily a better understanding of the old ways.

Sullivan also had a different idea about the importance of a patient's feelings about the analyst. He both removed himself as the object of the patient's attention and worked toward positive change through his use of behaviors that shifted the patient into new and better "operations." He did not believe that he had to keep in mind "inner" and "outer" manifestations of difficulties; rather, he stressed watching what happened. This shift of emphasis minimized his overtly corrective role because the illusory distinctions between language/thought and action/body were still subtly in place. While he was thinking about, and directing a patient to think about, the patient's everyday interpersonal relations, he was operating (tactically) on the patient's capacity to perceive more widely: what had happened, what could have happened differently, what might happen. Thereby, he was subtly moving the patient to connect imaginatively with new possibilities. In his view the "cure" comes from the patient's expanded ability to see things differently and to deal with interpersonal relations in new ways.

Perhaps because of his intense scrutiny of the visible manifestations of the self and self-system, Sullivan also conveyed confidence in the analyst's ability to be alert to, and aware of, what the patient needs to think about and do that parallels Alexander's certainty that he could construct the appropriate corrective experience. Sullivan (1954b) spoke about the need to be alert to "covert" processes (p. 54), and to think in terms of what the patient was trying to do "with and to" the analyst (p. 55). He was also optimistic about the analyst's ability to be in control of his own behavior through self-observation of behaviors that might hamper the interview. He believed that it was a straightforward process to move from understanding what was obstructive to ceasing to do it (p. 65). This self-control applied equally to the therapist and the patient. There is a symmetry between Sullivan's version of the role of learning in human development, his view of the analyst's role in promoting the patient's learning through doing, and his view of the analyst's ability to watch and to learn from what happens.

Yet another position on analyst action was developed by Klein (1927b, 1946). She did not aim to change the basic classical activity of verbal interpretation. She did, however, shift the area under investigation (as had Reich, 1949). As we saw in the chapter on patient action, Klein advocated concentration not on word content alone, but on all a patient's verbal and nonverbal behaviors in relation both to the analyst's interventions and to personal processes of thought, fantasy and perception. The new analyst activity that arose in this context had to do with the need to use countertransferential experience more consciously as partial evidence for what the patient was doing with and to the communications of analyst, since much of what was being understood was nonverbally presented.

Working through conceptions of the importance of drive, life and death instincts, and states of mind she thought were connected to drive development, Klein regarded not *what* happened to them, but patients' *reactions* to what happened, as most central in their difficulties. Kleinians address this aspect of each patient as it appears in the transference. In contemporary Kleinian thinking, the concept of transference is an expanded one, including not just repetitions of unresolved conflicts with oedipal figures, or objects of primary envy or love in the past, but also current, immediate expression of all the patient's ways of functioning including phantasy, impulse, and defense (Joseph, 1985). Contemporary thinking includes looking for a patient's active destructiveness or remorse at supposed destructiveness toward the analyst's interventions and toward their own perceptions and thoughts. The analyst may experience the patient's transference in anything said or done in the session: a reference to a wrong turn taken on the way, or a natural disaster may signal an inner wrong turn or catastrophe. How such references are to be understood rests on the analyst's experience of the patient at that moment. The subtle difference required, then, in the analyst's actions is the ability to *respond* in a full way to the patient's behaviors without non-reflective action. The analyst is required to register her or his reactions and make use of them to think about what is going on for the patient. The point is to understand fully each patient by making emotional contact and so to examine carefully how the patient gets in the way of this aim.[2]

---

[2]Contemporary Kleinians prize, and have devised a special way to develop, the analyst's ability to observe many levels of behavior. These include body-level phenomena (symptoms, postures), interactive to and fro, and subtle shifts of emotion and mental action. This method of training is the Infant Observation Seminar, a unique part of training at the Tavistock, the British Institute of Psychoanalysis and other psychoanalytic psychotherapy training institutions. Members of the Infant Observation Seminar visit a child and caregivers at home from birth to two years, one hour each week, and write out highly detailed descriptions of what happened—everything said, done, and shown. To be noted, of course, is that for roughly the first year and a half, the infant is a nonverbal, though highly active, participant. The observer's reactions—emotional and interactive behaviors—are also closely attended. From this base, a detailed and deep understanding of the baby's and the family's emotional life can be drawn. Interpretations of the detailed observations are based on ideas about the innate and context-generated experiences of the infant that must be well handled by the parents and caregivers if the infant is to be psychologically sound. In addition,

Klein's (1927b, 1946) very active interpretive approach was based on her particular view of what was "wrong." Klein believed that hate and love are innate and primary, and determined by internal factors, not just by reactions to environmental failures or impingement. She addressed the child's environment in a particular way, quite different from the way in which it had been addressed by Freud, Alexander, Deutsch, Reich, or Sullivan. She took note of the damaging effects of harsh treatment of children but saw in these, not the deprivation of the love, positive regard, and attunement essential for psychological development (which is what Alexander, Ferenczi, Winnicott, and Kohut saw), but, rather saw how such treatment stimulated the child's own hatred, causing sadistic fixations, excessive envy and guilt. She thought these negative feelings remained as barriers to receiving and accepting new and better experience inside and outside the family. It was these barriers she assertively addressed in treatment, not the lack of specific kinds of interaction or love shown the child.

Klein (1946) also thought that children could be born with particular problems she conceived of as excessive hatred or envy. She thought of parents as mitigating influences, only correcting or not being able to correct problems in the child's individual struggle with intense inner currents as she or he crossed developmentally from the paranoid/schizoid to the depressive position. Thus, a rationale was created for a different kind of analyst's action: a particular kind of focus of attention, and frequent interpretation of verbal and nonverbal behavior showing the patient's reactions to the work of the analyst and the hidden content of the patient's thoughts and feelings.

Klein's point of view on analyst activity was disputed by Anna Freud (1926–1927), who maintained that the analyst should wait for confirming language to develop before giving interpretations. She argued for a "preparation for analysis" and the establishment of positive rapport, transference neurosis being thought impossible in young children. Miss Freud thought that much more might be verbalized even by small children once the proper induction had been accomplished. Working along the lines of her father's recognition of the need for caveats, here, in terms of appeals to the ego,

---

students have the opportunity to experience much of what they will need as analysts before they are required to act. Indeed, the demand that they may only observe, not act, for two years, greatly enhances their abilities to notice their countertransference reactions, their identifications with baby, siblings, mother, or father, and the family's reaction to observation—the transference. These responses can be easily obscured by the anxiety to perform well as a therapist. This gives the therapists-to-be well-honed skill in reading themselves and the other to use in relation to their activity as analysts later (Miller et al., 1989).

Miss Freud thought that induction might require behavior beyond the ordinary analytic posture. She acknowledged some of these as tactics geared to gain the child's interest in or attachment to the analyst, to invoke the patient's "love." She gave three examples: (1) she promised cure to an obsessional little girl in order to gain her interest; (2) she offered herself as an ally in a child's struggle against her parents; (3) she exaggerated a symptom's severity in order to engage a child. She was working with the idea that children will fulfill obligations and, indeed, learn new socialized behavior only from those whom they love and respect. She did not make a strong separation between analysis and education, for she thought that children often learned for the first time in analysis which "infantile sexual impulses" (p. 60) are to be permitted and how, and which are not.

The analyst's role was to be that of beloved "ego ideal." To accomplish this, the analyst had to be regarded as a higher authority than parents in matters of the child's difficulties. Here again was a restatement of Freud's original caveat that the patient be granted enough gratification to permit the process of understanding to occur.

All the analyst actions explored so far are based on a supposition that the analyst can straightforwardly and correctly assess what is needed. This supposition continued in mainstream developments in Freudian circles that emphasized the "real" relationship between patient and analyst, as distinct from that which developed solely as transference distortion, bringing the past into the present. Greenson and Loewald were important figures in this development.

Loewald's (1960, 1986) position was that it is the actual relationship between patient and analyst that cures the patient, as much as the insight obtained from the content of the verbally expressed understanding of the patient's problems. Loewald's difference from Alexander's corrective emotional experience is that he did not advance ideas for change of technique or shift of role but, rather, stressed an expanded conception of what actually happens interactively (verbally and nonverbally) in the ordinary course of the analytic work and how the ordinary interactive processes relate to cure. He defined the curative in the relationship in terms of its organizing and regulating functions, its consistency and its positive regard, and the role of the patient's internalization of the analyst's function of understanding. Thus, he was recognizing the action within the interpretive behavior of the analyst and the importance of both the content of the interpretation and the interactive process between patient and analyst.

Greenson (1967, 1971) developed the concept of the "working alliance." This concept captured the idea of the patient's collaboration with the analyst apart from the transference distortions that might work against such collaboration. In Greenson's view, the analyst must behave in certain ways in order to establish and foster such a development. The analyst's willingness to explain the analytic procedures, as well as warmth, compassion, and responsiveness, are seen as central to the establishment of the working alliance. At the same time, Greenson thought that the working alliance arose at the moment of the first transference interpretation. In a more contemporary understanding, the moment of interpretation has to do with the analyst's being able to establish a difference between two possibilities: the patient's habitual conception of the other in the analyst and another interpretation of the analyst's behavior that Greenson called "real."

Greenson (1971) noted an additional aspect of the "real relationship," the fact that a patient could accurately recognize characteristics of the analyst and that these characteristics had an interpersonal impact. For example, one of his patient's shared his perception that Greenson was long-winded. Greenson recommended that this kind of awareness be simply acknowledged and its significance to the patient explored, rather than only funneled through a chain of presumed fantasy operations at a distance from the present.

It was in Winnicott (1955, 1958, 1960a, b, 1962, 1963a, b) and late Kohut (1971, 1977) that the "corrective" end of the continuum of thinking about of analyst action re-emerged explicitly, challenging accepted theory. These positions did not fundamentally alter conceptions of basic analyst action, but softened hard edges of neutrality and emotional distance. Previous efforts to shape the analytic method to special needs of patients explicitly or implicitly maintained the separateness of verbal and nonverbal behavior. In contrast, Winnicott intuited and Kohut stumbled upon the clinical significance of the intrinsic interconnectedness of words and actions. Winnicott (1955, 1960a, b, 1963a, b) and Kohut (1971, 1977) both addressed the question of how to help certain patients whose problems cannot be brought into the analysis without a significant shift in the analyst's point of view and behavior. Their positions started at a point similar to Sullivan's (1954b) view that some patients need an "impossibly secure relationship" (p. 87) with the analyst, but they go beyond Sullivan's tendency to regard this need as incidental to the more important one of learning how to relate to others beyond the analyst. Both Winnicott and Kohut can be seen as attempting to define in different ways "impossibly secure relationships," with the understanding that these were at least partially curative in themselves and certainly necessary to cure.

According to Winnicott (1954, 1958, 1960a), for some patients, largely nonverbal behavior with the analyst must come before the analyst can usefully initiate any talking "about." Coming into play here is the area of uncertainty that exists between the patient's and the analyst's ability to act and to know. Knowing, in the sense of being able to articulate an experience in the logical space of language, is dependent on one's ability to reflect on something that has occurred or is occurring in experience and that has been or can be differentiated from other experiences. Before that differentiation can happen, the analyst must sometimes provide what has been absent for the patient, the very possibility of meaningful discourse. In some cases, a reconnection to experiencing without interruption by thought or words must be instituted since verbal capacity developed discordantly with experiencing. Then, too, a differentiation of past experiences from present experience must be made palpable before it becomes thinkable. Necessary verbalizations in this context are felt, ideally, as part of *physical* attunement to the patient's dissociated dependent aspects.

Winnicott's (1949b) conception of what the analyst's activity should be came out of finding that the shifts in his own behavior beyond interpretation were crucial to the possibility of understanding and that the analyst delivered something behaviorally, physically, that translated, by ways of the body–mind connections of "phantasy" into something "mental." His recommendation for analyst activity unified his views on the connections between the body, nonverbal behavior, and thought and with the problem of coping with the patient's needs or demands for direct engagement. He took from Klein's (1946) extension of Freud's instinct theory the idea that the infant has an innate capacity for "phantasy," which is not resorted to only as a reaction to frustration, as Freud had suggested (1911), but was, as Klein believed, the basis for thinking (Isaacs, 1948). Within this theory of phantasy is the idea that an infant has innate, unconscious "knowledge" of objects of desire, such as the breast, mother, penis, womb, intercourse, birth, babies, which is based on instinctual action patterns that "imply" an object. The infant is thought to "seek" the breast, of which it has a set of expectations based on implied reciprocals to his or her own impulses. Because of such connections, not everything has to be or can be delivered verbally. Winnicott did not define the "something" delivered by behavior precisely, but located it in the analyst's presence and responsivity of body–mind.

Winnicott (1971) formulated an imaginary space for patient's meeting with the analyst's receptive presence of body–mind in his conception of "play." A transference, in its traditional definition, involves the capacity to reflect, to view experience as real or not real. Patients who cannot entertain the "unreality" of their experience, who cannot "play," are to be addressed at the level of this "major symptom" (p. 55).

The ability to play is a precursor to the ability to be "alone in the presence of someone" (pp. 55–56), which is the traditional transference state, and this state coincides with the ability to allow and enjoy mutual play, the overlap of the "play areas" of two people. To cure the "major symptom" of the inability to play, a person needs "a new experience in a specialized setting. . . .The experience is one of a non-purposive state, as one might say a sort of ticking over of the unintegrated personality [of] formlessness" (p. 64). In this context, one of Winnicott's emendations of the analyst's activity was the prescription of *inaction*, which is not the same as neutrality, nor is it really nonactive. He had in mind an analyst whose very engaged physical presence or state of being could be felt by the patient. Such an ineffable connection could allow the patient space and time in which to be formless and out of which to begin "a creative reaching-out" (p. 65). But this state was not something that the patient insisted on except symptomatically; rather it was an achievement of the analysis to reach an understanding of this need. The analyst needed to provide room for this state, the missing experience out of which the patient could begin to live authentically. It is for Winnicott fundamental to genuine communication.

Kohut's (1971) version of the "impossibly secure relationship" (Sullivan, 1954b, p. 87) pointed to still another kind of analyst action. In his view, interactive experience between analyst and patient can be thoroughly verbally mediated, but he implied that the analyst must go beyond the prescribed neutral, merely reactive, objective stance. His version of analyst action is tied to his concept of the process and function of "empathy." Kohut thought of experiences of self and other as revolving around the basic need for acceptance and idealization. He thought that the patient's deficits in this area, responsible for self-pathology, were reachable through the analyst's empathy, expressed in verbal resonance with the patient's experience. Yet there is a fundamental problem for psychoanalytic theory revolving around action and understanding brought most clearly forward in Kohut's concept of empathy. At times, it has been argued that it is "simply" a way of perceiving the patient and at other times it is maintained that it involves more—a kind of sympathetic behavioral resonating, outside the bounds of neutrality.

Kohut (1977) maintained that all developing human beings have unfolding intrinsic narcissistic needs that must be met by parental adaptation to them. He posited a necessary kind of relatedness between child and parents, aspects of which could be accessed within the psychoanalytic situation if the analyst were able and willing to reflect verbally the patient's own experience of needs in growing up and in the current analytic situation. He (1971, 1977) conceived of the patient as forming a particular kind of "selfobject transference," be it "idealizing, mirroring or twinship," whose features were originally recognized through the analyst's inevitable, but accidental, failure to complete the selfobject expectations generated by dependency in the analytic situation.

Kohut's view of empathy was thought to challenge the classical technical position. The issue his work raised is a subtle one: empathy is gratifying and thus not neutral. Empathy is directly gratifying of ego needs insofar as it is thought to be wrapped into a necessary layer of parental behavior that was missing in crucial ways and is now being "given" by the analyst. That is, empathy is a necessary ingredient in the processes of "understanding" that are inherent in both child rearing and cure. Thus Kohut's recommendations stirred up theoretical conceptions of verbal understanding or interpretation and introduced a different view that placed empathic understanding, conveyed verbally and otherwise, at the center of development itself. Understanding itself became a gratifying, "acted" not just verbally conveyed, interaction. (Instead we can say too that verbalization is also action.)

Although Kohut's (1977) recommendations were not defined within a "body" frame (indeed, he dropped the drive theoretical framework with which he had begun (1971)), he alluded to subtle nonverbal dimensions of relatedness essential to patient growth. The theory is ambiguous on this issue, which is related to neutrality. At first, Kohut (1971), rather like Fairbairn (1941, 1951), maintained that no change in analyst behavior was necessary but only a shift in what was reflected to the patient. That is, instead of interpreting along drive, oedipal, or ego-psychological lines, which underscore maturation (and contain an implicit critique of immaturity), the analyst needed to hear, not interpret reductively, the patient's experience. Nevertheless, Kohut hinted that, for this to be accomplished, some significant but hard to define shift in the analyst's state and attitude was necessary.[3] He (1977) said that, in order to recognize "the specific form of psychopathology of the narcissistic personality disorders," the analyst had to follow "the principle of analytic neutrality" (p. 250). But

> I do not attempt to approach a zero-line of activity. . . . The analyst's human warmth, for example, is not just an adventitious accompaniment of his essential activity—to give interpretations and constructions— . . . it is an expression of the fact that the continuous participation of the depth of the analyst's psyche is a *sine qua non* for the maintenance of the analytic process [p. 251].

Winnicott and Kohut struggled with a problem that was an artifact of the conventional split between verbal and nonverbal behavior. While they found ways around it clinically they were not able to escape it theoretically because they retained the conviction that normative practice was verbal

---

[3]Research on nonverbal behavior described in Part III indicates that this is certainly true, and further, that the analyst, like the patient, always assumes body attitudes that attend their conscious and unconscious intentions.

even though nonverbal behavior might be useful in specific instances or in circumscribed ways. The theoretical impasse is an important one because it leaves us without a framework for recognizing the physicality of verbal behavior and its impact in all verbal exchanges as well as in nonverbal interactions. Without reconceiving the relationship of verbal and nonverbal behavior as interwoven, it remains easy to imagine, falsely, that verbal interactions are complete in themselves.

The Widening Scope of Analyst Activity

The ideas so far explored about appropriate analyst activity beyond neutral verbal interpretation rest either on conceptions of expedience aimed at enhancing the possibilities of verbalization or on a sense that particular kinds of action are straightforwardly necessary to cure because some essential experience is too limited for reflection and verbalization "about" to be possible or helpful. As I have shown, these dimensions of nonverbal behavior have been explored implicitly and explicitly in psychoanalytic history. The discussion around these categorizations of analyst activity has gone on alongside struggles to change the theoretical explanations of pathology and cure. Fairbairn (1941, 1951), Sullivan (1953, 1954a, b), and early Kohut (1971) tried to deal with limitations in the practice of therapy by changing only their conceptions of what went wrong in a patient's development and by limited, if any, changes in analyst behavior beyond verbalizing.

Nevertheless, each shift of conceptualization of a patient's problem also necessarily entailed subtle and obvious behavioral changes in the analyst's activity. These changes were chiefly conceptualized along three main lines: (1) fostering the "real" relationship (Loewald, 1960, 1980, 1986; Greenson, 1967, 1971); (2) making behavioral shifts of an explicit but ambiguous kind (Kohut's 1971, 1977 empathy; Winnicott's 1954, 1971 nonintervention and "holding"); and (3) making definite behavioral interventions geared to getting to the right information (Sullivan's, 1954b, directed inquiry), and toward containing actions of large-scale (such as Winnicott's, 1954, 1962, 1963a) "management."

Recent views, for example, Gedo (1988, 1994) extending Kohut's thinking, and Lindon (1994) bringing Winnicott's idea of provision into the classical Freudian position, struggle to delineate the correct balance between analyst behaviors and the needs of their patients. This is a task they believe can be engaged, as it were, from the outside in. That is, they see themselves as making assessments of patient needs and responding accordingly.

In contrast, a development can be found within a quite varied group of interpersonal, Freudian, and Kleinian analysts who emphasize the hermeneutic dimension of practice. In this enterprise, the understanding of understanding, analyst action may be seen as always both shaping and responding to patient behavior and vice versa and as being only partly available to reflection at any given moment.

Gedo and Lindon explicitly argue that the nonverbal behaviors of the analyst should be designed and deployed to cope with unusual patient needs and their special inability to engage the classical approach. But they implicitly maintain the separateness of verbal and nonverbal behavior as they devise rationales for deviating from the classical approach in carefully defined cases.

Gedo (1979, 1988, 1994; Gedo and Goldberg, 1973) extending Kohut's thinking, made more explicit the kinds of departures from neutrality that he believes can and should be made because of developmental deficit requirements of the patient. He constructed a schema of appropriate types of intervention in relation to the developmental level of the patient at any particular moment. He included in it the tripartite and topographic models of the mind as well as models for the development of self (Gedo and Goldberg, 1973). That is, his view is that development is a step-by-step process with abrupt and short-lived, or prolonged, regressions and progressions on the road to maturity. According to Gedo, the analyst's repertoire should include "neutrality," but he sees this stance, or role, as one of many the analyst may need to play to address specifically the patient's level of development. He extends Alexander's (1963) project, "corrective emotional experience, " but attempts to avoid its pitfalls by adhering to a developmental biological model to which he tries to give clear differentiation and theoretical grounding.

Using his revised understanding of development as a guide, Gedo (1979, 1994) defines the goal of psychoanalysis as the completion of an incompleted developmental process. As such, it requires interventions "beyond interpretation." The analyst must function at times as an auxiliary self in order to help the patient learn what has not been learned. He gives examples of a range of his interventions: (1) speaking a phrase in French, "the mother tongue" (Gedo, 1994, p. 114) to signal, without excessive intellectual baggage, the connection of what the patient is saying with his experiences of his French-speaking mother; (2) hiding his anxiety in a very classically neutral response, to a patient's demand for a sexual involvement (p. 117); (3) making an angry outburst in response to a patient's obstruction of his every attempt to provide a reality check on the patient's paranoia (p. 121). In the last type of intervention, he counts on the patient's ability, which is not always available, to understand his intervention as partly his authentic response and partly a theatrical performance (p. 122), so that the analytic frame does not crumble into merely engagement and action without reflection. He emphasizes the needed space for reflection, as in Winnicott's (1974) theory of "play" but also notes that there are patients for whom "play" is not possible.

In Lindon's definition of "optimal provision" to meet patient need, he distinguishes need from desire and further narrows the scope of "need" to "a mobilized developmental longing" (p. 552). His position is in contrast to that of others who maintain a uniformly classical, neutral stance. These analysts include those working explicitly with nonverbal behavior in the Deutsch (1947) tradition, and maintaining the classical technique, for example, McLaughlin (1992) and Busch (1995). They emphasize the maintenance of analytic distance. For them, nonverbal behavior is of a symbolic kind that they believe can be usefully integrated within the classical analytic frame, adding material but making no demands for additional analyst action. The two positions are looking at two different sets of nonverbal behavior. Lindon is responding to patients who need extraordinary accommodation by the analyst. These provisions include, for example, seven days per week contact in a hospital, face-to-face sessions two to three times per day, longer sessions, food when hunger disrupts the patient's ability to think. He asserts that the purpose of "optimal provision" is "not to by-pass the patient's organizing principles, but to establish a context in which they can be investigated, illuminated, and transformed" (p. 560). He stresses that attunements are not therapeutically central, but tactical, and he warns against "subverting" analysis into becoming mere "provision" (p. 579).

Gedo and Lindon, like Alexander and Sullivan, make use of both the learning and the teaching dimensions of action, as well as the tactical dimension. They focus on the analyst's active, mostly consciously controlled manipulation of behavior to foster growth. They experience themselves as being in control of what occurs either immediately or soon after a lapse in awareness, and as able to monitor themselves, even while responding emotionally. In this, their work is strikingly different from that of those who frame their thinking as a hermeneutic stance.

This certainty that analysts can for the most part understand and control their behavior is in stark contrast to areas of theory being explored by some contemporary interpersonal, Freudian, and Kleinian thinkers. For example, from within the interpersonal school, Stern (1987, 1991) writes of the personal role of an analyst in formulating unformulated experience with a patient; Bromberg (1994) underscores the significance of an analyst's seeing and living with a patient's multiple selves. From a contemporary Kleinian point of view, Joseph (1989) writes about how a patient's living out his or her defensive system in the session and drawing the analyst into it, allows an analyst to note the minute shifts that need understanding. A Freudian, Spence (1982) challenges the idea that analysis "reconstructs" a patient's history; rather, analysis constructs it in line with the analyst's theories. And Schafer (1983), too, has defined the analyst's role as creating with the patient versions of experiences that are organized usefully. Although it is not always made focal by these different theorists, an important implication of their various conceptions is that an analyst will indeed be engaged in activity for some time without necessarily being either fully aware of or fully in control of it.

It is striking that these enlarged positions about analyst activity converge on questions of memory, perception, dissociation, and conception from generally opposite ends of the theoretical spectrum: interpersonal analysts from the point of view of the importance of the social field, and Kleinian and Freudian analysts, from the point of view of the importance of intrapsychic conflict and internal reactions to experience within a body-based field. Their convergence of focus is due to their parallel beliefs in the overarching significance of the interaction of patient and analyst in promoting and creating understanding. Where these positions differ on questions of certainty and the security of the analyst's point of view, the differences may stem from their origins in social theory or body theory, respectively; for there are long-standing affinities of thought that connect the idea of body with unchanging, hard fact, and the ideas of thought and social behavior with flux, freedom of construction, and imagination.

Such analysts as Levenson (1972, 1983), Gill (1983), and Ehrenberg (1992) believe that part of the analyst's activity should be to develop the patient's perception of the analyst as a central aspect of the dialogue. For example, Ehrenberg (1992) examines closely the shifts in relatedness of analyst and patient, with the view that the shifts must be acknowledged and not left to operate silently or to be interpreted only along historical lines (p. 34). She aims to guard against the dangers of mystification and also implicitly recognizes that understanding is not enough. She is concerned not with keeping analytic, neutral distance, but with understanding how the patient and the analyst are inevitably connected behaviorally. Her view is that both patient and analyst "act," and she calls "the intimate edge" at which the analyst and patient meet "a point of expanded self-discovery, at which one can become more 'intimate' with one's own experience through the evolving relationship with the other, and then more intimate with the other as one becomes more attuned to oneself . . . " (pp. 34–35). In this formulation, somewhat more weight is given to analytic engagement as a vehicle for experience leading to understanding rather than to repair, but with the implicit idea that understanding serves both as a vehicle for change and as provision in itself.

In general, within contemporary psychoanalysis, as it has been enlarged by the foregoing theorists, "coping" with patient's needs and the demands of the analyst and the analytic setting is accepted as a part of the central focus, rather than as a peripheral exception or caveat. Central concerns within this frame are the involvement of the analyst in creating as well as perceiving the transference and that countertransference must be present as the particular analyst's response to the particular patient; it is accepted further that there will inevitably be aspects of this responsivity that play both within and outside awareness. The degree and kind of acting played out by analyst and patient are understood to remain subtle and elusive more often than not. Clearly, powerful influences shaping the interactions of patient and analyst will also be expressed in their language—in their very choice of words (Spence, 1982).

Within this overall perspective, it is the analyst's greater capacity to repeatedly step at least somewhat outside the interactive engagement that allows things to progress as in a "bootstrap operation" (Levenson, 1972). This development occurs through the move to find a suitable perspective from which to examine and pose alternatives as well as to interact. Thus, the analyst's role is defined by her or his leadership in the activity of reflection. This role is analogous to the "real" relationship but stands it on its head (Sullivan, 1953, 1954b; Loewald, 1960; Greenson, 1971). In its early definition, the real relationship, thought to be distinguishable from the distortions of the patient, emerged as a clear space that was somehow uncomplicated, healthy, and growth enhancing. In the interactive view, the continuous pull into "acting out" or "in" is stressed, but not in opposition to "health." Health is thought to be a flexible and expanding view of differentiated options for behaving and interpreting, whereas problematic transferences and countertransferences are defined as a narrowed scope of possibilities overdetermined by the past experiences of both patient and analyst. The "reality" of the interaction is seen as a negotiable matter of joint definition, with each participant having a plausible view of the events. Such a shared definition means that the analyst lives in enduring uncertainty about the possibility of any easy differentiation between action (including both nonverbal and speech action) and verbalization (including thoughtfully mediated interpretation) or between coping and curing. The involvement of the analyst's particular view, shaped by theoretical position, history, state, and attitude is thought to be inevitable, not a matter of choice and not removable from the interpretive positions taken, which are as much influenced by the particular individual's character and state as is any "nonverbal act."

But the involvement of the analyst is then understood to be not just a necessary *evil*. It can't be avoided in fact, and also it is crucial in a pragmatic sense, for it is the only way one can have the full use of one's perceptual range. With regard to the ubiquitous characteristics of nonverbal behavior understanding necessarily takes place through involvement in interactive rhythmical attunement (see Part III). Neutrality, forced by and only conceptually possible within a theory-driven perspective, is itself one kind of involvement having a powerful effect on the patient's engagement, helpful at times, but, if held rigidly, likely to cause a stalemate. The analyst and patient *must* suffer unwittingly various engagements subtly drawn, as well as sometimes knowingly engage in "corrective emotional experiences" or various enactments that can be recognized by both participants as symbolic play. Certainty is acknowledged to be less secure, if not ultimately impossible. The actuality of engagement of the patient's and the analyst's activity is constituted in the very nature of what is brought up between the two, in the language chosen by each and in the newly produced action as well as the reproduced paradigmatic repetition of important interactive patterns. This state of affairs leads to a "never resting" position of continuing alertness for reactions to and shifts from what has gone on before in both the analyst and the patient.

Underlying many of the innovative perspectives just discussed is a new appreciation among analysts of the relevance of hermeneutics to the analytic endeavor. Hermeneutics seems to speak to the problematic of both analyst and patient necessarily being immersed in a mutually constructed frame of reference. One of the central theses of this book is that the study of nonverbal behavior can expand the means of definition indicated by the hermeneutic position, which is often seen as, and may in fact be, focused chiefly on language interacting with language. In the hermeneutic position, language is seen as part action/part reflection and subject to the same blindness as action. One of the originating polarities of psychoanalysis—action versus language—is thereby dispensed with (since language is action); but another polarity—body versus mind—maintains a shadow presence, through the absence of a broad and systematic inclusions of body behavior and experience in our theories of change.[4] We allow ourselves to "read" the body but not to include the physicality of expression in our theories of psychoanalytic practice.

We have seen that analysts do not escape to neutrality by talking, because the use of language and interpretation does not provide neutrality.

---

[4]Butler's (1993) *Bodies That Matter* is a response to critics of the hermeneutic position who ask the question, "What about the body?" She says that it is her purpose neither to presume nor to negate *materiality*: "To call a presupposition into question is not the same as doing away with it; rather it is to free it from its metaphysical lodgings in order to understand what political interests were secured in and by that metaphysical placing, and thereby to permit the term to occupy and serve different political aims" (p. 30).

Language is as shaped as nonverbal and speech acts by individual proclivities and interaction. Likewise we can use the nonverbal as a way to inform an understanding of interaction and of language. Insofar as the original frame is limited, expansion of it is an invitation to look more deeply into what is explicitly denied but recognized as a contingency—the nonverbal.

There is a dimension of interaction, in addition to that within language, that is not separable from language but also is not coterminous with what occurs verbally. This dimension of interaction is hinted at in the shadow discussion throughout psychoanalytic history. Even as theory rejected the body to allow thought to emerge and then rejected drive conceptions of "body" influence on "mental" processes to enhance perception of social influences, body experience continued to be experienced as influential. Nevertheless, none of our evolving theories has yet legitimated nor systematically incorporated the ubiquitous significance of nonverbal behavior.

PART III

✄

The Logic of Action
Studies of Nonverbal Behavior

CHAPTER 8

The Intrinsic-Meaning Position

≽⊂

*A*s in psychoanalysis, nonverbal research positions are taken along the lines of classical philosophical dichotomies: nature versus nurture, universality versus cultural difference, and intrinsic versus context-determined meaning. Debates within nonverbal research parallel those of competing psychoanalytic schools. The study of schools of nonverbal research has the advantage that the kinds of data generated in this research, unlike those generated from psychoanalytic case studies, allow a more detailed comparison among the different schools.

Examination of the data of these three schools of research yields two striking points. First, each centers on different kinds of behavior, discovered through strict centering on its focal point; second, each moves toward the others as it moves beyond its center of focus to explain features of behavior not containable within its predetermined philosophical set. The resulting different foci are both distinct and complementary.

Three basic schools of nonverbal research can be identified by their philosophical viewpoints: the intrinsic-meaning position, the cultural school, and the school of practical analysis. All three vantages, which originated at different times, continue to be developed by contemporary proponents. The roots of the intrinsic-meaning position are the oldest. The intrinsic-meaning position has its roots in Darwin's (1872) premise that there are innate, universally meaningful nonverbal expressions in animals and humans that evolved from originally noncommunicative action patterns to serve social adaptational purposes. This position is illustrated in the following examples.

Brushing by me, taking large strides, Barbara burst into my office as soon as I opened the door. She threw her arms upward, flinging them on a steep diagonal from her shoulders, and let them fall, to slap her sides, as she paced in large steps around the room. Her voice was loud, her speech rhythm staccato, her phrasing matching her pacing and turning. She turned suddenly and punched the air as she made a point about something that had particularly enraged her. Her eyes were wide, eyebrows lifted most of the time, alternating occasionally with a lift in the center. Her mouth was wide open. Then teeth bared and on edge, she closed her mouth. Gradually, she stopped ranting and sat on the edge of the chair. She had come here in this state because yet another man has left her.

In contrast, Nancy walked into my office carefully and precisely. She set down her bag neatly next to her chair, paused, pulled her close-fitting skirt under her, and sat down. She narrowed her arms against her body and sat with her knees pulled together tightly, or held together, as she slid one knee tightly over the other. All her movements typically occurred within a narrow space around her body, and they were precise, always as if she were carefully arranging a curl. Her face was also held in tightly: her lips pursed, eyebrows kept in place. Her feelings stayed within a very narrow expressive range. Her voice rose and fell precisely, with a little harshness and nasality. She complained that she has unexplainable outbursts of rage against her boyfriend, and she is afraid he will leave her.

Both women were angry but expressed their feelings quite differently. I could see the anger, and I could see, in addition, Barbara's wish to hide from her fear and Nancy's wish to hide her rage. Angry and distressed as each was, neither woman was expressing anger toward me. I recognized their anger—and that neither was angry toward me—through features in their expressions best described by the intrinsic-meaning position. The intrinsic-meaning position holds that the ability to understand others' nonverbal expression is innate and based on a body language substrate common to humankind (Eibl-Eibesfeldt, 1971, 1974, 1975). The case for this position follows from seeing that many aspects of body language, especially emotional expression, vary little from culture to culture. Moreover, there are striking cross-cultural similarities of body behavior that occur quite frequently, more often than mere chance could account for (Eibl-Eibesfeldt, 1971). On this substrate are built cultural variations that, to be sure, can impair our understanding. Culturally varying gestures may be quite disparate in form (La Barre, 1947), but they may nevertheless be understandable by members of other cultures because of their appeal to a kinesthetically and visually experienced "logic" of the body, which is common across cultures.

On one hand, the extreme cultural position is that body language, like spoken language, is arbitrarily determined and simply learned and that it is as egregious an error to attempt to understand nonverbal behavior through empathy as it would be to attempt to understand the content of spoken language through empathy. But the intrinsic-meaning position develops the idea that much of what we understand comes, indeed, through direct empathic connection. The expression of emotion is the clearest example of behavior patterns shared by diverse cultures that we can understand without question. Studies of deaf and blind children show that they use the same kind of expression of emotional range as sighted and hearing people. Beyond the similarities in basic emotional expressions, larger phrases of behavior show similar evidence of being intrinsic. For example, when people across cultures are angry, they all open the corner of the mouth in a particular way, frown and clench the fists, stamp on the ground, and hit at objects. This same pattern occurs universally in those born deaf and blind and even among children who were born deaf and blind and without arms, thus ruling out the possibility that they learned the patterns through touch (Eibl-Eibesfeldt, 1971) .

The biological basis and survival advantages of innate patterns of sociability and aggression is demonstrated by Eibl-Eibesfeldt (1970, 1971). In this theory, bonding and altruism, seen especially in cross-species responses to the infant gestalt (the specific structure of the infant's face and body that promotes tenderness across species) are the result of an innate releasing mechanism for parental care (Eibl-Eibesfeldt, 1971). In this frame, the mother–child relationship is the essential feature of human community, for the mother–child relationship's intrinsic and innate behavioral patterns are used to create and maintain social bonds, which then become extended beyond the primary mother–child unit. Such behaviors include kissing, touching and handling, rubbing, embracing, grooming, and feeding. This argument rests on comparative evidence that such behaviors cannot be explained by learning alone. Rather, they are built on innate structures that entail basic intrinsic connections to meanings. Thus, there are layers and steps in the creation of a "finished product" of meaningful behavior. First there are innate forms of expression. Then there are the elaborations of these as they are extended in use in different contexts. These elaborations and changes may be far-reaching and quite removed from their original appearance; behaviors can be segmented, and segments removed from their original whole, showing up in other places, juxtaposed by other kinds of behavior.

Examples from my own work come to mind in this connection. Some people pull at strands of hair at the back or side of their heads as they speak. They may do this in a seductively coy manner. Sometimes the behavior seems not to carry an interactive message but may indicate "state." It looks most to me like infant hair play, an accompaniment to nursing at breast or bottle. As such, it may be self-soothing, and reflect subconscious feelings going on in the session, for it is a remnant of a kind of unlearned early behavior, now fully integrated within conversational speech. I have noticed this behavior during well integrated stretches of communication. The patient conveys comfort, ease, give-and-take. Each has an individual style—one twists the hair around a forefinger and strokes the twisted strands; another works to free a strand, then twists with forefinger, thumb, and middle finger. Cultural forms are derived from innate templates, such as in these examples. One might wonder whether cultural forms of hair braiding and curling derived in part from this tendency to twist one's own and other's hair in grooming and self-soothing. Cultural variations in a wide range of socially relevant gestures, not specific to particular emotions or to biologically significant patterns, are also drawn from the common available, probably inborn, behavioral patterns in slightly different ways.

For example, the method of saluting by tipping the rim of the hat or lifting the hat is similar to the ancient practice of lifting the helmet as an expression of trust. While these are hardly universal gestures, depending, for one thing, on the presence of hats and helmets in a culture, many cultures have developed similar patterns (Heeschen, Schiefenhovel, and Eibl-Eibesfeldt, 1980). There is something in the gesture, beyond the accidental, that refers to a kind of intrinsic and intuitively grasped bodily logic that links "uncovering" with "trust." Another example has to do with signals for requesting and giving food among groups of people in a remote New Guinea village. The gesture for asking for food is to stretch out the arms at chest level and then to draw them back in a self-embrace. Food is also offered in a specific gesture, with the forearm vertical, as the offerer gazes at the recipient, who stretches out the left hand to reach for the food. Other standard sequences of a similar kind have been observed. While clearly these are ritualized and learned and very different from our own gestures, we can still understand and follow the logic in each gesture. This kind of argument is a variation of Darwin's (1872) suggestion that, although the kiss is a learned gesture and varies from culture to culture, it is nonetheless based on the innate pleasure of making skin contact with a beloved person. Firth's (1970) comparison of gestures and postures of respect in British society and in Tikopian society is based on similar reasoning. He offers the idea that gestures and postures in both societies derive from a shared kinesthetic logic that associates value with height, certain body parts, and particular positions in space in relation to others.

Thus, the intrinsic-meaning position proposes that the acquisition or invention of culturally specific gestures is guided (1) by adaptations of learning predispositions, which might be "innate releasing mechanisms" (such is the infant gestalt) that bias perception and experience, and (2) by drive mechanisms (such as hunger, sexuality, attachment), which direct behavior (Eibl-Eibesfeldt, 1970). Some body movement rituals so derived are subsequently passed down through teaching and become changed and independent of the once intrinsically meaningful basis while still retaining something of their intrinsic kinesthetic base. When this occurs, decoding is easier because of the reference back to these intrinsic forms. Yet other movement patterns may be quite arbitrary with the result that cross-cultural confusion may occur and gestures must simply be translated.

There is an additional route for variation: while the original form and meaning of a movement sequence may be intrinsic, cultural variations can also change its meaning while maintaining its form. The particular *use* of a motor pattern can be learned even when the pattern is derived from an adapted one and vice versa. A learned motor pattern might be invested with the meaning of an originally innate pattern for which it now substitutes. Cultural effects are built on an innate substrate, making the distinction between innate patterns and culturally transmitted patterns a complicated process. Likewise, the range of meaning of the same gesture across cultures may come from the cultural variations brought to bear on an intrinsically meaningful behavior.

For example, Roberta was speaking about her interaction with her mother. She was relating that she had had to go to Brooklyn from Manhattan twice on one Saturday because her mother had forgotten to tell her while she was there the first time that she needed a refill on a crucial prescription. Roberta showed some mild annoyance to me, but nothing of note. In the middle of her description of the events, she stopped and explained that her contact lens was out of place. She leaned over in her chair to reach for her lens solution in her large bag. She began to rummage through it very rapidly, searching for the lens solution. She had difficulty finding it and began to scatter her belongings on the floor. Though she herself was quite contained, her use of a habitual motor pattern connected with her handbag, a culturally determined structure, nevertheless seemed to be a temper tantrum. When I remarked on this possibility, she stopped short and said she was, indeed, furious but had only just then realized it.

The idea that there is any intrinsic meaning in human behavior is relevant to the question of whether or not there is a basis for a particular "good" kind of human adaptation. That is, is there a good life, and how do we define its range and degrees of freedom? Or is there a whole toward which human beings are programmed to strive in social and individual terms? Further, the existence of biological substrata shaping human behavior points to how we assess what is "good," whether determination of the "good" comes only from the agreement we can muster with peers, in a strictly cultural learning view, or whether there is an experiential basis for agreement that is not invented whole but dictated by biology. Holding the latter view does not mean that one subscribes to a narrow idea of "good."

Intrinsic-meaning suggests that there are innate connections to meaning and a sense of wholeness through which we structure interactive patterns and sense "goodness."

The intrinsic and inevitable "logic" of gesture has been pursued also in the laboratories of experimental psychologists. In this work, the individual is the focus of study, although the study of judging and observation, which becomes implicitly and explicitly a part of the research, brings a group or interactive aspect to it. The innate ability of judges to understand the "logic" of gesture, as shown in Eibl-Eibesfeldt's (1970, 1971) work, is assumed and relied on.

The following clinical experience of mine involves the sort of behavior elucidated by the research that is described next. Peter often appeared to have a vertically split face. One side of his face might show an expression of concern, and the other an expression of pain. This split was conveyed primarily in his eyes; one was fully open, directed in gaze, the eyebrow slightly lifted; the other eye was half closed, and the brow knitted down and inward toward the center of his face. The eyes seemed to look in different directions. As he spoke, Peter noticed that he felt frustrated at an inability to feel his feelings. That is, he could not *be* fully frustrated or fully concerned.

In research labs, as well as in the field, it has been shown that the basic patterning of expression and the capacity to comprehend emotion in others does not change cross-culturally.[1] Ekman and his collaborators have worked to validate universality in the expression of and ability to decode emotion. This research has extended Eibl-Eibesfeldt's work to analysis of muscular organization of the facial expression of emotion. Ekman's (Ekman and Friesan, 1974a, b, 1976, 1982; Ekman, Friesan and Tomkins, 1971; Ekman and Oster, 1979) systematic and narrow research focus, which includes the study of deception (Ekman and Friesan, 1974b) and the misapprehension of emotion, has shown both the multichanneled possibilities of expression of the body (O'Sullivan et al., 1985) and the social training of the face to hide as well as express feeling (Ekman, Friesan, O'Sullivan et al., 1980; Ekman, 1985). Further, they depict how cultural variations in expression exist on a continuum of possible options that typically involve restricting where, when, and how much feeling can be shown (Ekman, Friesan, and Ancoli, 1980) but not *how* feeling is shown.

---

[1]Ekman, Friesan, and Ancoli (1980) compared Japanese and American facial expressions in an interesting way: each subject was filmed alone and with another. The cross-cultural comparison was more similar when each subject was alone, indicating that display rules create cultural variation that is not present when one is alone. Observers in five countries were asked to judge the emotions displayed on photographed faces.

Differentiations among emotions are accounted for by the activity of separate muscles and muscle groups. Through analysis of the detail of facial expression, researchers showed what is visible to the observer in the process of "encoding."[2]

The "decoding" process involved in what the observer sees has also been studied (O'Sullivan et al., 1985), but separately. These studies have shown that untrained observers of both subtle and obvious facial displays can differentiate the emotional expressions of people from looking at their photographs (O'Sullivan et al., 1985). There are individual differences in sensitivity to perceiving them. For example, observers could identify 60% or more correctly in Ekman and Friesan's (1976) Brief Affect Recognition Test (BART), in which 70 slides of six posed emotions in the face were shown for 1/60th second each. The percentage of recognition depended on how long the slides were shown and on how well subjects attended. Interestingly, the scores were higher in psychotherapists as a group and lower for mental patients. The implication is that we have innate means of quickly decoding subtle and manifold emotional displays but that we do not always use this capacity; that is, we do not always pay enough attention or sufficiently trust our perceptions.

To detect deception, either conscious or unconscious, an examiner must exercise greatly increased attention and confidence. In film microanalysis (frame-by-frame examination), fragments of behavior indicative of feelings that are being withheld consciously or unconsciously are more easily visible (O'Sullivan et al., 1985) than in normal viewing but such behaviors are fleeting. Ekman and Friesan (1974b) found that, even when seeking to deceive an investigator and, more important, even when in a state of self-deception, people cannot completely erase the physical evidence of their feelings. While people may be more or less skilled at isolating and reducing the expression of "state" and "emotion" in the face, this research found their bodies generally less trained or able to omit expression. People may present contrasting emotions, for example, a drooping, limp body with an intensely smiling face or a frightened face and an angry, tense body.

There are a number of sources of leakage in deception: the morphology and timing of an expression, the location of the expression in the conversation, and microfacial expressions (O'Sullivan et al., 1985). Microfacial expressions may last less than 1/4 second and, though often unnoticed,

---

[2] In their studies of how emotion is expressed and how observers normally perceive the information conveyed, Ekman and Friesan (1974a, 1982) and Ekman, Friesan, and Ancoli (1980) developed the Facial Affect Coding Scheme (FACS), based on small facial movements or "Action Units," consisting of single facial muscle movements visible to observers and discriminatable from one another.

are visible to an observer who has had an hour's training. False smiles differ morphologically from genuine ones in that the former do not involve the upper face. They end sooner and may be used to suppress other expressions. Other morphological and timing clues to deception are blushing and the asymmetry of a partly controlled expression not well synchronized with the body.

Of course, picking up deception or noncentral aspects of a person's expression is an important part of the work of the psychotherapist. Using therapists and other observers, Ekman and Friesan (1974b) found that therapists were more skilled at detection than were non-therapist controls. But, even so, it can be difficult to pick up clues to deception. Since the face is more "trained" because it is more noticed as the seat of emotion, the body is often the best place to look for deception. In the case of a woman who was hospitalized for depression and later observed on film, those who viewed only her face judged her to be ready for discharge, whereas those who viewed her body judged her to be tense, withdrawn, and depressed. In fact, very sadly, after discharge she committed suicide (Ekman, 1985; Ekman and Friesan, 1974b).

This example points to another reason for the misapprehension of emotion—different parts of the body send inconsistent messages. The descriptions of Barbara and Nancy, at the beginning of this chapter showed some of these distinctions. In one case, Barbara's nonverbal acts, her flinging her arms and pacing, conveyed her anger, and her yielding to it. Her face showed very much the same feelings, and added very fleeting elements of fear. She was not at odds with being angry, but she was not as comfortable with fear. In the second case, Nancy's tightly held body positions contrasted with her facial expressions, which were, despite their constricted quality, of a pleasant or matter-of-fact kind in keeping with an introductory, rather businesslike conversation.

That we express nonverbally, and perhaps involuntarily, unwanted feelings and states means that the analyst as well as the patient reveals feelings even when seeking to remain hidden or neutral or when thinking of one thing while a feeling comes from a second, less central, concern. It is widely accepted that we must often pay attention to these secondary currents of feeling. This is not the case, however, when it comes to acknowledging that patients are aware, or could be aware, both of what we are experiencing and that we may be experiencing a dual focus.

Another area of study within the intrinsic-meaning position is the delineation of sets of behaviors used by senders and understood by receivers to convey interpersonal attitudes (Mehrabian, 1969, 1972; Mehrabian and Ferris, 1967). Interpersonal attitudes are conglomerates of behavior, including emotion, embodiments of a readiness to behave in a certain ways and not others toward another person. For example, if I say to a patient, "Maybe there is something more we can think about here," I can vary my message through differences in my posture, facial expression, and tone of voice. I inevitably convey an "attitude" toward the person with whom I am speaking. I can be straightforward, by using only that variability in tone which conveys the meaning of my words alone; and I can sit forward a little to convey added interest; and I can add some enthusiasm by accenting the "is" in my sentence, raising my eyebrows, and the like. Or I can convey a derogatory and patronizing attitude toward the patient by adding a questioning tone to the "maybe" and "think," while I sit back, my arms relaxed and outstretched at the sides.

Some interpersonal attitude is always conveyed, and what it means is quite discernible (Mehrabian and Ferris, 1967; Mehrabian, 1969, 1972). Mehrabian (1972) discerned the three dimensions of nonverbal behavior salient to interpersonal attitude: *positiveness*, *potency* or *status*, and *responsiveness*.[3] Positiveness refers to degrees of liking or disliking and is conveyed by demonstrations of "immediacy" in speech and in posture. People orient directly, lean forward more often, touch more and gaze more at people they like (although in intense liking gaze diminishes somewhat), and use language that suggests "immediacy," such as using the first person instead of "one." Potency refers to dominance and control versus submissiveness and passivity. This quality is obvious in the contrast, for example, between the demeanor of a dignified, snobbish person and that of a timid, overly reactive person. Dominance shows in greater relaxation, freedom of movement, and the decision to stop or start encounters, or alter the degree of proximity. A timid, intimidated person reacts too quickly, responds rather than initiates, and may not presume to use the immediate language that indicates intimacy. Responsiveness appears in the awareness of and reaction to the other and is connected to greater nonverbal and implicit verbal activity, such as nods, uh-huhs, and the like.

These three dimensions are variably significant and interact to convey meaning. Going back to my example, I can say, "Maybe there is something more we can think about here," with more positiveness and immediacy, but these aspects might be altered by my way of showing a need for more potency, and so my phrase comes out patronizing. Or I can speak it in a

---

[3]The analysis of how these dimensions were carried and conveyed was done through direct observation of interactions and factor analysis of judges' responses and also through experiments involving observed subjects' acting out various interpersonal attitudes toward a hat rack (Argyle, 1988). Argyle (1988) points out that, although Mehrabian used unrealistic situations, his findings have been corroborated by other workers studying real-life situations (p. 208).

way that emphasizes my potency and my lack of positiveness, with more or less responsivity. That is, I can be dismissing or engaging in my hostile dominance. Researchers could discern degrees of activity along these three dimensions and tended to analyze interaction according to these dimensions. The implication of their work is that people scan one another and make determinations about one another along these three axes. This conclusion would be true as much for the patient and analyst as for any other dyad.

Mehrabian and Williams's (1969) work on persuasiveness is a good case in point, particularly because this attitude can find its way into much of what we and our patients are doing with each other. Again, variations in gaze, vocal and facial activity, shoulder orientation, and degrees of relaxation/tension convey degrees of persuasiveness. Small shifts in behavior determine whether a message is delivered in an "informative" or a "persuasive" manner. People automatically make use of these variables in behavior and categorize behavioral cues as belonging to the positiveness, potency or responsiveness domains. Many persuasive behaviors are the same as those which convey positiveness (liking or reinforcement) in any attitude: gaze (weak effect), proximity, and, in males, less direct orientation. And other behaviors belong to the category of responsiveness to the recipient: faster speech, louder, more vocal activity (more changes in frequency and intensity range), and more facial activity. And a third group of cue variables in the potency realm forms what Mehrabian and Williams called the "relaxation repertoire": sideways lean, leg and arm asymmetry, and arm openness. Slightly relaxed is most persuasive in males, and slightly relaxed to somewhat tense most persuasive in females. Vocal cues are very important in persuasion: louder, faster, and more expressive voices were experienced as more persuasive.[4] Thus, variations of behaviors controlling position, emotion, pace, intensity, and tension level created varying impressions in the domain of positiveness, potency, and responsiveness that create a persuasive or not persuasive attitude.

Variations in behaviors in all three domains are salient, but, in addition, some channels through which attitude is conveyed are more important than others. In perceiving persuasion and other interpersonal attitudes, facial expression is given more weight than vocal cues, and vocal cues are given far more weight than verbal cues (Mehrabian and Ferris, 1967). [5]

[4]Argyle's (1988) reading of the literature suggests that these findings have been confirmed in more recent studies.

[5]A formula represents the order and weight given to different channels for liking and potency: Total liking, or potency = 7% verbal + 38% vocal + 55% facial. Thus facial expression and vocal tone, the nonverbal elements, conveyed attitude far more strongly than did worked content (Mehrabian and Ferris, 1967).

Particular postural dimensions occur in relation to more than one interpersonal attitude and not all dimensions occur to the same degree at all times (Mehrabian, 1972). For example, relaxation may be connected to dominance, but it can also indicate degree of positiveness. People can be moderately relaxed with those they like, but more relaxed with those they do not like, indicating dominance through indifference. Males, in another distinct set, were very unrelaxed with those seen as threatening. Going back to my statement, "Maybe there is more here that we can think about," we can now see that its meaning can be altered by changing eyebrow position, forward lean, head tilt, position in seat, and tone of voice to convey very different messages and attitudes toward the listener.[6]

Although Mehrabian's philosophical position places him in the intrinsic-meaning position, which has been seen as synonymous with "individual," his focus is unequivocally "social." Mehrabian is implicitly saying that an individual is always projecting to others and being perceived along the kinds of lines his studies have drawn. This statement implies that psychoanalysts need to be aware that their behaviors are being judged automatically along these lines and further suggests that it would be useful to inquire about patients' perceptions of the analyst along such dimensions. Given the strength of nonverbal features in conveying this information, it seems that it was not an accident that Freud and his followers, emphasizing neutrality, wanted to restrict the patient's visual exposure to the analyst. Certainly, on the surface of it, doing so aids the possibility of neutrality since, for example, 55% of the weight in a judgment of potency and liking comes from facial expression (Mehrabian and Ferris, 1967). Vocal expression is nevertheless still present and difficult to control and accounts for 38% of the weight of a judgment. Thus, the need for attention to the patient's actual perception of the analyst's experience is not removed by the couch.

In interpersonal communication, there is an interaction between these perceptions of attitudes, but Mehrabian (1972) examined one direction at a time in order to delineate the socially significant behaviors. He tells us what kinds of attitudes we look for, respond to, and project (positiveness, responsiveness, and dominance), but he does not examine how individuals

[6] The question of neutrality is relevant here. Can the analyst be neutral with regard to positiveness, responsivity, or dominance? If interactants are always judging each other along these dimensions, a studied neutrality that hides, rather than comes from, a relaxed listening posture creates problems for the patient. Ongoing assessment along these lines is clearly a contributor to countertransference and transference. Attempts to be neutral necessarily involve controlling our behaviors in these dimensions. Our approach ought to ask whether the problems raised for the patient by neutrality are useful in relation to the patient's needs. When, how, and why might we want the patient to be mystified about such attitudes?

use these behaviors to shape each other. This perspective is elaborated by the cultural school and the school of practical analysis, which we examine later.

Freedman (1977; Freedman et al., 1972) and Mahl (1968, 1977) change the question being asked. Both examined the relationship between nonverbal and verbal behavior in individuals. Like others holding the intrinsic-meaning position, both worked from the point of view that nonverbal behavior can be straightforwardly decoded by observers and that there are intrinsic connections among form, function, and meaning. They explored a third and fourth domain of the intrinsic meaning of innate nonverbal behavior, separable from the explicitly emotional or attitudinal. Each related nonverbal behavior to different areas of cognition and explicit verbal communication—Mahl to the function of memory, and Freedman to conceptual processes.

Mahl (1968, 1977) is a psychoanalyst who has concluded from research on the meaning of patients' movements during psychoanalytic sessions that verbal and nonverbal behavior are not in conflict. His work is in a direct line with that of Freud (1905a, b, 1923); Breuer and Freud (1893–1895), as well as that of Deutsch (1933, 1947) and shares fully this traditional psychoanalytic, intrinsic-meaning position. That is, Mahl does not question that he can discern centrally important information about a patient's "inner experience" through movement alone. Mahl's (1968) preliminary research, in fact, involved his recording all he could about patients being interviewed by someone else as he watched through a one-way mirror. His determinations of diagnosis, personality traits, and areas of conflict were found to correlate with the verbal content of the session and clinical records derived independently.

Mahl (1977) began with the Freudian idea that action is a "resistance" to verbalization and remembering, but he changed this view when he found instead that actions appear to be integral to recollection and remembering. In fact, he found that nonverbal behavior often anticipates the verbal content of dialogue, which emerges later in the analytic process. Mahl's detailed records of analytic hours showed that overt actions of the patient occur spontaneously and appear to be related to latent content of current verbalization that is verbalized later. That is, nonverbal behavior "tells" what present speech may only hint at. The time lapse between a gesture and the verbalization of what may have been connected with it ranged from seconds to several weeks. Actions he noted were not always large or overt. Sometimes muscular tensions and movement preparations for actions were recognized but did not develope into full action.

Mahl notes the following examples, which illustrate this kind of phenomenon. In the first, a woman spoke of her feelings of inferiority and inadequacy in relation to her husband. While she spoke, she placed her hand over her mouth, hiding it. Later she spoke about feeling uglier than her sister because she had buck teeth. There was, then, a direct, representational connection between the gesture and her feelings in relation to her husband.[7] In a second example, a woman removed and replaced her wedding ring while discussing her somatic complaints, weepy spells, and depression. Later, in an unrelated way, she spoke about tensions in her marriage. The link between her symptoms and her marriage was contained in her nonverbal act. A third example was produced by a man talking about going to visit his mother with his new wife. He was reluctant to go, he said, as he removed the pillow from behind his head. This action had not taken place before. Two sessions later, the patient recalled that his mother had taken away his pillow for four years as a punishment for finding him masturbating against it. The action was a preliminary step in remembering this important event. A fourth example is a patient whose movements over a long span of time were closely linked to his ongoing concerns in the transference. This man's behaviors were to wiggle his buttocks on the couch as he sat down, to remove his wallet from his back pocket, and to place his hands over his chest in a way that suggested breasts. These gestures preceded his relating experiences represented by them, such as feeling as though his "ass was on the table," problems about money, and issues connected to his mother's mastectomy. Mahl (1968, 1977) holds that self-touching evokes primary object representation. He suggests that transitions from motoric expression, to primitive ideation, to verbalization are continually occurring events in associative process.

Gestural activity is not just symbolic of the highly charged issues that may emerge within an analysis; it is also an essential aspect of the more general cognitive processing functions of nonverbal behavior (Freedman, 1977). For example, my patient, Carl (see chapter 12) made hand gestures as he lay on the couch that illustrated what he was speaking about. Here his gestures did not reveal a subtext but simply aided his expression.

Freedman's (1977) studies of the functions of body movement during speech challenged the Freudian theory that the inhibition of motor activity is necessary to the development of secondary-process thinking. Freedman contributed new data on the role of certain kinds of nonverbal behavior in information processing. He studied the relationship of movement, mostly of the hands, to aspects of cognitive functioning. Blind people move hands, head, or feet while they speak, emphasizing speech-accompanying

---

[7]Mahl does not note, though, the importance of the context of her present relationship to the analyst and the possibility of her fear that she may be ugly to the analyst.

movement's innate, unlearned dimension. Here the movement is intrinsically related not to the meaning of what is being conveyed but, rather, to the *process* of formulating and conveying thoughts. Body movement during discourse is necessary to support the processes of representing and focusing. Freedman's developmental studies indicate that there is evolving change in body movement and speech from childhood to adulthood, rather than a decline or inhibition of motoric behavior during speech.

Action evokes a *kinesthetic experience* that confirms existing cognitive schemata and connects image and word in a two-part process. One part is the activity of *representing*, which involves connecting image to symbol for communication, and always entails some intervening activity that sustains the image. It also involves the intention to share the image and so engages the representer in an object relationship. Another part is *focusing*, which requires retrieval, ordering, sorting multiple alternatives before representing can occur. The need to select or exclude alternatives requires the implementation of support activities and the differentiation of self from nonself. Both parts are visible in the movements occurring in an interpersonal transaction.

The basic communicative structures are "object-focused movements," linked to representing, and "body-focused activity," linked to focusing. Object-focused movement is movement of the hand accompanying speech, phased in with rhythmic and content aspects of the verbal phrases, usually directed away from the body (Freedman, 1977, p. 113). Body-focused activity involves self stimulation. An example illustrates the definition and function of these two activities. A 10-year-old asked to define a word such as "vase" or "hammer" will make object-focused movements depicting the shape of the object or the action that illustrates its use as he or she speaks. When more difficult cognitive processes are involved, self-touching is evoked. For example, during the Stroop Color-Word test, children asked to name the color of the blue ink in which is imprinted the word RED, touch the head or shake their hands while groping for the answer. This example of a confusion in ordering or selecting illustrates self-touching's function as an aid when there is added difficulty with focus of attention. Tactile stimulation here regulates sensory input and confirms the boundaries of the self when the sharing of thought is also required.

A child's object-focused movements depicting action schemas or representing objects occur before verbalization and can be seen as a sort of cognitive rehearsal. Different kinds of object-focused movements have different functions. Some are "beatlike" accompaniments to thinking, such as finger rubbing, foot tapping, that seem to keep symbolizers in touch with the sensory stuff of their mode of representation. These accompaniments are called speech primacy motions, carrying no message content but occurring at the onset of a clause.

Movements of all kinds tend to bunch, not at the beginning of any clause, but at the beginning of what is called "fluent speech," whether this occurs at the beginning of a clause or after some nonfluency within the clause. There are individual differences in the amount of movement, but this factor does not change the timing of the movement. Also, more movement occurs in nonfluent clauses than in fluent clauses. By inference, such movement bears on the behaviors of people searching for language. As people search for language, they search for units larger than words, units containing both meaning and syntax, and movement is an aid to such a search. Thus, there is less information carried in the relationship between speech and movement in fluent clauses than in nonfluent clauses (Dittman, 1972).

Body-focused activity seems to arise in two ways (Freedman, 1977). In one experiment, the stimulus was interpersonal uneasiness. Subjects interviewed by a cold, disinterested interviewer showed more self/body touching than did those interviewed by a warm interviewer. Here verbal encoding had to continue while feelings of distraction, fear, or anger were endured. The self-touching was interpreted as aiding the subject to hold to verbal encoding while avoiding the interference brought by the interviewer's behavior. One might imagine that self-touching replaces the nonverbal reassurance looked for in a listener. In the case of tasks that themselves present some interference with straightforward encoding, as in the Stroop Color-Word test mentioned earlier, all subjects used more self-stimulation overall and those who used most showed fewer errors than did those who used least.

Thus, developmental and diagnostic studies offer further evidence that action and thoughtful verbalization are not incompatible. Instead of activity decreasing as verbal ability increases, developmental observations of children aged four through sixteen years of age showed a straight linear increase of object-focused movement (Freedman, 1977). At college age, those students who used more object-focused movements were judged to have a greater range of associative imagery than did those whose movements were less frequent. Also body-focused movement increased up to 10 years then declined, though there was still quite a lot of self-touching at 14 years. Changes with development in body-focused movements showed a refinement of its thought- and verbal expression-enhancing character. With development, self-touching narrowed from bilateral, covering large areas of the body, to lateral, covering smaller areas of the body. In its most advanced form, the hand acted as an agent on the body as subject, and movement was usually one sided, as in the hand gestures of a skillful orator.

Besides changing developmentally, various kinds of body-focused movement appear differentially in diagnostic groups. Bilateral self-stimulation (for example, rubbing eyes and face with the hands, crossing arms and rubbing upper arms) was noted in cases of agitated depression where a continuing need for defining self-boundaries might be presumed (Freedman, 1977). Finger and hand motions (such as shaking loose hands and fingers when one cannot think of a word, rubbing thumb and first finger together) were a prevalent response among those who are vulnerable to stimulation that would interfere with thinking, for example, field-dependent people under stress, chronic schizophrenic patients even under conditions of interpersonal support, and congenitally blind persons.

Mahl (1968, 1977) and Freedman (1977) describe complementary and overlapping processes. Their studies firmly show that nonverbal and verbal expression are far from intrinsically in conflict. Motoric free associations are not always directed toward communication explicitly but come from loosening the need to formulate precisely for someone else or precede the ability to formulate precisely. Stress adds to the need to gesture and touch the body when communicating. It is possible to distinguish between the failure of verbalization due to vulnerability to interference (which might come from anxiety aroused by the analyst's behavior, for example) and that due to difficulties in connecting to thoughts (which might be inherent in the person's structure). In chronic schizophrenia, where there is both a known vulnerability to interference and a highly tenuous sense of self, pervasive bilateral self-touching is more prevalent. In contrast, in hysterical or anxiety states, where there is no primary focusing difficulty, there are instead difficulties in connecting image to word due to repression. In these cases, there appear vague, rather than precise representation gestures and various kinds of associative discontinuities (Freedman, 1977).

Keen observation can determine a therapist's choice of intervention. It evokes questions about the usefulness of the sitting up or lying down posture. Observation of a patient's communicative process could be helpful in determining how to facilitate it: for example, one patient became aware of her need to guard herself from her attention to my responses which was interfering with her ability to reach her own feelings; another patient very much needed my nonverbal support to get to his feelings at all. Obviously, the couch was very helpful in the first instance, and the chair in the second. These body positions and differing relationships to communication bring forth different *behavior* from patients and from ourselves and therefore call forth different kinds of content. The interactive process has its own set of behaviors, the need for which the couch reduces. The couch can allow a patient to use symbolic processing unconstrained by the demand to make conventional sense or to be interactively responsive in ordinary ways.

While remaining within the intrinsic-meaning position, Freedman

(1977; Freedman et al., 1972) and Mahl (1968, 1977) dispel one of the fundamental ideas of the original developers of this tradition (Darwin, 1872; Breuer and Freud, 1893–1895): they make clear that the languages of the body and that of the mind are not fundamentally distinct or organized hierarchically along an axis of emotional and irrational to intellectual and rational. Further, early adherents thought that secondary process could occur only with the suppression of action. The more recent findings discussed clearly suggest that this is not the case. On the contrary, certain degrees and kinds of actions are central to the development of thought. Eibl-Eibesfeldt, Ekman, Mehrabian, Freedman, and Mahl have all demonstrated a range of ways of seeing nonverbal behavior that I have designated the intrinsic-meaning position. The researchers have brought certain kinds of issues and behaviors into relief and have trained our "eye" and kinesthetic sense in particularly useful ways.

From this point of view, universal innately/biologically determined meaning is intrinsic to at least some body-mediated patterns of expression. Subtle or obvious movements of facial and postural muscles create patterns that others recognize and on which they base responses. Practiced *attention* enhances the capacity to recognize these behaviors, especially in instances of deception or out-of-awareness trends. Cultural variations occur along the lines of "when" and "for what" purpose rather than "how" a feeling is expressed. Facial and bodily display-discrepancies, as well as verbal and vocal display-discrepancies, are quite salient. Often the least trained aspects (body and voice tone) are the most revealing in situations in which there is a need to subdue or hide expression. Training allows for some hiding and deceit, but it is never complete. In addition, there are innate language- and thought-processing behaviors that develop in a way parallel to the development of language use. These movements are thought to enhance cognitive and verbal capacity. Other movements that have a symbolic aspect (e.g., representational of objects or "pieces" of situations) seem to be inherent in free association, memory retrieval, and verbal communication. These findings suggest that action and thought are not antithetical, but are intrinsically related.

CHAPTER 9

The Cultural School

⋙⋘

*A*sharp break with the intrinsic-meaning position was made by the linguistic anthropologist Birdwhistell (1952, 1970), who may be considered one of the originators of the cultural school. Birdwhistell was struck by the fact that the sets of movements used by speakers of different languages are as distinctively different as are the spoken words. He formulated the idea that body movement and nonverbal communication are coded—learned as language itself is—and therefore in meaning and form are socially determined rather than innate or biologically endowed. Called "context analysis," his approach spawned a great deal of research.

The context-analytic approach frames the following: father, mother, and four-year-old child are in the waiting room. As I enter, the child is insistently demanding a lifesaver. His mother says, "No, you already had two. Don't you think that's enough?" Her manner is gentle, despite the child's forcefulness. The child whines, very unpleasantly, "But I *want* one!" Father says, flatly, "Listen to your mother," when the child whines for more. As the father finishes speaking, mother gives the child one more. Gobbling that speedily, he asks for another, and when mother says, "No" in an angry tone, he grabs for them and hits her. I am told that he often hits his mother.

In another instance, Marla, a 40-year-old woman, is talking to me about how she might explore her options in her work life, which is at present quite unsatisfying to her. I have begun to notice a repeating sequence in our interaction. As we arrive at a point for further exploration, Marla abruptly stops talking to me, tilts her head down to gaze at her fingernails, and picks a little at them in an absent-minded way. I feel suddenly dropped from her awareness; she seems oblivious to anything beyond her fingernails. She stays in this state until I insert myself with a question. As this behavior is repeated in later sessions, I find myself feeling puzzled and increasingly reluctant to continue it by asking a question.

These scenarios involve behaviors that are culturally determined. They depend for their occurrence on the presence of a group or dyad and on aspects of experience that are culturally, interactively determined. In the first case, the behavior was of a whole; no part can be singled out as "the central one." All three people were equal participants in the whole. In the second vignette, the cultural and interactive significance is perhaps less obvious. I associate Marla's gesture with that of a person waiting—for a bus, perhaps, or for an appointment in a waiting room. I wonder if she is waiting for me to take her somewhere. These are the kinds of behaviors and questions, among many others, that can be illuminated by the nonverbal researchers I call the cultural school. This position is distinguished by its focus on interaction and study of the dyad or group and by its emphasis on the learned and culturally determined aspects of body movement behavior.

Birdwhistell (1952, 1970, 1973) said forcefully and seminally that it was not possible to understand and interpret behavior without reference to culture, that is, systems of interaction between people. In developing his own approach, kinesics, he formulated on certain principles: that audible and visible behavior (i.e., words and actions) are united aspects of every interaction; that an individual can be viewed only within patterns of inter-communication; that body motion and facial expression are part of a learned, coded system which varies culturally (Birdwhistell, 1970). He set out to show that the meaning of body movement can be derived *only* from con-text, *not* from reference to an intuitively derived inner, universal core. The meaning of any bit of behavior, Birdwhistell (1973) said, is "the behavioral difference occasioned by the presence or absence of a particular cue at a particular level of context" (p. 289). That is, the meaning of a behavior can be deciphered only in a group of two or more people from the reactions of the receivers of the communication. This statement implies that, even if we could know definitively that a particular behavior were "innately wired," its meaning would still depend on its impact. In its strongest form, this position disregards the possibility that a bit of behavior might derive mean-ing from more than one source.

Giving meaning to the unnoted obvious and underscoring the link between audible and visible behavior, Birdwhistell (1970) showed that a bilingual Kutenai tribesman moved in a consistently different manner when speaking Kutenai than when speaking English.[1] The Kutenai man was not

---

[1]In contrast to Freedman's (1977) perspective on speaking behavior, this one shows the stylistic differences that occur cross-culturally in all movements, rather than within kinds of speech behavior (e.g., thought-processing). Freedman's work

simply "imitating a white man" but, rather, following the rules deriving from an existing "systematic relationship between audible and visible communicative behavior" (p. 28). It is primarily the link between language and behavior that Birdwhistell set out to define. He delineated a "language" of movement comparable to, and integrated with, spoken language both in its structure and in its being part of a systematically ordered "communicative system" (p. 26).[2] He specifically countered early, simplistic intrinsic meaning conceptions about language and nonverbal behavior suggesting that words and logic carry what the speaker says, whereas style, tone of voice, vehemence, and so forth, carry how the speaker feels about what he says. He noted that such separation of word and feeling was naively fostered by a sense that formal situations, having affinities with formal speech and words, felt "artificial," while informal situations, affined with feeling, felt "natural." Instead, he viewed social relations of all kinds, artificial and natural, as patterned and learned. In his view of behavior, one learns the behaviors one performs in a natural way as much as one learns those performed in an artificial way. For example, Birdwhistell (1970) spoke of his early study of smiling:

> Smiling, it seemed to me, provided the perfect example of a behavior bit which in every culture expressed pleasure . . . [but] it became evident that there was little constancy to the phenomenon. Middle class individuals from Ohio, Indiana, and Illinois, as contacted on the street, smiled more often than did New Englanders with a comparable background. . . . The highest frequency of smiling was observed in Atlanta, Louisville, Memphis and Nashville. If I could have maintained my faith in the smile as a natural gesture of expression, an automatic neuromuscular reaction of an underlying and "pleasurable" endocrine or neural state, I would have had a sure measure to establish . . . [the frequency of occurrence] of pleasure with which to map the United States. Unfortunately, data continue to come in [pp. 29–30].

Here Birdwhistell noted the cultural rules and variations of when and for what purpose action schemas may be performed. This is what Eibl-

---

suggests that there are structural and functional identities relative to language processing within these stylistic differences.

[2]Birdwhistell was looking closely at what we informally notice when we speak of cultural stereotypes and, for example, imitate an "Englishman" or an "Italian." We may dismiss our intuitive grasp of the link between movement and language until, perhaps, we attempt to learn a foreign language. At this point, the advantage of attaining the whole body language, and thus the fact of its existence, becomes evident.

Eibesfeldt (1974) noted as the use of an inborn behavioral scheme for symbolic, interactive purposes. Where Ekman and Friesan (1982) looked at the behaviors involved in the creation of different kinds of smiles, Birdwhistell stressed the rules of "how much" and "when" of emotional expression over the innate aspects of this basic human response. Birdwhistell used his observation as a mandate to study solely the cultural creation of meaning at all levels. And this focus produced a radically different, highly useful way to see behavior.

Birdwhistell's (1952, 1970, 1973) method of movement analysis ultimately breaks movement sequences into their smallest units (kines), down to eye blinks. Indeed, these units have no inherent meaning any more than the smallest unit of sound in language (phone) has meaning by itself, and so each can be understood only in larger groupings, which constitute levels of context. On the basis of this breakdown into meaningless kines, Birdwhistell (1973) eschewed efforts to pursue what he called the "phantom of meaning" (p. 287), insofar as this term refers to the access a behavior may seem to give to an "inner state." To maintain his radical position, he went beyond the level of analysis that Ekman, for example, performed (e.g., Ekman and Friesan, 1976). He reduced emotional expression to smaller units of movement or stressed the cultural rules of expression over the emotion itself. This radicalism seems to have been necessary in order to provide a new perspective, that of watching what happens not so much within discrete behaviors as between behaviors and behavior microunits, and between interactants.

Different cultures, Birdwhistell (1970) found, emphasize different aspects of the human range of body motion. He noted that even the most discrete facial expression (a smile or frown), or the most obvious gesture (a nod or head shake), or most indicative posture (sag or military uprightness) relies on other behaviors for its meaning. His analyses of filmed sequences call into question "naive" observer reports of behavior, which he says can be only impressionistic summaries of quite complex and systematically varying particles of activity. The naive observer cannot be relied on to report in detail what goes into these movements and cannot interpret them outside of context. This point of view seems to contradict what Mehrabian, Ekman, and Mahl, of the intrinsic-meaning position, assert. The significant stress is on the much finer detail that Birdwhistell disembeds and on his attention to what goes on *between* two people rather than *within* one person.

His vantage point rests on the analysis of American body communicative behavior, which, through context analysis, he separated into tiny segments (kines). He arrived also at a "grammar," which orders the discerned "vocabulary" or particles of movement, and showed how these operate together to frame meaning. Birdwhistell (1970) demonstrated that even a five-second segment of behavior performed by two soldiers hitchhiking a ride showed a patterned, culturally defined system, as highly formalized as speech, reducible to components that are seen in other sequences:

> Just west of Albuquerque on Highway 66, two soldiers stood astride their duffle bags thumbing a ride. A large car sped by them and the driver jerked his head back, signifying refusal. The two other soldiers wheeled and one Italian-saluted him while the other thumbed his nose after the retreating car [p. 173].

This brief description is followed by a fuller one, a narrative about six times as long that gives the details of facial expression and more exact position changes, and then two pages listing the kines, the tiny, submeaningful movements of all body parts. In the fuller narrative, Birdwhistell says:

> Without apparent hesitation, the boys right-stepped posteriorly, one of the boys moving in echo following the movement of the other. Facing the retreating car, one of the boys raised his upper lip to expose his teeth, furrowed his forehead, lowered his brows, contracted the lateral aspect of its orbits, and flared his nostrils [p. 176].

The point of this demonstration, characteristic of Birdwhistell's approach, is in the first instance, to point out how for him the individual kines (exposed teeth, furrowed brow) take on meaning only within the overall complex of behavior. For Birdwhistell, meaningful behavior is constructed out of micromovements that are not meaningful in themselves. At the microkinesic level, he disembedded movements of lips, trunk, shoulders, eyebrows, fingers, at first grouping "nothing" as a unit (p. 174) except in context. Birdwhistell regarded the grouping of these behaviors as culturally defined in a languagelike expression. Salient movements occur in regular, orderly, and predictable ways, for example, in head nods and sweeps, eye blinks, small chin and lip movements, and the like. For example:

> As I reviewed head nods in my filmed material, I noted that certain moments contained one head nod, others two head nods, and still others from three to nine such nods. Certainly, on the level of pre-kinesic skeletomuscular activity, the individual nods in these activities seemed the same. . . . However, context analysis quickly revealed that one head nod was distinguishable as a stem form . . . from a two head nod (when there was no sustained rest at either the highest or lowest point of the down and up and down and up movement sequence) as a stem [p. 160].

It seemed to him that the units of body movement, such as nostril flaring, raising the upper lip, or sidestepping posteriorly, have the same variability of semantic function as do letters or words.

Birdwhistell attempted through context analysis to isolate the significant forms of communicative body motion behavior in our culture and gain perspective on the levels of context in which these forms function. The kine is defined as "an abstraction of that range of behavior produced by a member of a given social group which, for another member of that same group, stands in perceptual contrast to a different range of such behavior" (Birdwhistell, 1970, p. 193). The existence and range of meaning of a particular cue is governed by the range of contexts in which the cue can be observed to occur and the range of behaviors it evokes. He envisioned a division or segmentation of a whole of continuous body movement of which each social system makes use, within limits governed by physiological structure. For example, he says, a member of culture A will report two degrees of lid closure, whereas culture B may recognize and teach five.

Having broken down movement into essentially meaningless basic units, Birdwhistell defines the next level of structure as the kinemorph, "an assemblage of movements (kines)" in one segment of the body. (For example, contrast kinemorph A, opening the hand and fingers, extending palm upward as the forearm moves downward, with kinemorph B, holding the fingers closed, thumb side upward, with the first finger extended.) Kinemorphs function in body language as word parts function in verbal language; complex kinemorphs function like words (p. 101). Context analysis showed that different cultures segment the body into different areas (Americans into eight areas, e.g., head and neck, face, shoulders and trunk, right arm, left arm). According to Birdwhistell, all cultures have characteristic kinemorphic constructions. For example, speakers of French bulge their lips forward (kinemorph) and, with that, tilt their heads along with particular hand gestures (kinemorphic construction). Kinemorphic constructions occur through (1) synchrony, in which component kines and kinemorphs are simultaneous; (2) serializing, in which kines follow one another; and (3) mixing, in which both synchronic and series features appear. In complex kinemorphs, kines from two or more areas form a complex, which, under context analysis, behaves like a kinemorph. The next order of combination is the kinemorphic construction, the simplest being in parallel or series or in kinemorphic compounds, in which complex kinemorphs combine. Marla's looking at her nails is a kinemorphic construction, a serial and synchronic composition, involving hand, shoulder, head, neck, and face. It is a recognizable and often repeated sequence—a sentence, as it were, placed within the ongoing interaction.

In addition, Birdwhistell (1970) proposed that *stance* is another level of

linguistic grammar and syntax that holds together kinemorphic constructions. Stance refers to an arrangement of the whole body that contrasts
significantly with another stance; that is, it creates "a marked shift in the
total message" (p. 200). A stance is sustained through time, and within it
one or a series of kinemorphic constructions takes place. For example,
Nancy might shift from a stance in which she is seated in a particular way,
with two feet on the ground, arms on the arm rests, while she is looking
and speaking directly to me, to another stance in which she crosses her
legs, tilts her head to one side, and looks at her fingernails. Another patient, Richard, lies on the couch with his legs crossed at the ankles, arms
with elbows bent across his chest, and fingers laced. He sometimes makes
small movements with his hands and feet as he speaks, but his basic position remains for a time. Then he moves his left hand (arm nearest the wall)
behind his head, and turns his right leg so that the knee is bent more and
points away from the couch. The total picture appears different and has a
different "feel." Several such shifts occur during the session. These are
stances. Shifts in stance occur in transitions on the construction level. These
are also patterned in a culturally salient way, as evidenced by Birdwhistell's
discovery that people react to "too many or too few" stance shifts (p. 201).

Birdwhistell contrasted kinemorphic constructions, which tie together
the tiny kines, with "body base" and "body set" behaviors, which tie together large amounts of interactional information. These seem to derive
from a group's conceptions of physiology and constitute the basis for an
internalized and generalized image of other group members. It is against
this baseline that individuals make judgments along the lines of position,
sex, age, state of health, body build, rhythm phase, territoriality, mood,
toxic state. Birdwhistell brings these presumed judgments into his system
because they are evident in behavior, for that is his only basis for inclusion.
Birdwhistell illustrates with an example of an interaction between a 63-
year-old chairman of the board and his 35-year-old junior vice president.
Here stressing the elements of age and territoriality, "body set" puts in
relief such elements as the younger man's "interaction-centered" behavior
and the older man's "movement projection into the whole room" (p. 207).
The salient behaviors have to do with control of the space with visual focus
and more individually determined use of space. These uses of space seem
partly determined by social protocols, attitudes dictated by status, as well
as by more biologically determined variables, such as age, and so are situation dependent, a chemistry resulting from a mix of factors.

"Motion qualifiers" are another distinguishable set of variables. These
modify the kinesic meaning of a kinemorphic construction by altering intensity (tenseness or laxness), duration (staccato or allegro), or range (narrow, limited, or widened or broad). The integration of these qualifiers creates

the manner of expression of affect, from "flattened" as in the psychiatric definition, to "fattened," in Birdwhistell's (1970, p. 213) terms, to signify an individual's narrowing or widening of the range of a piece of kinesic behavior.[3] This category of behavior relates to individual differences. Birdwhistell (1970) allows that such differences exist, but he couches his admission carefully to maintain the greater salience of cultural definitions:

> The particular biological system and the special life experience of any individual will contribute idiosyncratic elements to his kinesic system, but the individual or symptomatic quality of these elements can only be assessed following the analysis of the larger system of which he is a part [p. 184].

This thesis, of course, is questioned both by the and by the school of practical analysis. It well served Birdwhistell's (1970) aim to put in relief the learned and visibly perceptible shifts in the body that constitute the communication systems of particular societies or subgroups. Kinesics stresses the salient "what happened" aspect of movement, the spatial displacement of all parts of the body in short or long body-movement units. (Some longer forms, some taking minutes, even hours to complete, have been studied by Scheflen, 1965.) Motion qualifiers in Birdwhistell's system are noted to deal with "how" movements are performed, but these do not form a central concern for Birdwhistell because they move into the arena of individual variation, which he acknowledged but did not address as his main interest. Birdwhistell asserted the singular significance of context analysis.

Birdwhistell's point of view is interesting in that it is consonant with the hermeneutic position, now influential in psychoanalysis, which holds that meaning is interactively determined and context bound. But Birdwhistell offers a potential enrichment of the hermeneutic view, since he focuses attention on the nonverbal; whereas most of the influence within psychoanalysis has been drawn from studies of linguistics, philosophy, and literary criticism. Birdwhistell's approach offers a broader, enriched conception of context, incorporating not just the audible, but also the visible, that is, body behavior. Yet, Birdwhistell (1970) was not a clinician, nor was he interested in clinical understanding; his examples are taken from naturalistic observation, not the consulting room. Consider the following:

> As a speaker of English may use pronunciations characteristic of a variety of dialects, so the actor may from time to time, stimulated by

---

[3]This category of behavior is most highly elaborated by the school of practical analysis that is reviewed in the next chapter.

the special situation, put into motion responses which signal a different milieu. For instance, while the actor cannot, of course, simultaneously sit like an upper status New Englander and sit-slouch like a recent migrant from the Appalachians, he may, in the course of a given scene, utilize both of these postures. The fact that he sit-slouches but once in a long scene is obviously of special interest to the investigator. But whether this is a slouch of "despair or rejection" can only be determined by extensive contrastive analysis. With no more information than that provided by the kinemorph count, we have no more justification for such an interpretation than we do for the contradictory assumption that the sit-slouch signals the only time he "really relaxes" in the whole scene [p. 185].

The sense of embeddedness that informs this observation is palpable—but it remains for clinicians to see how the same approach may be brought to bear in the consulting room. To a large extent, the clinical implications of Birdwhistell's work have been explored by Scheflen (1963, 1964, 1965).

A psychiatrist and also a researcher, Scheflen produced several studies making use of the concept of context analysis. Scheflen studied the psychotherapeutic exchange by delineating the significance of complex kinemorphic constructions. He applied Birdwhistell's methods of identifying repeating sequences of behavior, some quite extended. Scheflen hypothesized that sequences of interactive behaviors within psychotherapies could be discovered that might last days, months, or longer. Scheflen (1965) analyzed a film of two family therapists, named Whittaker and Malone, working with a schizophrenic girl and her mother. The results of his analysis yielded a complex series of interactive behaviors made up of smaller and larger "chunks," or phrases. Scheflen examined the relations between behavioral items to find out which sets or clusters occurred together regularly. These behaviors could be categorized as (a) "regulatory behaviors, which serve to maintain or re-direct behavior and interaction" (p. 65), (b) complementary and reciprocal performances, which maintain group cohesion, or (c) complex rules, mechanisms and procedures by which interactions were organized.

One example falling into all three categories was a completely out-of-awareness signal that involved the use of the pipes that both filmed therapists smoked. When Whittaker was about to make a shift toward one of the patients, he would light his pipe. But not until Malone had responded by lighting his pipe would Whittaker make his postural shift. The signal function of pipe lighting was confirmed when, in a later session, roles were reversed, but pipe signaling continued. In one session, Malone was the initiator and began to make a shift without waiting for the confirming pipe lighting from Whittaker. But he did not complete the move toward the patient, and returned instead to his original position. Then, several minutes later, when Whittaker did light up, Malone completed his moving-in shift. This signal occurred without the awareness of the therapists, though when it was pointed out to them, they recognized it. They simply had not been alert to its occurrence or function. This is a stark example of the fact that often we all may do something quite significant without being aware that we do it or why.

In context analysis, Scheflen considered a number of factors. He isolated subunits of behavior and indicated their level in a hierarchy of sets[4] through their occurrence as part of a sequence that repeatedly produces a behavior difference. Logical types were separated: sound and movement make up the communication behavior unit, so Scheflen eliminated abstracted qualities that are judgments about or evaluations of behavior, for example "goodness" or "masochism." He aimed to make a sharp distinction between what occurs and the inferences we make about that.

Rather than make judgments, Scheflen (1964) identified sequences of positions and the transitions between them. Positions were, for example, "listening and questioning," "contending," "lamenting," "intervention and interfering," and so on. This way of organizing observations is comparable to Mehrabian's (1969) approach preserving meaningful chunks. But Mehrabian's observations were confined to displays of attitudinal information, whereas Scheflen's "positions" referred to various kinds of actions, some affecting the process of an interaction and some communicating emotion. That they are actions does not preclude that they may also convey interpersonal attitude. Scheflen's (1964) "positions" are identified by their repetition by therapists and patients in different circumstances throughout a session or over a course of sessions and by their creation of behavioral differences in each participant. Interpersonal attitude, as defined by Mehrabian (1969) may contrast with other attitudes but may or may not create a behavioral difference in a particular session or within a particular dyad of therapist and patient; but it might in another session or for another dyad.

Scheflen identified certain behaviors, actones, as those which con-

---

[4]Subdivisions beyond what seemed salient to the situation were not made. For example, Scheflen thought that in this situation there was no point to subdividing a gesture such as raising the palm to the chest into handraising and handlowering, nor to put in foot waggling just because it happened to cooccur. This limitation in observation distinguishes his approach from that of the school of practical analysis, which catalogues all movements, not only those which create an obvious interactive difference. Also Freedman (1977), of the intrinsic-meaning position, notes foot waggling as preparatory to speaking and thus shows showing a third, contrasting point of view on the same occurrence.

tribute to another main event. Main events, for example, might be dressing or having lunch. Actones relate to the main event and function to maintain the transaction but can also change it. For example, pipe lighting, nose blowing, picking up a tissue, touching, clothing adjustment, and stroking can all be seen to service a main event, or to be a transition between positions or places where engagement will occur. In one case, when one of the patients stroked her thigh, one of the therapists would invariably stroke his chair in synchrony. The question of what this gesture might "mean" may follow from noting its function as servicing, transitioning, or maintaining engagement.

At times, body segments were engaged differently, creating different channels in simultaneous operation. For example, one person would be watching or speaking to someone, aligned facially, and at the same time the torso would be turned in another direction, say to hand someone else a tissue. In Birdwhistell's language, these are contrasting and simultaneous kinemorphic constructions. In this case, the two channels carried the symbolic in speaking and the actonic in the hands. One of the patient's positions was dual channeled. She would lament by her speech and head and shoulder movements but with her lower body showed courting behavior, in an actone, maintaining engagement. Other layers of analysis showed representation sequences, such as dominance and submission displays, and quasi-courting. About multichanneled communication, Scheflen (1973) wrote:

> People have a number of different modalities and bodily regions to work with in maintaining the communicational process. They use each of these in a multi-channeled system and features of each modality are integrated in a communicative unit like the position. Multiple simultaneous communicational relationships collectively maintain the group and constitute the social organization [p. 83].

Scheflen (1965) also wrote on "courtship" behavior as a model for all human interaction, including that between patient and analyst. He found, again by studying films of therapists and patients, that all participants used what seemed to him to be "courting" behaviors. Preening, hip rolling, presenting and caressing the leg were present even though there seemed to be no overt sexual intention given or received. Scheflen interpreted this behavior to indicate a state between immediate sexual preoccupation and marked sexual inhibition, which enhances attractiveness, enabling a person to be compelling. Further, he suggested that we manipulate these "courting" behaviors to create optimal levels of relatedness. He found that these behaviors occur in all therapies, even in psychoanalysis, although in the latter he thought it occurred more covertly.

The issue in psychoanalysis is not only "covertness" but the fact that there is a great deal of action that is *attenuated,* on a small scale, because of the positioning of the patient and the analyst, and less noticed because of the heightened attention to speech and its accompaniments. Nevertheless, since speech and nonverbal behavior are as linked as research so far indicates, action's attenuation does not hamper the operation of nonverbal factors. The analyst, according to Scheflen, adjusts the level of involvement and the transference or the level of sexual or dependent involvement. Quasi-courting, he thought, might be one of perhaps many devices for engaging or cooling off the relationship.

But it is important to note in his statement about "courtship behavior" that Scheflen moved somewhat away from Birdwhistell's (1952, 1970) strict context-analytic approach here. This move shows how difficult it is to eliminate "intuitive" interpretations of behavior based on an implicit assumption of intrinsic meaning, even when one is starting from an opposing theoretical commitment. That is, to follow Birdwhistell's approach strictly, I believe, would be to say that there are two situations in which similar behaviors are significant interactively. In the first situation, the behaviors are received as a sexual message; in the second, the same movement sequence is perceived as lacking the sexual component. This should mean that all such behavior would be placed in a higher order category—perhaps *behaviors that serve to establish and maintain connection.* If this is not done, Birdwhistell's method of contextual determination of meaning has not been followed; rather, meaning has been determined through reference to "intuitions"—what Birdwhistell claims are learned meanings and what the claims to be understanding based on intrinsic kinetic connections to meanings. Scheflen does not look to the minor aspect of Birdwhistell's system, "body-based motion qualifiers," which might give the missing details that further distinguish the two movement sequences. (These could be more fully delineated by the school of practical analysis, which puts them in center focus.)

Without disconfirming our intuitive connection of the two behaviors, we would do well to press forward Birdwhistell's aim here, whatever the basis for our understanding of meaning; we might therefore learn something new about sexuality and attachment. But Scheflen's use of "courtship" shows how difficult it is, even for one of the cultural school, to be rid of an immediate, "intuitive" response to nonverbal behavior.

Scheflen (1965) proposed that the expression of a certain degree of involvement, including quasi-courting behaviors, was necessary to "provide an environment for the learning experiences which psychotherapy must be if it is to be successful" (p. 195). Scheflen's emphasis adds to our understanding of the therapist's effect on the patient. Further, he stressed the importance of new learning in the relationship over "uncovering" what is unbearable to the patient. Scheflen's research reinforced his point of view and provides an important corrective to a singular focus on the individual. Scheflen indicated that, even when people do not know that they are enticing, or distancing, their behavior inadvertently moves in these directions in a dyad. It seems, then, that the larger, more intentionally performed behaviors of Alexander (1963; Alexander and French, 1946), Ferenczi (1919, 1926, 1931, 1933), and Winnicott (1949a, 1960a, 1962) are but extremes along a continuum. This idea is consistent with contemporary views that emphasize the interactive aspect of psychoanalysis and the inevitability of countertransferential as well as transferential "acting," but it has not eliminated the significance of intuitively grasped meanings in behavior.

Pointing out a limitation in Birdwhistell's approach (and by implication that of Scheflen), Kristeva (1973), herself a language theorist, criticized Birdwhistell for not going far enough in his work with the nonverbal to get beyond the thrall of language. Because Birdwhistell used linguistics as a structural frame for understanding body language, she thought his work fell short of where it could go in allowing body behavior to inform linguistic analysis. In my view, this problem may stem partly from an inherent paradox. Communicative exchange about body language occurs through linguistic discourse. Yet it is only when verbal content is put aside that all language, even written, can be seen to be a part of nonverbal expression. That is, even written, and certainly spoken, language carries the rhythmic intensity and even spatial attributes paralleled by the writer's bodily expression. But the direct attempt to view all language as nonverbal expression has not been made yet, although Birdwhistell (1952, 1970, 1973) and Scheflen (1964, 1965) went far in this direction by stressing that the verbal and nonverbal are under the same cultural constraints.

Yet the cultural school has also generated work that does seem to move toward seeing how language exists *within* nonverbal connectedness. Condon (1980, 1982; Condon and Ogston, 1971; Condon and Sander, 1974) and Byers (1976, 1982) forged a link between social interaction, and intrinsic, biological systems affecting interaction and in so doing they allowed for a refinement of what we mean by cultural and intrinsic, which also has implications for understanding language use. Their work is illustrated by the following clinical examples.

Mary starts out sitting straight in her chair, both feet touching the floor, and I start sitting slightly to one side, my legs crossed. At some point later, I notice that we are both sitting, legs crossed, mirror images of each other. Another patient, Bob, on the couch, moves simultaneously with my movements or a fraction of a second later even though he cannot see me.

I find also that my movements serve as a question might. I need not ask, "What are you thinking?" I need only shift my position to stimulate the patient to speak.

Condon and his colleagues and Byers demarcated an aspect of interactional behavior that they found to be based on biological, not learned systems. In Condon and Ogston (1971) we find an examination of the group that leads through their initial focus on the social aspects of behavior into biological underpinnings and "innate" meanings of a kind different from that set down by the original . Still, their approach, like Birdwhistell's, emphasizes interaction and the elimination of the distinction between the verbal and nonverbal aspects of behavior.

Condon (1967, 1982) and his collaborators (Condon and Ogston, 1971; Condon and Sander, 1974) are known for their delineation of the concept of self- and interactive synchrony. They found that body movements occur in synchrony with the rhythmic patterning of speech, both one's own and that of someone to whom one is listening. Their work emphasizes the rhythmic attributes of language and body movement and the way that interaction occurs like a dance at a level not always apparent. The hiddenness of this level of engagement may be due to the fact that it is basic to all other communication to which we do attend. Condon (1982) found also that pathology may be defined in terms of the inability to achieve self- and interactive synchrony. Holding to the cultural school's emphasis on learning, Condon proposed that infants begin to learn the culture's rhythms in the womb. But he also defined an interactive effect between the culture's selection of a particular language and rhythm and the necessary biological substrate; it is this effect that makes learning possible.

According to Condon (1976, 1980, 1982), the nature of self- and interactive synchrony, and their link to a biological explanation, is illuminated by the fact that the speed of reaction required for synchrony to occur negates the possibility that it could be learned. This process is claimed to be regular and salient at a microlevel of analysis (occurring in fractions of seconds). That is, a speaker's body movement is rhythmically coordinated with speech: changes in the body of a speaker occur in precise timing with changes in the structure of his or her speech. Further, listeners' movements entrain, within .05 seconds, with the speaker's speech and body rhythms. One study showed infants responding in this way to their mothers' speech (Condon and Ogston, 1971).

Condon (1967, 1976, 1980, 1982; Condon and Ogston, 1971) discovered this process by observing movement's continuity rather than its segmented quality, as had Birdwhistell (1970) and Scheflen (1963, 1964, 1973). For example, after long observation of a family dinner on film, they began to note such phenomena as the wife's head moving at the exact moment (within .05 seconds) when the husband's hands came up. Such synchronous events occurred throughout the film. Condon (1982) began to see body motions "in bundles;... [such that] as a person is talking, there's a changing and moving together of the body parts which are precisely synchronized with the articulatory structure of his or her speech" (p. 54). This observation led him to believe that communication occurs not as exchanges of discrete gestures but as an on-going *modulation* that takes place between people in a continuous fashion. There is never any absence of communication, according to this model. The listener's body frequency modulates within 50 milliseconds to the incoming sound structure of the speaker's speech and, in fact, can do so to any sound.

Condon found that humans entrain and "lock in" even inanimate sounds within 50 milliseconds. He established that there is a myogenic (muscle) response to sounds within 10 to 50 milliseconds. This response occurs without awareness. The body–mind "attends," but another part of the mind is otherwise occupied. These muscle responses depend on the synchronization of on-going muscular, tonic activity to speech which again occurs within 10 to 50 msecs of onset (p. 57).

Condon (1982) postulated that the rhythm of the speaker becomes anticipated outside awareness by the listener. He interpreted this phenomenon as suggesting that interactional synchrony is, for one thing, an early phase in the auditory perceptual process for most organisms. Body motion, then, seems to be formed of "process units: or bundles of movement, where the body parts change and sustain motion together" (p. 61).[5] There also appears to be a one-second rhythm cycle in speaker behavior, in which the phrasings of speech and body motion can be seen to occur at approximately one-second intervals. This observation is viewed as support for Birdwhistell's (1970) idea that there are basic units of body movement of a particular duration.

Condon (1980, 1982) has suggested, too, that a consonant-vowel-consonant (CVC) pattern exists in body motion as in speech. The CVC distinction is fundamental in speech. When a speaker articulates a word, there is

---

[5]Kendon (1970) extended the concept and showed how movements of different body parts correspond to different units of speech. The larger the speech unit, the more body parts are involved in a "speech preparatory movement." Also, larger movement waves fit "over" larger segments of speech, such as words or phrases, and smaller movement waves, contained within the large one, fit over the smaller segments such as syllables and sub-syllabic tone changes. Later Kendon (1972) demonstrated from the microanalysis of a film of four men conversing in an informal setting how the boundaries of the movement waves of the listeners coincide with the boundaries of the speakers. A listener may not be mirroring the speaker's shape, but he is moving his hands or eyes or even blinking in a synchronous rhythm.

an initial onset or releasing sound that rises in intensity and then falls to an arresting sound form, ending the word. This releasing sound creates a pulse. Condon (Condon and Sander, 1974) found that the body is precisely locked in and integrated with this flow so that the body will hold quietly on a consonant and speed up on a vowel, and this rhythm occurs within other rhythms.

Where such rhythmic coordination does not occur at all, that is, in the absence of self- and interactive synchrony, something hard to define but significant seems "off" (Condon, 1976). In pathology neither the body nor vocal patterns follow the CVC pattern, and they do not synchronize with each other. Condon (1982) reported on a film of Eve Black, who was diagnosed as a multiple personality. Usually able to view a film for four to five hours a day, he found himself falling asleep when viewing this one, a sign to him that something was wrong dynamically. He noticed after a while that as Eve talked, one eye shifted over to the camera and the other stayed on the psychiatrist, a dramatic example of self-asynchrony, interfering with the viewer's ability to synchronize with her.

Condon (1982) stressed that a biological substrate for interactional behavior is essential for learning to take place. Condon (1980) believed that this aspect of interaction involves an ethical dimension, since he found that human communication affects the "inner being" of others. Nonverbal and out-of-awareness posture sharing occurs in all kinds of dyads and groups. Posture sharing creates a state of "communion" for good or ill. Nonverbal posture sharings, what might be referred to as "the vibes" in a group, is a metaphorical rendering of what Condon and Ogston (1971), and Byers (1976, 1982) delineated. We recognize "the vibes" when we realize that the mere presence of a particular person in a group has an impact on the group's overall feeling and dynamics.

Others have followed Condon and Ogston (1971). And while the frequency of interactional synchrony is not always confirmed, its presence is. A study by McDowell (1978) of the frequency of interactional synchrony in groups of six people, a mix of male and female, friends and strangers, did not find interactional synchrony to be as frequent as originally suggested. But he did find that there was a tendency for synchrony to be more frequent where "the interaction flowed more smoothly" (p. 973), thereby confirming an important aspect of Condon and Ogston's (1971) theory about the importance of synchrony between speaker and listeners for "good" communication.

The existence of a related phenomenon, "posture sharing," broadens the possibilities in this domain. La France (1979) examined not interactional synchrony but postural synchrony (a phenomenon first identified by Scheflen, 1966) and found a connection between "posture sharing" and rapport. She studied this connection in classes of 15 college students in relation to their professor: she made 10 measures per session, and two sessions were recorded. Posture sharing was found to be a moment of posture mirroring. For example, the professor with his right hand under his chin was mirrored by students using their left hands under their chins. In these sessions, La France found that posture sharing and rapport were positively related. That is, reported experience of rapport between students and professor corresponded with higher amounts of posture sharing, which was out of their awareness but seen by the researcher.

If interactional synchrony and posture sharing occur with positive results for communication and rapport, the question for analysts is what this relationship implies about communication with patients. Assuming that they are is different in each case, we need to ask what inhibits or enhances their occurrence with each patient. First, by all indications, interactional synchrony cannot be consciously executed and postural synchrony usually occurs without awareness. Therefore, these behaviors cannot be construed as a "signal," although they may be signs and concomitants of being "with" and "open to" each other. They are as much a product of being open and connected as they are a means to openness and connection. Second, the existence and significance of these phenomena point to the importance of the body in interaction. To move with another is to show that one is with another, and it may simply be that we cannot *fully* understand another unless we can be with in this way. It is not that we show we are with and then communication takes place, but rather that we must *be with* in mind and body as communication takes place. If there are blocks to being with, then full communication is not taking place, except the communication of a major or minor blockage. To be sure, interaction of some kind and feel is always taking place. Yet equally certainly, the extreme pathological self-asynchrony of schizophrenia noted by Condon (1982; Condon and Ogston, 1971), to take an example, would drastically inhibit interactive synchrony or posture sharing. There are other degrees of difficulty that get in the way but that should be noted and worked with. In my clinical experience, there are different reasons for this problem: some patients have rigid physical defenses preventing easy mutual adjustment; others speak so fast or so slowly that the pace of their speech interferes with attunement. Kestenberg and Sossin (1979) have demonstrated temperamental matching and clashing, which also contribute to the ease or difficulty of communication in a dyad or group.

Related studies by the anthropologist Byers (1976) of speech and movement behavior corroborated the cross-cultural occurrence of interactive synchrony in groups. In addition, he added usefully to these concepts. Very significant for analysts, Byers's (1976, 1982) research amplified what Condon

(1976, 1980, 1982) has said about interactive synchrony. Byers (1976) added the idea that individual variation creates irregularities, which become information for each participant through comparison with the standard set by each individual's own temperamentally defined rhythmic propensity. Regularities and irregularities can be seen as a basis for transference and countertransference reactions, that is, the structure on which subjective experiences of one another are built. First, Byers demonstrated that speech and movement share underlying organizational properties and that appropriate segmentation, that is, phrasing into meaningful units, can be derived either from the vocal track or from movement. He cited evidence that there are two primary brain rhythms, with frequencies of 10 cycles/second and 7 cycles/second, that act as pacers or integrators of motor activity, of which speech is one kind. All behavior is, then, seen as lying along a hierarchy of levels of organization with rhythms specific to levels. In support of this point is his analysis, mentioned earlier, in chapter 3, of films of the Netsilik Eskimo, the Bushmen of the Kalahari Desert in Africa, and the Maring of New Guinea. Looking systematically at what other workers with such films had noted informally, he corroborated that changes of one sort or another (for example, changes in the direction of movement, pacing, repetitions) normally occur at five- or ten-frame intervals.

This sort of analysis is quite complex, since body movement is "multichanneled" such that a mover/speaker may be acting in relation to more than one other, for example talking to one, glancing at another, and waving to a third, while caressing a child or carrying out another task. Also, some aspects of body movement are related to adaptational purposes, such as opposing gravity, maintaining balance, and the like.

In all, Byers noted, in a film of Eskimos watching one group member skinning a seal, that, while there was minimal movement in space and mostly small shifts in weight or idle movements of sticks that individuals held in their hands, a common rhythm or beat, 10 cycles per second, underlay all the movements. In the film of the Maring of New Guinea, a dozen people, members of two clans, were arguing about the killing of one clan member's dog by a member of the other clan. While he did not have independent data identifying clan membership, Byers found that about half the group moved in synchronous relation with a given speaker. The third film, of Kung of the Kalahari, documented a ritualized storytelling practice. One Kung tribesman talked a "story line" while listeners imitated part of his gestures in a prescribed way and added comments over his speech and repeated syllables of his speech at the end of certain segmental or syntactic units. Analysis of underlying rhythms revealed two intermixed, out-of-phase sets of speech bursts, each falling at 0.2-second intervals. (This 0.2-second rhythm corresponds to the other measure of 10 cycles per second brain rhythms.) These findings underscore the rhythmic continuities between people that cooccur, providing room for synchronization.

Second, Byers (1982) noted that there are individual variations in rhythm that also provide an asymmetry or irregularity against a regular rhythm. His point relates individual personality to group interaction. He described a conversation between two people as an oscillation that moves between regularity and an irregularity or asymmetry assignable to the differing personalities of the individuals and to the state of their immediate relationship. The states of the individuals and the state of their relationship could be described in terms of temporal measurements of their behavior, singly and conjointly defined. This information is continuously available to persons in face-to-face relationships, although the only reference or comparator that a person has available is his own state-modulated rhythm.

Byers cited for corroboration Chapple's "interaction chronograph," which emphasizes temporality in measurements of the interaction behavior of a subject in a controlled interview. Chapple (1976) found that certain properties of the interactional behavior of individuals do not vary and that these properties are tied to rhythmic characteristics. The invariant properties are (1) the amount of interaction the person requires, (2) the habitual frequency of interactions, (3) the origin–response ratio (how often he or she initiates or responds), (4) the rhythm of his or her interaction rate, and (5) her or his ability to synchronize or adjust to others. Differences in these dimensions may produce asymmetries and lack of synchronization at change points between moments of synchronization or, more generally, may work against synchronization.

A third point is Byers's (1982) conclusion that groups of people reinforce synchrony as a way to support connection and discourage aggressive behaviors. He postulated that groups of people engage in synchronous and phase-related behaviors (ordinary conversation, marching, dancing, singing, etc.) as a way of supporting, reinforcing, or leading individuals toward adaptive interrelationships and away from maladaptive or lethal relationships. He concurred with Chapple's (1970) argument that interpersonal synchrony–dissynchrony has biological concomitants that the individual experiences as feeling good (synchrony) and bad (dissynchrony). Feeling good, Byers said, is therefore not just an internal matter (biologically or psychologically) but an internal concomitant of being in a synchronous, or phase-related, connection with the environment, both physical and social. The rhythms are biologically determined, and the two rhythms that Byers delineated correlate with brain waves and the upper limit of human movement frequency:

I have found a 7 c/sec rhythm in speech traces when the speaker is performing speech instead of talking with another person. When, for example, a Maring at a ceremony shouts to his dead ancestors to come to the ceremony, the underlying rhythm is 7 c/sec. When one Yanomamo shouts to a group of others to help him sweep the village plaza in preparation for a feast, the rate is 7 c/sec. But when a villager shouts back and the two "talk," the rates are then 5-10 c/sec. I have recorded and processed radio news broadcasts, and found again that this performed speech shows an underlying 7 c/sec rhythm. When, however, a person anywhere in my film data is working at a task—chopping, hitting, paddling a canoe, hoeing, etc.—the rhythm appears to be task-related and is not otherwise predictable. But even when a person is carrying out a repetitive task at a task-related rate, and another person comes along and engages the first in conversation, the shared rhythm invariably shifts to fit the 5-10 c/sec frequency [p. 158].

Since each person is then phase related to another on multiple levels, and the rhythms are modulated by and reflect the state of the human organism, information is constantly available to each interactant about the multilevel states of the other. This information is not processed as a message from one to another, but operates through the joint modulations of rhythms that are a reflex of total mind–body states, and the modulated rhythm is an accurate representation of the participants' states.

Stern (1982a, b, 1985), a psychoanalyst and also researcher in infant and mother interaction, gives a different emphasis to interactive rhythms, which he calls interactional rhythmicity, a term he favors over interactional synchrony. His work delineates the significance of irregularities of rhythm in mother–infant interactions. His work and that of other infant researchers offer pictures of interaction that help to explain the following clinical vignette.

For several months, Ann would arrive at my office in an very low-keyed state, barely able to talk. Her behavior called forth from me a set of behaviors that would gradually "bring her up." Feeling at first concerned about her lack of aliveness, I would sit at the edge of my chair and say little, but speak in a low voice and with a light manner. I might repeat, for example, "You seem very low today. It seems something's bothering you." Initially, she would seem barely to notice me. I might say, "Perhaps you don't want to, or can't take me in today" at moments when she took a breath. I varied my volume and intensity slightly each time I spoke, and gradually there was a gradient upward in my volume and intensity, as she began to follow me, moving a little in her chair as I spoke. Eventually she began to liven up just enough to talk and interact with me.

Stern (1982b) suggests that, through entrainment, infants and caregivers mutually regulate the interactive level of excitation, rising and falling, through both regular and irregular rhythmic interaction. He came to this model as a result of examination of the way maternal initiative in establishing certain rhythms functions to maintain an optimal level of arousal and positive affect in her baby.

To demonstrate the nature and importance of interactional rhythmicity, Stern (1985), Tronick, Als, and Adamson (1979), Beebe et al. (1982), Gianino and Tronick (1985), Tronick (1987), and others have shown, by analyzing short, filmed interaction sequences, that very young infants have the capacity to regulate social engagement through behaviors that seek out and invite or discourage stimulation. Baby and mother engage in a complex interplay of initiatives on both sides. Stern et al. (1977) developed the Infant Engagement Scale, used to judge infants' reactions to mothers' initiatives on an axis of "engagement" to "disengagement," based on observations along a continuum from sustaining to disrupting face-to-face contact. Beebe et al. (1982) observed that the levels of relatedness are thought of as both degrees and modes of interpersonal relatedness across a continuum from high positive engagement to inhibition of responsivity. The kind of infant behavior noted is, for example, "a limp head hang," a sudden cessation of activity toward a motionless limp state, or movements of the head in horizontal (side-to-side), vertical (up-and-down), or sagittal (frontward and backward) planes as the baby scans, looks at, or looks away from mother.

While studies (Tronick et al., 1979; Beebe et al., 1982b) have documented that regularity and repetition of microrhythms are characteristic of maternal stimulation, Stern (1982b) contends that it is also in veering from the *expected regularities* that expression has an effect. A regular, and generally slow, maternal rhythm of behavior best enhances positive affect; with too much irregularity, quickness, and no sustained repetition, infant engagement and pleasure drop off. Periods of regularity allow the mother and infant to synchronize, with the resultant good feelings this produces when properly timed; irregularity operates against synchrony for a change or break in rhythmic synchronization. The particular tempo and degree of variance seem to be important in these formulations.

According to Beebe et al. (1982), an optimal range of tempos may be demonstrable in individual infant–mother pairs. Mothers can and do learn to alter the tempo of their movements and speech to come more into attunement with their infants. On the basis of these kinds of regularities, Stern (1982b) demonstrated the importance of irregularity. He showed, for example, how, in a game they often play with babies, mothers repeat, "I'm gonna getcha" several times, each time stretching the interval between phrases until the surprise, quick ending, "Gotcha!" The affect and excitement are not generated by more stimulation, but by playing against the expectation of regularity, involving cognitive operations of the baby. Similarly, Stern observed that rhythms for sustaining soothing have a precise, slow tempo and regularity. But the slow, steady tempo achieved is not the only essential. Typically, the mother goes above the baby's rhythm first and brings baby down in tempo. Thus, an irregular tempo initiates the soothing and gradually leads to the steady tempo that maintains the baby's quiet state.

Irregularities, built on expected regularity of rhythm between baby and others, allow baby to attend to speech but not to habituate to it, which would lessen impact. Stern (1985, pp. 108–112) found that babies and mothers do the same things kinetically as they do vocally (confirming Birdwhistell's, 1952, 1970, 1973, contention that the visual and vocal aspects of behavior are of the same structure). Stern (1982b) used voice spectrograph analyses to show how vocal pitch contours worked in interactive situations. For example, he showed how a baby's attention was gained by mother's sharp rise in pitch as she said, "What's the matter, huh?"

It is with the irregularities of rhythm that the mother qualifies her intentions. For example, she can intensify a sense of urgency by gradually shortening the time it takes to raise her tone in subsequent bursts as she says, "Come on, come on, come on!" Such a variation in the expectable is a signal that something needs attention or change.

The communicative significance of rhythmic changes in pitch parallels kinesic changes of shape, intensity and timing that are continuously occurring, as is pitch change (Stern, 1985). These dimensions, again, are relevant cross-modally, applicable in sight, sound, touch, kinesthetic awareness, and the like. For instance, all standard, or what Stern calls "categorical affects" (happy, sad, angry, etc.), whether expressed in voice, facial configurations, or movements, can be described through characteristic changes in the dimensions of shape, intensity, and timing. For example, "happy" is affined with rising intensity, quickness in tempo, and indirectness spatially. Stern postulates that, beyond the "categorical affects," there are many qualities of feeling that do not fit into the existing lexicon of affects which are

---

[6]These ideas are also to be found in the work of gestalt psychologists Asch and Arnheim. Arnheim (1949) said, "expressive behavior reveals its meaning directly in perception" following the "principle of isomorphism, according to which processes which take place in different media may be . . . similar in their structure" (p. 308). Asch (1958) said, "There is apparently no aspect of nature that does not serve to express psychological realities. Light and darkness express the conditions of knowledge and ignorance, while the action of rivers and storms and the change of the seasons are the images in which we describe the vicissitudes of life and the data of inner experience. Conversely, there are, it seems, hardly any psychological terms, *sui generis*, denoting psychological operations exclusively. . . . Our language

captured by more dynamic, kinetic terms such as "surging," "fading," "exploding," "drawn out" (p. 54).[6] These can be analyzed dimensionally as changes in intensity, time, and shape, and they are felt within oneself and experienced through observing the behavior of other people, as in a rush of anger or joy or the flooding of light. He calls these "feelings of vitality" and posits that they may be experienced by a baby visually, when baby sees mother fold diapers, or felt, for example, when mother picks up baby and performs the range of ordinary daily functions. So the manner of performance of a parent's act expresses a "vitality affect" as well as whatever "categorical affects" might be involved. The dimensions of experience of intensity, time, and shape find further delineation in the school of practical analysis (see chapter 10).

Proponents of the cultural school give equal weight to nonverbal and verbal behavior in analytic therapies. For example, Stern's (1995) concept of the "protonarrative envelope" (p. 202) delineates how experiences of affect and nonverbal behaviors are integrated in interactive patterns of being with another. The details of "what it is like to be with someone in a certain way" (p. 202), which may or may not be recategorizable into concepts of drive, other motivational systems, or self and other, are usable in themselves to elucidate what is happening and what may have happened. These points are directly relevant to the construction of narrative history and to the understanding of transference and counter-transference formation.

Other findings of the cultural school pertain to the technical realm of psychoanalysis. Condon, and his colleagues, Byers, Stern, and others demonstrated that the speech alone of the analyst has present dynamic impact as well as possible transferential meaning. Changes in pitch are analyzable according to variations in intensity, shape (sound is often experienced spatially, for example, full, thin, high, low, deep) and time,[7] all of which are also salient dimensions of change in other sensory modalities (besides hearing, also sight, touch, taste). Stern (1985) has shown evidence that infants generalize from one sensory mode to another through these abstract dimensions.[8] Such a process has relevance to the infant's, child's, and adult's

---

has not established a distinct vocabulary pertaining exclusively to psychological phenomena. To be sure we possess many terms that have become specialized in a psychological direction (e.g., hope, jealousy, wrath). However, their etymology reveals they once had a clear physical reference" (pp. 325–326).

[7]These dimensions were noted by Birdwhistell (1970) as the dimensions of "motion qualifiers," and the school of practical analysis performs movement analysis based on these same categories (Laban and Lawrence, 1947).

[8]Many studies cited by Stern (1985) showed that infants as young as three weeks have cross-modal fluency. For example, infants could discriminate visually between

capacity to construct an internal model of the interactions with objects and others through sensorimotor experiences that become generalized. This capacity implies that new internal models of analyst and patient interaction might be built through the extension of the qualities of speech alone (and, of course, be augmented by visual experience) and be generalized to other sensory dimensions (touch, e.g.), forming a whole interactive scheme experienced in fantasy in all modalities. Thus, the dimensions of an analyst's speech indicate what the analyst is like in other modalities. Patients may use their experience with this aspect of the analyst to create fantasy interactions that can serve to repair missing experience, redo bad experience, and yield more knowledge of the analyst.

Data from infant research (Stern et al., 1977; Tronick, 1987), in conjunction with findings about rhythmic interactive patterning in all human groups (Condon and Ogston, 1971; Condon and Sander, 1974; Byers, 1976, 1982; La France, 1979), point to self- and mutual regulation processes in the psychoanalytic dyad. These findings suggest that both analyst and patient are engaged in nonverbal management of their own states, and simultaneously, of the interaction between them, which in a circular fashion contributes the processes of state regulation of each individual (Lachmann and Beebe, 1997). This picture of interaction suggests that analyst and patient are nonverbally influencing one another at all times.

---

two pacifiers of different texture (one smooth, one nubbly) after having sucked on only one of them and not having viewed either one. It is thought that the mode of transfer of information between modes of perception occurs through the abstract categories of intensity, timing, and shape.

CHAPTER 10

The School of Practical Analysis

※

The school of practical analysis, having originated the work of Laban (1950; Laban and Lawrence, 1947), falls chronologically and theoretically between the other two. It addresses in-depth aspects of nonverbal behavior that are touched on but not dwelt on by the intrinsic-meaning position and the cultural school. In bringing them into central focus, the school of practical analysis lays out details, not yet seen, pertaining to how attunement is accomplished and what in nonverbal terms constitutes the individual. The following are cases in point.

Each session with Abby would begin with a friendly, relaxed tone. But inevitably, she would become very angry at me. She would complain loudly, "You don't understand what I'm saying." I never saw the anger coming, because I always felt quite comfortable with her, and it seemed she with me, before her outburst. As we worked on these moments, it became clearer that it was not what I said that provoked her, but how I said it.

In another therapeutic encounter, with a couple, I could see a similar interactive problem between them. The wife moved with light, direct, and gradually changing tension. She also had a fine touch and was capable of sustained thought with a flexible, sometimes hesitant approach to decisions and action. She moved and thought very differently from her husband. His movement was strong and alternately gradually changing and abruptly changing in tension flow. He was indirect in his movement in space and in thought. He did not directly counter arguments but brought in new information or moved to another concern. Neither could explain how the husband enraged the wife, but she felt repeatedly enraged and helpless.

The school of practical analysis operates outside the extreme polarities from which the intrinsic-meaning position and the cultural-school ideas originated. This position is *not a synthesis of the other two, but is a third,* independent point of view, which nevertheless has lines of connection to the two previously discussed.

While Laban began with a practical task of finding a way to record movement and its dynamic qualities in fine detail, he discovered that there were regularly occurring links between them and "attitudes." How a person moves has bearing on adaptation to the environment, to other persons, and to self-experience.

Not a research scientist, Laban was a dancer and choreographer. A major difference in his work begins with this fact and with his aims, which were practical as well as theoretical. He wanted, first, to establish a way to record dance accurately and, second, to analyze movements involved in manual labor in order to aid efficiency. He was not initially investigating the meaning of movement, but rather movement per se, the relationships between movements, and the "fit" of particular movements and movement qualities to actions on the environment. His work evolved from that point into a highly detailed phenomenology of movement and mind. The differences among the schools create three spheres of overlapping sets that together offer a detailed picture of nonverbal behavior. Laban looked at individuals' movement and how movement affects interaction with people and things and framed questions from that vantage: what are the dimensions that define movement within its own parameters; how are movements to be distinguished from one another; how can terms be developed to define efficient and inefficient movement behavior; how may people be characterized through the dimensions of body movement they habitually utilize; how do the movement characteristics of two or more people interact?

I am emphasizing two aspects of Laban's (1950; Laban and Lawrence, 1947) perspective that are especially helpful in developing the psychoanalyst's visual and kinesthetic senses. Since he studied movement from a production and practice starting point, the first aspect to be noted is that he did not give precedence to nonverbal behavior's sign function or communicative dimensions (as do the other two schools). Rather, he started from a person's adaptive style with things and with other people as physically, not only psychologically, experienced objects. Second, he found an intrinsic connection between subjective experience and the dimensions of movement. Laban elaborated the correspondences he observed between movement repertoires and the attitudes of the individuals he studied, in what amounts to a phenomenology of movement and mind, as we will see.

Laban began his work 20 years earlier than did the researchers of the other two schools, but his approach was rejected as a research tool by members of each group for different reasons. The reasons for this rejection provide a beginning framework for understanding it. Indeed, part of the task of understanding Laban's work is to recognize that it belongs to a different logical order from that of prior research discussed. First, Mehrabian (1972) complained that it did not allow "meaningful units" of behavior to be isolated and recorded but that movements are recorded as such, without prior reference to what they signify.

This claim is true, for Laban did not focus on defining any particular body language or emotional, attitudinal state. Rather he developed Labanotation, a method for the detailed notation of *any* sequence of movement. For this reason, Labanotation and Effort/Shape (E/S) analysis—a system for classifying *how* movements are performed—together could enhance but not replace a detailed analysis of the motion factors that proponents of the intrinsic-meaning position, such as Ekman and Friesan (1974b, 1976, 1982); Ekman et al. (1971, 1972, 1980 [both]); Mehrabian (1972); Mehrabian and Williams (1969); Freedman (1977); Freedman et al. (1972), and Mahl (1968, 1977) delineated as salient in "emotion," "attitude," "symbolizing," or "representing," since they point to a different level of movement analysis. For Laban, the grouping of characteristic nonverbal patterns came first and the link to meaning came second rather than first as in the methods of the intrinsic-meaning proponents. (The intrinsic-meaning proponents look to find emotion, attitude, symbol. Laban *looked to find* movement.)

This latter aspect of Laban's approach should have recommended it to Birdwhistell (1970) and Scheflen (1963, 1964, 1966, 1973), who regarded the intrinsic-meaning position's intuitive determination of meaning as without adequate basis. But Birdwhistell objected to Laban's theory of the concordance and continuity between inner state or attitude and movement. Birdwhistell related that he had studied Laban's methods, but set them aside because he thought they assumed what he wanted to investigate. Although this conclusion is understandable it was an error, since Birdwhistell set out to define a method of discovering a particular culture's body vocabulary and grammar, whereas Laban set out to define a recording system that could be applied to any movement sequence without prior reference to its cultural or individual character. This Laban analysis does not exclude "context analysis." In fact, Laban's work relies on framing distinctions in movement according to the contexts they create for one another. Laban-derived analysis can augment understanding of movements defined as salient within the context-analytical approach. Further, one part of Laban's system, the Effort/Shape dimension of analysis, is comparable to minor features in Birdwhistell's (1970) system, "motion qualifiers," "parakinesis," or paralanguage, indicating individuality. These features are defined by degrees of intensity, frequency, extent, and duration of movement or as stance, posture, and style (e.g., flaccidity, rigidity, tone). What had only been glanced at by Birdwhistell, because he concentrated on cultural forms not on the individual, was in fact already highly differentiated by Laban.

Stern (1985), who continues in Birdwhistell's tradition, has also not made use of Laban's work. He seems to misunderstand Kestenberg's (1975a; Kestenberg and Sossin's, 1979) use of Laban's work to delve into aspects of the individual and of interaction that Stern did not consider. He does not recognize that in his definition of "vitality affects" (pp. 53–61) he has made use of the same movement dimensions defined by Laban, without reference to Laban's systematic delineation of them. This aspect of movement is found in its intensity and shaping changes, and rhythmic patterns. Laban's work details how group rhythmic structures can evolve from varying individual patterns, and hence his work connects also to Condon's (1980, 1982) and to Byers (1976).

At no time did Laban make the assumption that a particular *gestural* "body language" is innate. Rather, Laban's work suggests that body-language systems work with innately and intrinsically meaning-leaning kinesic qualities and relations between parts, which he elaborated. It is the conjunction of meaning tendencies inherent in kinesic qualities in particular contexts that constitutes meaning. Hence context is crucial to the ultimate meaning. At the same time, he recognized that context also calls forth certain kinds of movement qualities, so that there is a natural dynamic interaction between contexts, behaviors, and meanings. For example, light, bound, flexible movement with sustained tension is appropriate for placing delicate objects, but strong, free movement with abruptly changing tetension is appropriate for hammering a nail. Also, the kinesic qualities in certain combinations and contexts carry an experiential component that gives not just a meaning that comes from context, that is, a salient signal to another, but also a subjectively felt component. One feels different doing each of those activities. And two people who use these dimensions of movement habitually are experienced differently and have distinctively different approaches to and experiences of themselves in the world of objects and other people.

It is the analysis of "effort" that yields this kind of information about an individual. "Effort" analysis has evolved into "Effort/Shape" analysis, which is a systematic categorization of *how* movements are performed rather than which particular movements are performed. Which movements are performed is scored by Labanotation, a very complex system for recording the details of any sequence of body movement, analogous to individual sounds making up words or to "kines" of body language making up "kinemorphic constructions" (Birdwhistell, 1970). Instead of delineating positions and position changes as such, the effort system focuses attention on the qualitative aspects of movement performance, their attributes of energy change. In the realm of language production, the analog to the qualities of movement is tone of voice and pitch change, rather than the word content of speech. Effort/Shape categories can be usefully applied in this arena as well.

Effort is analyzed into four component dimensions, not all of which are necessarily present at any given time, but whose "absence" is nevertheless significant. For it is the proportion and balancing of each dimension that provides efficiency in a task and conveys attitude. The four component dimensions are found in what Laban called the approaches to or attitudes toward *space, weight, time*, and *flow*. To illustrate, I take you back to the two women I discussed at the beginning of the intrinsic-meaning position (chapter 8). They were opposite in attitudes toward *flow* and *space*: the first woman was free and fluent, making use of all the space available to her, and the second was always ready to stop, and narrow in her use of space. The woman and man of the couple described at the beginning of this chapter differ in their approaches to weight and space: the woman is light in her movements, regardless of weight and gravity, while the man uses strength, engaging or "contending with" weight and gravity. She is direct and he indirect in approach to space. Because she has little or no access to strength or an indirect approach to space, she has little ability to follow him, to hold him and keep him from wandering (in his conversation with her and in his overfull life), so their arguments leave her feeling helpless and misunderstood. He, on the other side, cannot or will not attune to her, although he appreciates her superior ability to focus and be steadfast.

Thus, flow can be "bound," ready to stop, or "free," fluent, without regard for stopping. A person's quality of effort in the approach to weight can be with strength (which might be expressed as engaging and using, or fighting with, weight) or with lightness (which is regardless of weight and gravity, as if they do not exist). To determine the approach to space, it is asked whether a person is usually *direct*—moving straight to somewhere— or *indirect*—going nowhere in particular or moving all around a space. The effort analysis of time questions if the person moves with *sudden* changes, a get-there-now approach, or through *sustained* gestures and qualities, less "getting there" and more "taking my time." These poles can be characterized as attitudes: on one hand, a person can "fight against," "contend with" weight, space, time, or flow, producing the strong, direct, sudden or bound effort elements; and on the other hand, a person may "indulge or luxuriate in" the dimensions of weight, space, time or flow producing lightness, indirectness, sustainment, and fluency. People combine factors, some indulgent and some fighting, creating a rich display of many degrees of attitude toward the various motion factors.[1]

Combinations of the variables in these four dimensions create eight basic efforts: punching, slashing, wringing, pressing, dabbing, gliding, floating, flicking (that is, punch is composed of movements direct in space, strong in weight, sudden in time, and free in flow; slash, by movement indirect in space, strong in weight, sudden in time and free in flow; wring, by movements indirect in space, strong in weight, sustained in time, and bound in flow; etc.). Any other dynamic experiences can be categorized in the same way and have affinities with one or more of the basic efforts. For example, a rush of joy would be an indirect, strong, sudden (closest to "slash") experience. (This kind of analysis is thus a more detailed and systematic way to approach what Stern, 1985, noted as "vitality affects" and categorized generally through the same experiential dimensions.)

A movement shape of any part of the body, or group of parts, can be varied through effort changes by adding, for example, more of a "punching" or "floating" effort quality. "Punch" in E/S is recognized by its being strong, sudden, direct, and bound; whereas "float" is recognized by being light, sustained, and indirect, and free. A punch *shape* will lack punch in effort if it fails to have sufficient strength in the weight dimension, because it trails off into indirectness in the space dimension, or because it is not sufficiently sudden in the time dimension.

The shape aspect of E/S is analyzed according to use of movement planes (vertical, sagittal, and horizontal) and directions (upward and downward, forward and backward, side-to-side). Here we are still analyzing "how" in movement, not the exact positioning of legs, arms, torso, and head that is done through Labanotation. In shape analysis, the aim is to look at the frequency of the use of planes and directions in shaping and how well coordinated it is with effort for particular tasks. While culture also necessarily defines the use of these elements to a degree through the gestural-postural repertoire, there are nevertheless noticeable degrees of freedom of expression within the culturally determined gestural body language. For

---

[1] If it is difficult to visualize these dimensions, the following stereotypical images might be helpful. *Weight*: Contrast a wrestler's strength, always contending with gravity, and ballerina's lightness, a seeming lack of concern with gravity. *Time*: Contrast how people quickly walk on a weekday morning, fighting with time, with how they stroll on a Saturday, luxuriating in time. *Space*: Contrast the way a child may sprawl and move all around a room before coming to a stop, luxuriating in space, and the way adults to a greater extent (though still variably) will enter a room and locate themselves, contending with and limiting access to space. *Flow*: Note how some people speak in an endless stream, while others say the bare minimum and must be prodded to talk.

example, a person may show a preponderance of movement in the side-to-side direction, even while being "fluent" in American body language. Such a person will shake hands perhaps by coming first to the side of another person and moving her or his arm across from side to center and then stepping sideways into the greeting. Another might be more of a forward–back mover and approach frontally along the sagittal plane. Still a third might bob up and down in a greeting and handshake.

The approach of Laban and Lawrence (1947) to "attitude" was to observe just this: that people differ in the kind of movement dimensions they prefer habitually or overall. In addition to having varying ways to approach to space, some people may generally use a combination of strength, directness, and quickness when not constrained to do otherwise and can easily be differentiated from those who use lightness and indirectness or flexibility and sustainment. Or a person may combine strength with sustainment and will be seen as quite different from a person who combines strength and abrupt change in tension. Because of their habits, based on temperament, Laban and Lawrence found people to be better suited or ill suited to certain kinds of activities.

In addition, people may have certain difficulties due to one-sidedness, for example, as Laban and Lawrence suggest, when one-sided and exaggerated strength results over time in crampedness (think of the stereotypical weight-lifter—even when he puts down his weights he seems to hold himself in readiness to lift) or one-sided and exaggerated lightness results in sloppiness (think of a excessively light, perhaps "dithery" person who could not possibly raise the window or even the tea tray). This kind of analysis can be done for each of the effort elements. One element may predominate over others in a person. For example, the predominance of the time element will give one the character of hurriedness (the stereotypical New Yorker) or indulgence (the stereotypical Southerner) in time. People whose dominant characteristics are in their approach to space will either circulate through space and enjoy the space around them (the cocktail party wanderer who gets "caught" briefly by someone and then is off again) or be quite sparing in their use of space (the cocktail party clinger who goes to one spot and finds one person to talk to at a time). Finally, in the dimension of flow, some people enjoy letting their movements flow (a person who is continuously moving and shifting position), and others show a reluctance to do so (those who hold still and shift infrequently). Thus, each dimension can be discriminated and seen in combination, and the combinations of "preferences" or temperamental leanings in approach to space, time, weight, and flow have implications for relationships with other people as well as with the environment.

These basic approaches to weight, space, time and flow structure the

individual's involvement in and experience of certain activities and interactions, defining some as pleasurable and others as troublesome. They also
constitute "attitudes" that can be linked to character. Thus, Laban showed
how meaning is constructed from these movement features and how their
combinations are involved in the expression of intention, attitude, and
emotion. Laban also noticed that one's basic approaches to space, weight,
time, and flow are consistent over time and situation and so form a recognizable, enduring character or personality. Outside this system, it is understood that there are learned contributions to the personality. But the Laban
system helps us see that learning takes place in the context of a particular
set of behavioral dimensions that are most comfortable for the individual
and comprise that person's temperamental "talents" and "occupational
hazards," if you will.

Laban's work has been employed by other researchers interested in its
application to psychotherapy and psychoanalysis. For example, Bartenieff
and Davis (1965), dance therapists using the work, have observed significant differences in the movement patterns of schizophrenics and other
hospitalized patients. The following patient description shows the kind of
detail available through the application of Laban's methods:

> His movement was actively restricted in many ways: postural shifts
> and gestures were mainly sagittal [front and back], two-phasic,
> segmented: Head and face were often immobile as he spoke;
> dynamically the movement was very even in flow, with occasional
> instances of lightness or quickness. . . . However, for all of this
> restriction, Martin was far from inert in his manner. There were
> glimmers in the foot tapping and hand fidgeting, for example, which
> were fairly intricate and rhythmic patterns. Also the fact that he
> looked actively controlled in the postural shifts and gestures (and
> not inert or set in a neutral tonus) suggested that he may have more
> vitality when less anxious [Davis, 1970, p. 67].

Bartenieff (1980), working in a hospital setting, accurately diagnosed patients solely on the basis of their movements as defined by Laban's system.
Davis (1970) did the same. Both researchers generated data supporting
highly specific correlations between gestural patterns delineated in E/S and
states of mind, both in individual assessments and in initial aspects of the
patient–therapist relationship in interaction assessments. Dance therapists
make use of this work to understand levels of restriction of repertoire (e.g.,
the inability to perform strong movements) as well as layers of meaning in
movement. They next turn to reaching people through movement within
their range and to expanding range of expression physically and, it is hoped,
psychologically and interactively.

Lamb (1965; Lamb and Watson, 1979) and Kestenberg (1975b; Kestenberg and Sossin, 1979) have expanded Laban's original framework to deal with their observations of additional aspects of movement. It will be useful first to follow the development of Laban's work undertaken by his student, Lamb; Kestenberg built on the frameworks established by the methods developed by both Laban and Lamb.

Lamb's work was geared to understanding skill or aptitude as it related to innate temperamental qualities and character, the environmentally and interactively adapted temperament. This dimension of movement is relevant to showing how people with similar or differing aptitudes may work together or be at odds in certain ways, depending on the parts of action sequences that are emphasized by each and the context in which they function together.

Applying Laban's (1950; Laban and Lawrence, 1947) concepts, Lamb (1965; Lamb and Watson, 1979) showed how individuals' characteristic movement patterns have specific predictable relationships to decision making and action taking and how these patterns affect interactions, particularly those involving coaction. For example, if one member of a team, marriage, or family is a very good communication/exploration type, and another an operation/decision-making type, these differences may promote a symbiotic tendency in which one explores and the other acts on the analysis but is inhibited somewhat in exploring, and vice versa. Alternatively, the two might argue about what is most important in a particular situation, exploration, or operation, and whose point of view is the right one. Lamb makes use of this point of view to train people to work well together, taking into account their different predilections in movement qualities. This kind of assessment would be able to reveal, for example, why the members of a couple are often angry at each other's ways of dealing with responsibilities. For example, the husband's action profile shows his tendency to be accelerating, increasing pressure and moving with directness, and the wife's to be decelerating, decreasing pressure, and moving with indirectness. His is a "get it done yesterday approach," hers, a "let me see approach."

Lamb (1965) discovered the correspondence between predominant attitudes and the amount of "posture/gesture mergers" (PGMs) that occurs in each of several movement categories in every individual. A posture-gesture merger is noted when movement of part of the body flows into whole body movement or vice versa, for example, as when a person emphasizes a point and on the third sweep of movement of an arm up and down, the person steps forward onto the right leg, thus involving movement of the whole body. Segmented movements, gestural only, may occur when one is conflicted or restrained, or artificial or unsure, but PGMs are thought to show the truthful and stable aspects of the personality, including the structure of cognitive functioning. Such integrated movement is thought to be "committed." These moments represent the most comfortable and authentic (Winter, 1987). The "Action Profile" developed by Lamb (1965) records the amount of PGMs that appears in the four dimensions of effort and shape.

The four dimensions of effort and shape through which PGMs are categorized are the same as those Laban set out: space (indirecting or directing; spreading and enclosing), weight (diminishing or increasing pressure; rising or descending), time (deceleration or acceleration; advancing or retiring), and flow (freeing or binding, growing or shrinking).

In this form of analysis, it is not the kind of gesture (such as hitting the top of a desk or sweeping away dust) or the "emotional" or "attitudinal" stance taken that is picked up as the salient feature, but the dimensions of movement in PGMs that the individual uses most often (e.g., rising, descending, increasing pressure, acceleration, bound to freeing, as in hitting the desk, or spreading, diminishing pressure, acceleration, as in sweeping away the dust). From these elemental data, interpretations can be made of action and cognitive predilections, interpersonal attitude, and emotional range. The first three dimensions, space, weight and time, have a link respectively with three affective/cognitive attitudes of exploration, intention, and decision making, which Lamb has delineated as steps in action taking. The fourth dimension, flow, shows degree of adaptability or malleability.

Most people show a preponderance of PGMs in one of the dimensions (e.g., space/exploration or weight/intention or time/decision making) with less in each of the other two. Fewer people show a balance in each category, although all action must use, to some extent, each of the categories of movement. That is, a person who has more PGMs in a particular dimension of effort and shape is more concerned with aspects of experience that are touched by activity in that dimension than with aspects related to the other dimensions—such a person may be geared to looking around, "weighing matters," or alternatively, acting and reacting. As Lamb (1965) puts it, persons who show most PGMs in the first category, "communication type" (relating to space, the horizontal plane, indirecting and directing), are said to show a broad span of attention and observation, to be attentive to others, and to be good listeners, difficult to take by surprise, and clear in exposition. Those showing more PGMs in the second category, "presentation type" (emphasizing weight, the vertical plane, lightness, and strength), can be said to be forceful, determined, highly resolved, dedicated, able to give a convincing demonstration, confident in self-presentation, easy in their expression of authority, and always clear about where they stand. And people in the third category, "operation type" (emphasizing time, the sagittal plane, accelerating and decelerating), are decisive, ready for action and commitment to carry through a program, clear in stra-

ready for action and commitment to carry through a program, clear in strategic planning and immediate organizing, and naturally systematic. Lamb (1965) summarized these characteristics under the following headings: Communication (exploration), Presentation (intention) and Operation (decision making/action taking).

Lamb illustrated by describing a greeting made by each of the three types. The *way* in which a full action is completed by each type is determined by the emphasis on one aspect of the action. The Communication type stresses the initial meeting of eyes and subsequent attention. Such a person is most involved in observation and puts himself or herself on the same plane with the other. The next stages of greeting, the "turn and approach," followed by shaking hands or an embrace, are less emphasized by the Communication type and happen simply as an extension of the initial Communication. In contrast, for the Presentation type the initial gaze is but a fleeting moment on the way to the more important "turn and approach" segment. The Presenter underscores the *act* of presenting self to the other. This attitude is maintained through the handshake or embrace, which is conducted so as to give emphasis to the face-to-face encounter. It is not, however, the attention being given or the handshake or embrace itself that is paramount but, rather, the presence of this person with the other that is stressed. The third, Operation, type, makes much less of the meeting of eyes or the "turn and approach," but much of the handshake or embrace. The actions of coming together are uppermost. Lamb (1965) notes, "Two operation types meeting each other give an impression of great industry, almost overpoweringly so to people who are not themselves operators to any extent" (p. 151).

Among the additional, overarching categories within Lamb's system is the effect on others of persons who have great variation in the kind of behaviors at their disposal. Such people are in more "keen physical communication" than are others, irrespective of degree of intensity, as in shouting or affectionately demonstrative behavior. Those with higher than average ranges of E-S behavior and the coordinated use of affined elements of effort and shape, promote communication. With their higher loading, they "contaminate" those people who have a lower "loading" of physical behavior. This effect may not always be experienced as pleasant by those around them, and it is independent of variations in aggressiveness or extroversion, which are more obviously highly influential. Such persons may be quite shy or introverted but are nevertheless experienced as powerful and persuasive, for good or ill.

Lamb (1965) applied his system mostly to people working together and to couples and families. The same tendencies toward symbiotic functioning or clashing that coworkers and married couples are prone to are operative for the psychoanalytic dyad. For example, patients of mine whose functioning reflects most the time dimensions (advancing, retiring, and acceleration or deceleration) and least the space dimensions (indirecting or directing, spreading or enclosing) cause me to experience a clash that I register in different ways: as discomfort, as anxiety in response to their action schemes, or as an effort to halt their action with my interpretations. I operate more than such people in the space dimensions, and these patients challenge me continuously. While they may need help in the exploration phase of action taking, the question arises at what point action taking needs to dominate. For one patient, the trial-and-error approach was his only mode of operating. Even short spans of forethought were difficult or impossible. While his mode of operating made me enormously uncomfortable, he could not be expected suddenly to forego a way of dealing with life that had worked for him to some extent. Lamb's point of view offers understanding of the ways a person might expand his or her repertoire, but it also helps the analyst see the ways in which the patient's mode of operating has been adaptive and successful as well.

Kestenberg (1975; Kestenberg and Sossin, 1979), extended Laban's and Lamb's work to psychoanalytic thinking. In so doing she provided a framework for discriminating what is temperamentally innate and what changes people have incorporated in arriving at the defensive and adaptive positions that they use most often and most comfortably.

By adding the concept of "tension flow rhythms" to Laban's and Lamb's systems, the Kestenberg Movement Profile (KMP) (Kestenberg and Sossin's, 1979) permits distinctions to be made between temperamental, innate trends and later-developing characteristics. These distinctions are discerned through the analysis of the affinities, clashes, and balance or imbalance between areas of functioning depicted. In addition, comparison of profiles shows areas of matching and clashing between two or more people, an aid in understanding experiences of compatibility or conflict. For example, they describe one of the children Kestenberg observed from infancy to young adulthood as follows:

> Charlie's early preference for the diverse [i.e., clashing, nonaffined] attributes of high intensity and graduality was ameliorated when he attuned to his mother and could become less gradual [by adding more abruptness to his repertoire]. Later on he became less intense, but his original predisposition for conflict—seen in his [clashing elements of] tension flow—expressed itself in his frequent use of vehemence [a pre-effort of strength] with hesitation [a pre-effort of deceleration] and of strength with deceleration. The conflict between activity and passivity persisted, but took on a new form [p.76].

The developmental studies of Kestenberg and her colleagues (1975; Kestenberg, 1975b), conducted longitudinally, led them to the formulation that one is born with preferred tension-flow rhythms whose attributes are, like handwriting, distinctively one's own, subject to some alteration consciously and unconsciously through life, but always reflect basic unchanging dimensions. Charlie, it appeared, was born with a tendency toward conflicts: between activity, expressed in his high intensity and vehemence, and passivity, expressed in his graduality and deceleration. His mother added some abruptness to his repertoire, which could be used better with his high-intensity vehemence to get him going. Adding lower intensity later would help him be more adaptable.

Tension-flow rhythms are ascertained from watching the patterns of alternations between "bound" and "free" flow of movement that occur continuously from before birth:

> The newborn infant's toes stiffen periodically in bound flow. His legs fling and bicycle in spurts of free flow. An influx of suddenly emerging free flow may bring his fist near his mouth, and the ensuing bound flow may enable him to hold his fist there for a brief moment. Soon, however, the repetition of free flow derails the hand. In every movement of child and adult alike, one can detect a regularly occurring alternation between free and bound flow of tension, as well as a repetition of their attributes, *i.e.* evenness or fluctuation of levels, high or low intensity, abrupt or gradual change of tension. This highly differentiated self-regulation is already present in the newborn [Kestenberg et al., 1975, p. 196].

Thus a baby's individuality shows at birth in the distinctive patterning of certain movement attributes, higher or lower intensity range, stretches of evenness or more rapid fluctuation of bound or free tension, and abrupt or gradual change between high and low intensity. Tension-flow recording depicts the continuous changes from freedom from muscular tension to bound tension in an infant's movements, an oscillation that is continuous in most states.

In the KMP (Kestenberg and Sossin, 1979), tension-flow recording augments the recording of the changes of fully developed "efforts" that require a clarity of definition of movement not present in the newborn and not continuously present in the adult. Rather, full effort expression is achieved over time, through development and adaptation. Tension-flow rhythms are present from birth onward and can be traced in adults along with (a) "pre-efforts," the precursors and tentative versions used in defense or in learning of the developing full efforts, (b) "efforts," motion factors expressing changes in attitudes toward space, weight, and time that operate in the engagement with the external world, (c) "shape-flow," the changes in body shape, through expanding and shrinking symmetrically and asymmetrically, that express changes in affective experiences of objects in the environment, (d) "shaping in planes," two or three dimensional shapes sculpted in space by a person's movement that may include two or three of the spatial planes (horizontal, vertical, sagittal), and (e) "shaping in directions," movements in space to localize distant objects or to defend against stimuli and objects (Kestenberg, 1975b; Kestenberg et al., 1975; Kestenberg and Sossin, 1979; Lamb, 1965; Laban, 1950). Movement characteristics, according to Kestenberg, are not so much outgrown as augmented and refined through interactions with the environment and with other people.

Kestenberg (Kestenberg et al., 1975; Kestenberg, 1975b; Kestenberg and Sossin, 1979) categorized tension-flow rhythms in terms of the stages of psychosexual development defined by Freud (1905a, 1915c) and Abraham (1924). Her observations led her to add a urethral phase after the anal, and an inner genital phase after the urethral. Each of these phases has an indulging, yielding aspect, "libidinal," and a fighting, struggling aspect, "sadistic." She embraces Freud's theory of phase development, and designed the KMP to augment Anna Freud's (1965) developmental assessments. As a result her work has been subject to criticism both by Freudians concerned about her extension of Freud's original concepts of drive and by non-Freudians who reject drive theory.

Kestenberg's work has, of course, run afoul of those who object to Freudian drive theory and find no usefulness in conceptions that might be influenced by it. This bias is unfortunate and unnecessarily limiting. Tension-flow rhythm units are useful constructions through which to view behavior. In addition, they may be thought of in terms of their qualifying attributes alone. Kestenberg and her collaborators (1975b; Kestenberg and Sossin, 1979) were careful to say that these rhythms are not the "drives." Rather, they were named after drive phases because they represent rhythms found in muscular activity of organ zones as well as in other behavior, including speaking behavior. Also, such systematic categorization allows variations within the same person to be compared meaningfully and also permits differences between individuals along these lines to be drawn and understood.

On the other side, Freudians have disputed the association of "drive" with motor rhythms (Kestenberg and Sossin, 1979, p. 46) because the classical Freudian position does not locate drives within the body. Freud (1905a) defined drive as a border concept between mind and body. These critics have misread Kestenberg. While she "reembodied" drive, she is not, as they feared, denying its border status and its psychological aspect. She shows how drive manifests as physical behavior, not only as fantasy, and how it shapes interaction as well as thought.

The eight tension-flow rhythms of the KMP can be described as follows: "sucking," for oral libidinal, or "biting" for oral sadistic; "twisting," for anal libidinal and "straining," for anal sadistic; "running," for urethral libidinal or "run- stop–go," for urethral sadistic; "undulating," for inner genital libidinal, "swaying," for innergenital sadistic; "jumping," for phallic libidinal, and "leaping," for phallic sadistic (Kestenberg and Sossin, 1979, p. 46). Indeed, Kestenberg adhered to a strict Freudianism when she said this nonpsychoanalytic language was "in no way as accurate" as the one derived from psychoanalytic terminology (p. 47). In fact, this assurance flies in the face of her own pioneering work, in which the categories "oral," "anal," and so on do not describe anything by themselves but, rather, are further described by their attributes. In her formulation, the drive terms provide images that may be useful prototypes for the rhythms but are not a detailed account of them. Nevertheless, Kestenberg's classification of rhythms according to Freudian drive theory (Freud, 1905a; Abraham, 1924) and her combining these ideas with Laban's (1950; Laban and Lawrence, 1947) and Lamb's (1965; Lamb and Watson, 1979) has far extended them. She has shown drive phases and zonal development to be more complex, observable, and interactively salient in children and adults than theory has before attested.

Kestenberg's films of groups of children from infancy through adolescence (viewed in her classes in 1986), show concretely 1) the behaviors that can be linked with psychosexual stages of body–mind development, 2) the developmental links between mental and physical functioning, and 3) the interactive impact of the changing psychosexual stages. Drive stages are distinctive and apparent in the movement of children of different ages. During each phase, all broader functioning bears the rhythmical signs of the dominance of the particular zone that is developing. For example, in infancy, oral rhythms of sucking and biting predominate. This is a period during which orality is the chief mode of engagement with the world, but it is the whole body, not just the mouth, that is involved in this experience. Just so with each of the rhythms. In the anal period, the child's squirming, straining, stubbornness, and anal toilet development are linked kinetically and structurally. Kestenberg shows the link and adds that it is not that the stage's behavior is to be reduced causally to an organ link with the development of the anal sphincter; rather, behaviors of whole body–mind and body part are linked by the function of, for example, the "straining" rhythm (repetitive abrupt rise in tension, holding evenly, and release), common to controlling the bowels, standing up, pushing on heavy objects and refusing to cooperate. The movement attributes of the anal stage—high intensity achieved abruptly and sustained—all appear as new possibilities at the same time.

Freud's early reductivism (1912b), relying on the motivational force of drive alone to explain behavior, is not necessary for understanding what is happening in Kestenberg's formulation, but she made it clear that neither is it correct to say a person's range of behaviors is attributable only to the interactive set at the time. The body–mind link has to do with the way action and mental functioning become structured by developing physical capabilities, and how action both reflects and simultaneously creates a way of thinking and interacting. The link between the body and socialization comes through the ways in which the developing child's new body–mind behaviors require new behavioral responses from caregivers, whose reactions, in turn, have lasting effects on the child's subsequent behaviors and the development of an individual movement repertoire. This movement repertoire, in turn, affects the body and its functioning and solidifies the child's ongoing expectations of responses from others.

This conception reflects a complex state of affairs. There is the interaction of the child's early preferred tension-flow rhythms with newly emerging rhythmic trends within his or her body–mind. In addition, involvement with significant caregivers brings into play other rhythmic forces requiring active and passive adaptation.

Preferred pattern of tension-flow are conceived as basic to a person's temperament, and they allow temperament to be described by characteristic alternations of free and bound flow of muscle tension in the body. Attributes of tension-flow can be divided between "fighting" or "contending" elements, and "yielding" or "indulging" elements. The "fighting" elements, even level of tension, high intensity, and abrupt changes in levels of intensity, are associated with states of frustration, anger and opposition. The "yielding" elements, frequent adjustment of tension level, low intensity of tension, and gradual changes of tension, are associated with states of satiation and relief. Thus, rhythms of tension-flow and their attributes are thought to reflect bodily needs and wishes, and in addition they are associated with different subjective states for example, of caution and ease. Kestenberg and Sossin (1979) illustrated the concept of temperament along tension-flow lines as follows: even flow is evident in people who are unruffled, phlegmatic, or even tempered; flow adjustment, in the pliant, twisting, restless, or shy; high intensity of tension, in people who are excitable, easy to anger, or to frustrate; low intensity, mostly noted in people who are low-keyed, depressed or calm, and not easily frustrated. Abruptness of tension change is a sign of impulsivity, impatience, irritability or alertness; and gradual increase or decrease of tension is characteristic of deliberate people who need long preparation before they become involved or before they can give up involvement (pp. 159–160). The descriptive power of the

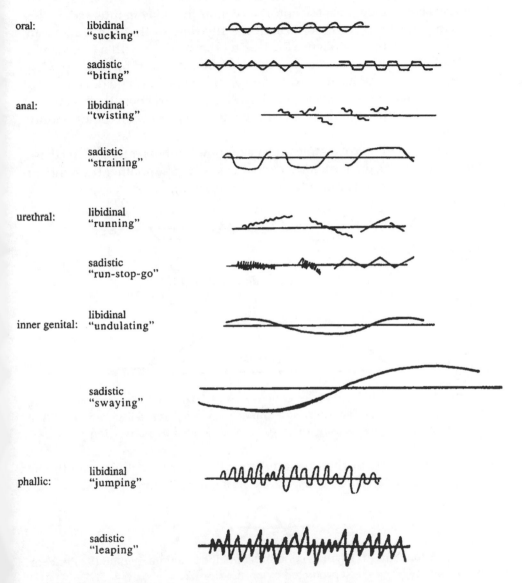

Figure 2: Basic tension-flow patterns (Source: Kestenberg and Sossin, 1979, pp. 7–8. Reproduced by permission).

movement observations that go along with tension-flow description is sufficiently developed to capture an enormous amount of detail about a person and also to show how tension-flow comes into play in interaction.

On page 157, I have duplicated the rhythms so that the reader can have a visual depiction (Figure 2). Tracing the rhythms with a pencil, and feeling their "timing" as you do so, would be helpful in picking up what Kestenberg is after. The upward movement is to free flow and downward is to bound flow. The greater the amplitude in either direction, the higher the intensity. "Neutral" intensity is at the center line, neither free nor bound, but flaccid.

The following two examples of tension-flow rhythm patterns show these rhythms following on one another and mixed with one another (Kestenberg and Sossin, 1979, p. 5, reproduced by permission):

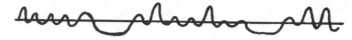

Figure 3: Phallic, anal, oral, and inner genital/feminine rhythms mixing with and following on one another (Kestenberg and Sossin, 1979, p. 5. Reproduced by permission).

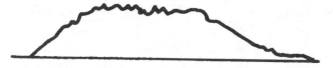

Figure 5: Large organizing unit (inner-genital sadistic) of gradually rising and falling intensity "containing" other shorter rhythmic units (oral, oral-sadistic, anal, urethral units) (Kestenberg and Sossin, 1979, p. 11. Reproduced by permission).

The bulk of adult rhythms are "mixed" rather than "pure" rhythms. Some are easily categorized, as, for example, phallic-inner genital:

Figure 6: Adult "mixed" rhythm, combining phallic and inner-genital (Kestenberg and Sossin, 1979, p. 11. Reproduced by permission).

Others are mixes of all units, or uncategorizable:

Figure 7: Uncategorizable "mixed" rhythms (Kestenberg and Sossin, 1979, p. 11. Reproduced by permission).

In the Kestenberg Movement Profile[1] tension-flow rhythms are re-corded and the amounts of each attribute and kind of rhythm are tallied. Movement sequences are analyzed for numerous levels, components, and loadings of movement factors: pre-efforts, full efforts, shaping, and PGMs. Tension-flow rhythms are coupled with and have affinities with rhythms of "shape flow," that is, changes in shape of the body. Shape-flow is found not in the gestures and postures per se, but in the overall flow of the body into and out of varying dimensional configurations, that is, widening, narrow-ing, growing, shrinking, rising, sinking, advancing, retreating. As with ten-sion flow, shape flow changes reflect subjective states of comfort or dis-comfort and simultaneously a relatedness to the environment as attraction or repulsion. Affined dimensions have been delineated between tension flow and shape flow: for example, free and bound flow in tension have an affinity for "growing" and "shrinking" respectively in shape flow. But ten-sion and shape flow may operate independently, for tension flow can occur without shape changes, and shape flow can clash with its affined tension flow characteristics (that is, instead of growing and free flow, growing may be seen with bound flow, with a change in the subjective and objective experience of the movement).[2] The rhythmic alternation between growing and shrinking and their dimensional attributes (narrowing, widening, ris-ing and shrinking, advancing and retreating) create the structural basis for interaction with the environment and with others, and for the expression of feeling tones and specific needs or "drives." The resulting experience and meaning come from the combination of context created and received through these movement qualities.

Thus, the Kestenberg Movement Profile (KMP) interpreter can put together what in a person's adaptation has been in accordance with tem-perament, what within temperament has clashed or has been harmonious from the beginning, and what has been added or altered through adapta-tion to and identification with others. In addition, the KMP can be inter-preted to show how phase development of the body–mind has dealt with

---

[1]The Kestenberg Movement Profile (KMP) consists of (1) a Laban-derived system of categorizing basic movement qualities, (2) a method for psychological assessment through observation and analysis of movement, (3) a theoretical framework which guides interpretation of movement developmentally, and (4) guidelines for prevention and therapeutic treatment of psychological, physical, and cognitive problems (Kestenberg-Amighi et al., 1999).

[2]It would be useful here to try to make a "shrinking" shaping with the hand or arms in either free, falling inward, or bound, pulling inward, flow, as well as a "growing" shaping in free, flinging, or bound, controlled pushing, flow to try to experience these as options. In free flow, there is no resistance to movement, and in bound flow muscle groups oppose each other.

sexuality, object relations, and sense of self (Sossin, 1987). The following discussion of Glenda, one of the children Kestenberg (Kestenberg and Sossin, 1979) studied from birth to adulthood, illustrates how these aspects of a person may be gleaned from the study of profile attributes.

Glenda and her mother had considerable clashing in "shape flow." Mother tended to comfort Glenda too much and in a misattuned way: "When Glenda needed comforting, mother would apply her own method of doing it by widening and thus expressing her generosity. Glenda did not seem to be able to adjust to this method too well. She tended to feel constricted and used to combat the constriction by literally lifting herself up. . . . " (p. 23).

Glenda periodically attuned to her mother, and this created a tendency to divide her functioning rather than integrate her mother's approach with her own: "The biphasic solution—akin to doing and undoing—made her more dependent on external circumstances and passing states, and diminished her capacity to internalize punitive codes" (p. 23).

Hence her mother's influence was not as useful as another's might have been in helping Glenda to modulate some of her behavior, which had been troubling for her from birth:

> Glenda's original preference for phallic rhythms carried with it a predilection for abrupt changes of tension which often reached a high intensity of release in free flow. In the newborn nursery she stood out because of her ability to fling her legs up and initiate locomotion [movements] while supine. She would spend herself in such activities and would need a rest. Whether present from the beginning or added later, snapping "oral sadistic" rhythms would frequently fill the intervals between flings. Biphasic functioning of this type permeated her behavior-day and could be noted during short periods of observation as well. She would become involved in an exciting activity in an abrupt fashion, and would pursue it briefly to give it up as abruptly as it started. After a short rest or a period of fiddling she would resume her carefree flings. . . . At the peak of the phallic phase "phallic-sadistic" rhythms became prominent while her biphasic functioning receded throughout the phallic phase. Instead, a quality of continuous excitement [at that time] gave her behavior a frantic tinge [p. 36].

Her frantic quality appeared later in difficulties in doing her homework. Her mother's consistent influence, though, helped her get through them, but with much difficulty:

> Throughout her development, Glenda responded to maturation and to her mother's influence by decreasing her abruptness in comparison

with other attributes in her tension repertoire. During latency, she became more patient and controlled, and used biphasic functioning to make a compromise between needs and external demands. Vivacious exclamations would be followed by lip-biting and fiddling— especially when her mother criticized her. . .the preference for "phallic" rhythms influenced her choice of such ego-controlled defensive and coping mechanisms as suddenness and acceleration, in making decisions [pp. 36–37].

As Glenda grew through adolescence and into maturity, phallic rhythms were less prominent, as anal and inner genital-libidinal components helped her contain the more frequently oscillating rhythms:

Glenda continued to use abruptness as well as suddenness (a sequel to abruptness of tension and a [pre-effort] of acceleration) and acceleration as her favored patterns. This could be correlated with her impulsivity, her learning in spurts, her counterphobic behavior, and her ability to get conflict-free tasks accomplished on time. Before her pregnancy, she would employ vehemence (a sequel to high intensity of tension and a [pre-effort] of strength) and resorted to strength very sparingly. During her pregnancy, the complexity of her [pre-efforts] diminished considerably, she reduced her vehement actions and used more strength than before, combining it now with directness. . . .This was in keeping with the clinical observation that Glenda, during her pregnancy, became [phase appropriately] fearful, reduced her defenses, and was able to function with determination in planning the surroundings for her child [p. 65].

Kestenberg's (1965) understanding of the workings of interaction rests on her conception of motoric and kinesic, as well as emotional attunement. She considered the timing, quantity, and intensity of nonattuned interactions very important in adding to a repertoire, since too much, too quickly is merely jolting and ultimately destructive to an infant's developing ability to be a self and to have a sense of self. In Kestenberg's view, as in Winnicott's (1960a), an infant must be allowed to experience his or her own ways and patterns as dominant at first, so that adapting to others adds to, rather than detracts from, self-functioning.[3] For example, a baby who is generally high intensity with a lot of abruptness must be "met" by the caregiver and

[3]If we couple tension-flow rhythms with Condon's (1976, 1980, 1982), Byers's (1976), Stern's (1982b, 1985) and Beebe et al.'s (1982) views of interactive rhythmicity, we can see how the individuality of participants makes a difference in the achievement of synchrony, and of well-timed alteration of synchrony. Some couple and groups will be better than others at achieving synchrony.

gradually helped to modulate in ways that do not interfere with the innate rhythms too much but are enough when help is needed. This aspect of her work connects with Stern's (1982b) conceptions of interactional rhythmicity. But also she noted that a baby's naturally occurring rhythms may be problematic for the baby. For example, very abrupt tension units may jerk the baby awake, a problem that can be resolved to a great extent by closeness with a caregiver who can override abrupt and jarring rhythms with gradual increases and decreases of tension in breathing and rocking that contain these frequent rhythms within a slower, more regular rhythm. Babies can present other conflicts that are innate and especially challenging to any caregiver, since attuning to such innate conflict is difficult and uncomfortable.

The work of Kestenberg (1975a), Lamb (1965; Lamb and Watson, 1979), and Laban (1950; Laban and Lawrence, 1947) does not constitute a synthesis of the two other positions within nonverbal research, but represents a third, independent way of seeing nonverbal behavior. This work does not include the same kind of interactive phenomena that the cultural school, Birdwhistell (1970), Scheflen (1964, 1965, 1973), and Condon (1980, 1982; Condon and Ogston, 1971; Condon and Sander, 1974), documented, or behavior that the intrinsic-meaning group, Mehrabian (1969, 1972), Ekman (1985), Ekman and Friesan (1947b, 1976, 1982), Ekman et al. (1980 [both]), Mahl (1968, 1977) or Freedman (1977) studied. The school of practical analysis began with what can be observed in body movement itself. It delineates dimensions of movement per se, without prior designation of purpose, be that the expression of emotion, attitude, or thought or the participation of a movement in a culturally defined body language set or interactive set. Thus, the school of practical analysis culls another, different layer of nonverbal behavior that may be applied usefully in addition to the others, even though it touches the edges of both.

Laban-derived analysis rests on a conception of "wholeness" that links it with the intrinsic-meaning position through the idea that there is a subjectively experienced and objectively observable whole set of movement behaviors toward which people become oriented and that serves as an orientating point in interaction with the social and physical worlds. There is also a connection with the concerns of the cultural school, for there is a dynamic tension implied between the individual's innate relationship to the whole of movement, his or her particular range of movement, and the perceived wholeness of the group. The group wholeness may be felt and seen; that is, it comes to "be" internally and externally, since it is felt in efforts to do all that is possible and seen in the activities and achievements of others with whom one identifies. Adaptation occurs within this repertoire of wholeness as human organisms use selections from the whole repertoire to serve particular ends. Unlike Birdwhistell's (1970) delineation of American body language, which he derived from context analysis of interactively salient movement cues in one culture, Laban's aim was to derive a movement analysis in relation to interaction with the physical environment and with other humans as physical objects. A different context analysis performed by Laban (1950; Laban and Lawrence, 1947) aimed to catalogue the range of humanly possible movement irrespective of its interactive significance. The interactive significance of *all movement* was thus discovered. An individual's movement is seen in relation to that of others as well as in relation to self. Questions such as how an individual copes with various emotions, drives, excitations as well as with other people can be approached concretely in physical as well as in psychological terms.

Thus, all points of view that I have described in Part III are needed for the full picture of nonverbal behavior and interaction to emerge. Any single perspective is too limited to constitute literacy in nonverbal behavior; then again, these viewpoints are not in conflict and do run toward each other at the edges of their central focus. They together, but not separately, represent a broad framework available for a visual and kinesic literacy.

CHAPTER 11

Toward Complementarity

⧓

At this point it is useful to bring to the foreground again my reasons for undertaking the discussion of these three schools of nonverbal research: first, to bring together in one frame the various kinds of data emphasized by each approach in order to make available useful points of view for understanding nonverbal behavior; and, second, to use the arguments among the schools of thought of nonverbal behavior to put into new perspective the parallel polarities that beset psychoanalysis.

The data generated by each school of nonverbal research entail different aspects of nonverbal behavior; the behaviors at the center focus of each school of research are quite distinct. These views do not negate each other but, rather, work with coexistent behaviors and levels of behavioral operation. Despite hot debate about the salience of theoretical rationales and explanations among the three positions, the data they draw upon are not contradictory. Their data's compatibility is perhaps more obvious in the field of nonverbal behavioral research than might be a similar proposition about psychoanalytic schools, because the data found and examined by nonverbal research are more discrete and thus, more easily comparable than the data of the psychoanalytic case study can be. Researchers' questions and reasons for identifying their data are explicitly stated and particular kinds of answers are sought quite directly with distinct methods.

Within the field of nonverbal research we can see that grouping facial muscle movement as evidence of what constitutes a genuine or false emotional expression does not contradict the fact that emotional expressions can become part of a culture's prescribed ritual. Nor does such information dim the significance of the use of, say, pipe lighting as a signal for a set of movements of a partner, or the significance of the intensity, timing, and direction factors of movements to understanding the temperament, current needs, or wishes of an individual person. Different kinds and levels of behavior with different orders of significance are not *intrinsically* more or less *important* in any given chunk of interaction or movement.

Like the various research approaches to studying nonverbal behavior, psychoanalytic theories, as I showed in Part II, search out and choreograph different kinds of nonverbal encounters that lead to different and partially predictable pictures of behavior. The linkage of theory and behavior is not avoidable or problematic in itself. In fact, in clarifying the linkage, we can create more options. In light of the additional interpretive avenues opened up by nonanalytic and analytic researchers, the question for the clinician ought to become, what is salient now? Other questions follow: what is being created between me and this patient; what is the best theory and practice to fit it; is what is happening useful or is it producing undue stress by missing another aspect of behavior on which it would be better to center?

Looking at research approaches to nonverbal behavior can offer a range of views of behavior to scan, to broaden where one is looking and where else one might search. The intrinsic-meaning position details the prelinguistic encoding and decoding of emotion, interpersonal attitude, and symbolizing. These are the experienced endpoints of interactive processes. Their detailed examination aids in deciphering dominant and subthemes in patients' behaviors, enhances our ability to see deceit and simultaneous messages; further, the latter may be conflictual or complementary (as, for example, in differences between what the face and the body are signaling or between what is said and what is done). The intrinsic-meaning position also makes clear that the analyst, too, is revealed nonverbally. Small reactions and subtle attitudes (i.e., indications of positive or negative feeling, power or responsivity) kept in check by neutrality, while not necessarily consciously noted by patients, will be felt and have an impact on what the patient feels and can bring forward to be engaged. The analyst would do well to foster the patient's capacity to note and articulate what he or she perceives in the analyst's invariably present body attitudes.

Within the intrinsic-meaning position falls the discussion of parallels and complementarities between speech and action motoric patterns, both symbolic and paralinguistic. These action patterns enhance memory retrieval and verbal representation and presentation. This aspect of research dissolved an early intrinsic meaning position's misconception that action necessarily disrupted the ability to think and put experience into words. Before the intrinsic-meaning position made this correction, the cultural school developed its own corrective view that aspects of nonverbal and verbal behavior are two parts of a whole, both learned and coded.

Both the cultural school and the school of practical analysis make finer divisions in the behavioral stream and so picture it with different details that can correct overconfident assumptions and too narrow a focus on the supposedly innate. The cultural school trains our eye to look for behaviors that occur *between* two or more people. It instructs us to test our unavoidable intuitive leaps of imagination about the meaning of behavior by finding first *the behavioral difference in others occasioned by its occurrence.* This research refocuses on entirely new sets of behaviors and demands that we include ourselves in what is observed and understood. But, ironically, proponents of this school find evidence that aspects of social engagement itself are biologically programmed, for rhythmic coordination between people seems to occur in ways that cannot be learned in any ordinary conception of learning. Indeed, this rhythmic coordination seems to be the base on which learning may depend. This means, too, that the analyst cannot remain outside. The analyst must, simply by being present in an interaction, enter a dance with the patient if anything meaningful does occur and most important, if learning (both by analyst and patient) is to take place. This will be true even if analyst and patient believe they only speak. For speech itself, even the written word, involves, in addition to content, rhythmic and intensity changes with which the listener/reader must engage in order to understand. Learning is constituted by behavioral change; that is, change does not happen after the "mind" changes. If change is to happen, behavior is involved throughout.

Yet, despite the emphasis on and detailed analysis of the culturally defined aspect of nonverbal behavior, which, like verbal behavior, is understood to be coded and learned, the cultural school does not entirely avoid intrinsic-meaning interpretations. At the edges of its lamplight it finds, for example, synchrony of movement, intuitively understood to mean or constitute connection and openness; judgments of engagement and disengagement based on the gaze behavior and emotional display matching of mother–infant dyads; behaviors identified in the context of sexual courtship, which are assumed to mean something similar in a very different context. The power of the intrinsic or intuitively understood is felt even by those who correctly conceptually resist such a process.

Further understanding of this phenomenon is offered by the school of practical analysis, which helps us understand the power of phenomenological affinities between aspects of movement at another level of nonverbal behavior: that of the dynamics of how movement is performed. The intensity (weight dimension), direction (spatial dimension), frequency (time dimension), and flow of movement, as well as its spatial shaping, carry meaning tendencies that come from their immediate and intrinsic link with environmental and physical interactive adaptation. These links seem to be "in" the movement attributes, for they are made intuitively, without learning; in fact, learning is often necessary to undo the powerful assumptions that aggregate the concepts' underlying affinities. For example, angry feelings are affined with aggressive defenses (defined by fighting pre-efforts such as vehemence and suddenness) and with aggressive modes of coping (fighting efforts, directness, strength, and acceleration). Pleasant feelings are affined with peaceable defenses and with accommodating types of coping with the environment, both drawn from the "indulging" end of the effort and shape categories exemplified by Kestenberg and Sossin (1979), as flexibility, gentleness and hesitation or indirectness, lightness, or deceleration (pp. 133–134). It takes learning not to assume the aggressive intention of aggressively affined movement elements or the nonaggressive intention of indulgently affine movement elements. For example, a hunter stalking a deer does so by attuning to its gentle, decelerated steps, and when a destructive person pretends friendship it is through attunement. Also, it may be difficult to recognize that a person who uses light, indirect, and gradual movements may nevertheless quite aggressively harm another.

In addition, the school of practical analysis provides a way concretely and philosophically to see individuality, which neither of the other two schools provides. Both intrinsic meaning and cultural determination have difficulty accounting for the individual. Intrinsic-meaning positions rest on assumptions that we all share a structure for coding and decoding information that is significant specieswide. The cultural positions rely on what is learned, and what becomes significant within a culture, subgroup, or dyad. Practical analysis shows how even within culturally distinct body language or within the range of behaviors that are innate, there are individual variations that have a significant impact on the individual and the group. Individual variations raise questions about the motivation for, or function of, behavior. To some extent these two aspects are independently variable—that is, what may motivate behavior may not be its entire functional result.

Let us look at an example from infant observation. Culturally inspired infant observation theories (e.g., Gianino and Tronick, 1985; Tronick, 1987) specify that infants have a dual task and motivation to regulate both inner experience and social interaction factors. The social goal is portrayed as the creation of reciprocity and a state of "mutual delight," signaled by feelings of joy and freedom from anxiety, endpoints recognized and detailed by both the cultural school and the intrinsic-meaning positions. But in either school what defines the internal set goal remains conceptually difficult to grasp. It cannot simply be "positive affect," because this is noted to be a biproduct of interactive mutuality that is well-balanced. But at this point we are left wondering what internal marker lets each participant know what good balance means. "Positive affect" seems to "exist" only in an in-between place. The baby is happy if the connections are good between baby and mommy, and vice versa. Neither the cultural nor the intrinsic-meaning positions has recourse to an explanation of what is used as a guide by the infant. Without a concept of "inner self-experience" and some notion that there is a set of experiences, distinguishable from others, that seems right or wrong from the start of life, the aim of mutuality prescribes mere compliance as the simplest route to it. Even then one is left asking, "Compliance to what?" The answer can only be the other's learned and internalized patterns. Certainly this kind of circularity is documentable where, for example, a person has been unable to identify or act on her or his own sense of what feels right. But this conception permits very little room for understanding the sources of authenticity or initiative that are not understood as the rearrangement of givens or random experimentation. Also, there is no place in these two views for an understanding of psychopathology that takes account of the individual.

The school of practical analysis adds the suggestion that an infant's signature, innate way of being is a continuous thread through kinesthesis, an ongoing lived and motorically defined "me-ness-in-action" that has a critical role to play in guiding interaction. This signature way of being is observable in movement from birth and persists, often despite hardship, although sometimes quite hidden. Ideally it exists in dynamically maintained balance with the environment and with other people. Disturbances brought about by poor attunement of caregivers can certainly be observed in an infant's behaviors. The critical feature of good attunement is the maintenance of the individuality of the participants, which is distinct from the recorded sum of prior experience or of innate, species-wide givens. Individuality can be understood against and within a cultural body language repertoire, but it may also be usefully viewed against and within the "wholeness" of the conceived range of the human potential for environmental adaptedness, about which the school of practical analysis informs us.

Thus, we see that the three schools of nonverbal behavioral research are not arguments against one another but together form a picture of a range of ways of looking and seeing. The issue that emerges for the clinician is in what realm of nonverbal engagement we find ourselves with a particular patient. Observation of ourselves and our patients is the window through which we may see what we are dealing with: for example, rigid interactive patterns, frozen drive expression or body attitudes, behaviors symbolic of prior experience or new behavior unique to the analyst and patient. But, for this vantage point to emerge fully, the analyst needs openness to and familiarity with a widening range of behaviors that constitute and signify various levels of salience—in short, a developed "eye" and kinesthetic sense, as well as an "ear."

PART IV

≫≪

The Logic of Action
in the Clinical Setting

CHAPTER 12

The Matching and
Clashing of Temperament

✣

*I*n the next 4 chapters, I draw attention to aspects of nonverbal behavior that were central in each of 7 cases: (1) the matching and clashing of temperaments, (2) rigidities of body attitude that obstruct communication and change, (3) the experience of dominance of "drive," (4) the effect of speech rhythms on communication.[1] The message of nonverbal research is that we must often frame conceptions of what is happening after we live in an interaction for some time. In any dyad, pivotal dimensions of nonverbal behavior—what allows for good communication and understanding or becomes an obstacle—are particular to that dyad since interactive dynamics arise from the individual characteristics of each of the participants.

As we turn now to the first topic, matching and clashing of temperament, recall that when parents and caregivers attune to babies, and when adults attune to each other in conversation, they are attuning to tension-flow patterns that move along over the synchronizing beat of interaction. From the beginning, babies affirm some behaviors in caregivers and attempt to suppress others by responding with pleasure, comfort, and engagement or with crying, withdrawal, or discomfort.

Strong differences or similarities between a baby's and a primary caregiver's tension- and shape-flow patterns can create difficulties in

---

[1]In all the cases that follow in Part IV I have narrowed the scope of description to highlight the influences of my understanding of nonverbal behavior. I have not tried to identify the possible connections with psychoanalytic concepts except when these derive from nonverbal research itself. My aim is to focus on the nonverbal interaction in order to broaden psychoanalytically trained patterns of observation and experience.

attunement that may cause damage to the relationship and to the baby's growing sense of identity or self. Ideally a baby's tension-flow patterns can first be met by the active adaptation of caregivers, who, regardless of their own inclinations, can see and experience what the baby feels and needs. When early attunement is good, gradually the baby's need for such close matching lessens. With development of perceptual and motor skills, the baby can learn to attune to the patterns of family members.

Unfortunately, all too often good-enough attunement is thwarted. For Abby and Beth, the two women I discuss in this chapter, the absence of consistently good attunement with their parents compromised their feeling good and lovable and their capacity for attachment and loving.

Abby: Temperamental Clashing

Abby entered treatment in her late 20s with the pronouncement, "My life is not working." She felt that she inevitably made the wrong choices for herself both in work and in love. When she entered treatment, she was at a loss to know what to do next to develop her career or to find an appropriate mate. She felt she had been failing in both areas of life. Abby complained that she felt "bad," and did not feel heard or "met" by anyone. Her experience of these feelings with me was initially a serious threat to our work. Helpful change, hard won, was to rest on our discovery and exploration of the fact that our temperamental characteristics were clashing in a hidden way that felt hurtful to Abby.

Before we came to understand our problem in this way, our explorations began with her describing problems with her present love interest, who seemed to Abby to repeat numerous others: lovers and friends who did not take care of her enough or required her care and ministration. She *managed* her friends and lovers. She seemed always to be listening to their problems, organizing their lives, and accommodating to their schedules and needs. She knew this pattern had been built on how she operated with her mother. She understood that she was overcontrolling and that this habit was built on her mother's nonverbal demand that Abby understand her needs, expressed as depression, helplessness, and self-denigration. Abby energetically tried to lift her mother up in the vain hope that she would return this nurturance. She readily confirmed my suggestion that she might be expecting me to fail her too.

Similarly, in her career, Abby's mentors regularly disappointed her when they turned around and asked her for advice. Hence, she set a pattern of continually leaving jobs and even her career path.

I quickly evoked her disappointment in me for not solving her problems rapidly enough. She felt bogged down in thinking about her patterns of blame and feelings of guilt when she believed she should be *doing*—making changes in her life. She said that she was very depressed about how our work was going. In tears, she said, "I just keep feeling that this isn't helping me—I just want somebody to get me past this, and you don't seem to be able to do it." She felt that we had had enough time to figure out what she should *do* (three months of twice weekly sessions had passed).

I could barely hold her with the idea that we had to endure the difficulty until we could understand it better. She responded, furiously, "Yes, I know that's your point of view—to look into something—but so what. It doesn't get me past *this*. You seem unable to get me past *this*—as though you don't know how. And that scares me. And I don't want to talk anymore. I talk too much."

My wondering and inquiring stance was unbearable for her. She wanted certainty and action. When we could get a bit of distance from her outbursts, we thought about Abby's avoidance of understanding her problems as a replay of her identification with, and similarity to, her father, who she thought was like herself, a "doer." If she felt upset, he would "slap his hands on his knees and shout, 'Let's go!'"—and they'd take off to the park. He always made her happy. This obviously felt better to her than her mother's vapid "haze," which offered nothing or, worse, the "excuse" of her own personal problems in response to Abby's needs. She felt that our work was just like her mother's approach: an endless thicket of complicated talk when what she really needed was "body work, a massage, or maybe acupuncture." I was able to keep her hanging on by showing her that her repeated action sequencing of momentary excitement and engagement followed by disappointment and leaving were not solving her problems. These were repetitions of sequences of behavior through which her father had "saved" her by removing her momentarily from the problem, but they had not solved anything. His temperament was more like Abby's, and so she felt better with him. But his tendency, like hers, to do something impulsively did not address the area that needed to change: she still returned to her pattern of overattuning to her mother. I repeated that we needed to look more closely into the details of our interaction—which she thought was all talk.

As Abby's angry feelings intensified, I started looking at the nonverbal dimensions of our relationship for some explanation. Abby's temperamental tendencies, described in tension-flow terms, favored high intensity of muscle tension, with both small adjustments in the tension, and abrupt and large changes from low to high intensity. She used strength, directness, and acceleration frequently—she was intense, mercurial, fast-paced, and on-the-go. Also, her movement had a high loading in two spatial planes, sagittal and vertical—she was a performer, presenter, and operator. She often sat forward, even stood up to make a point as she talked. In contrast, my tendencies are biphasic, that is, I move into phases of high intensity and flow fluctuation; but, when I am working, I veer to low and moderate intensity, long stretches of evenness of tension or gradual change of tension, alternating with shorter stretches of flow fluctuation. At work, I am more an explorer (movement in the horizontal plane) than Abby and much less an operator (movement in the sagittal plane). Fortunately, we shared the vertical—an ability to "present," and thus to confront. My words also reflect my temperamental exploring. I say, "I wonder if. . ." and tend to present alternatives. This verbal and movement style was difficult for her transferentially and, she insisted, *really*.

Once attentive in this way, I could understand our potential for symbiosis or clash and the difficulty of achieving joint interactive rhythmic flow. But I had not felt the problem sooner because I had not seen how Abby attuned to my movement and rhythmic characteristics most of the time. That is, during our "talks," she would slow her pace and lower her intensity to match my movement attributes, although she felt miserable doing so. It took some time for me to catch on. Although, in fact, she alternated between attuning to me and complaining loudly about how she felt, she did not know anything about her option not to attune to me or even that she was doing so.

At times, nonetheless, she could be very much "herself": for example, she would use her own preferred rhythms and intensities when she told stories, which she loved to do. But in our usual back-and-forth interaction, she kept to *my* rhythms and so did not create the rhythmic gradient that would allow me to join *her*. Had she moved and spoken in a faster pace, I would have felt the pull to follow, and we would have come to a comfortable, negotiable exchange. But at this point, without knowing it, she made sure that I felt comfortable—until she blew up in despair and rage.

Abby would erupt when she could no longer bear to absorb our difference and acutely felt my discontinuity from her. Then, disrupting her attunement to me, she reverted to her abrupt, high-intensity manner. At such times, she felt more "herself"—liberated from her too close accommodation to me. But that very fact made her feel ashamed, since she concluded that it was her true, basic nature to be angry. Then she would feel guilty and unworthy for breaking the intimacy that she desperately wanted. She was filled with remorse and terrified of loss, wanting desperately to mend the rupture at any cost to herself. Hence, a vicious circle was established, in which after an outburst she fully reverted to her attunement to me and moved away from herself, not leaving room for my adjustment to her.

After one of our blowups, Abby came into the following session softly apologizing for her outburst. She sat up straight in her chair, on the edge as if she were going to launch into a speech. Then I saw on her face very fleetingly a self-conscious expression as her eyes darted swiftly from right to left to me. After that, she sat back, where she continued to speak in a quiet voice, with gradual changes of intensity, more like mine. I noticed her fleeting expression, and thought of it as a conscious effort at self-control, which initially I did not want to question. In the beginning of treatment I was glad for these reprieves, fearful of her leaving before we could understand and get hold of what was happening. In retrospect, it could be said that her sense of self as "bad" seemed to rest on her anger, which made her feel comfortable and free, but which she always condemned.

Abby was not inauthentic: she did not construct a "false self" (Winnicott, 1960a) in relation to me, nor had she lost awareness of her own most comfortable way of being. Her relationship to her father had helped her preserve her sense of how she functioned most comfortably. Rather, her overattunement to me felt like work to her, much as a teacher feels relating to her pupil or a parent to a child. She extended her range to fit the most obvious range of my rhythms that matched her expectations based on the way she had related to her mother.

While she did not know it consciously, certain attributes of her angry expression—high intensity, directness, and abruptness—were by no means confined to angry behavior. They were part of her temperamental style. She was extremely passionate in her interests in people and in her work. And she had moments in which her humor exploded as unexpectedly as her anger. But her self-assessment did not include the fun along with the difficult moments.

One day Abby came bounding into my office, about 15 minutes late, laughing; she threw down her bags and sat forward, leaning her elbows on her knees, on the edge of her chair. As she pulled up one sleeve and then the other, she announced, "I just had a 35-minute fight. I was in an elevator with my mother—she's buying a new couch and she *needed me*—can you believe it—and the elevator got stuck for 35 minutes! Naturally, she still couldn't decide what couch she wanted. Actually, it reminds me of your elevator—which kind of says, 'Oh—You wanna go to 12?'" Here she settled back in the chair and continued at a slower pace: "Oh—sure—well—let's see—[very drawn out]. I guess I'll get you there—yeah, uh huh—just hold on a minute—we'll be taking off—any time now." Of course, this was also her caricatured experience of my physical presence and movement characteristics. The truth was, she could make me laugh as easily as she could make me feel concerned about her anger.

My acceptance that our problems were in part "real" and not only a matter of her *distorted* association of my behavior with her mother's meant that we could recognize that her mother was really similar to me, but far more extreme in her movement qualities and difference from Abby. This realization helped us to come to a more comfortable interaction. But this view by itself made Abby feel she should let go of her anger, that it was misplaced and childish. As it turned out, this was an incomplete accommodation and disregarded the need for us to do something differently in order to better understand each other.

Going into the minute details of how I reminded her of her mother in my physical movements came next; it allowed us to discriminate what was difficult about her mother from what was similar or different about me and how these similarities and differences affected her. For example, Abby experienced any "lightness" on my part as weakness. Lightness is an "effort quality" (Laban and Lawrence, 1947) having an affinity with low intensity, a "tension-flow rhythm attribute" (Kestenberg and Sossin, 1979). Unless I have a reason not to, I often "explore lightly" and wait to see what a person picks up on. My words and my tone are "up in the air," so to speak. Abby and I understood that her fear of involvement with me was formed by her experience of her mother's lightness, which was extreme and uncompensated by other movement and tone factors (by quickness or loudness, for example) or by adaptation to Abby through matching. Also her mother used lightness in defensive uncertainty, and disengagement and so was unable to take a firm position about anything. Her mother retreated from engagement, as when she blamed herself as a way to avoid responsibility. "I know, I'm a failure," she would say with a sigh, lightly retreating from Abby's frustrated attack and hidden yearning for a stronger engagement. My lightness and my range were as yet untested, because what was visible to Abby served as a signal that she should quickly take charge or leave, either way losing out on being contained and met by my attunement to her.

Further, we established that Abby had adapted to her mother by creating a symbiosis in relation to action (Lamb, 1965; Lamb and Watson, 1979). To some extent, mother and daughter were aware of this symbiosis. For example, Abby's mother became upset with her when Abby could not attend a dinner party because, as her mother said, "You're the only one who talks! It'll be dead without you." In other situations, the process was more subtle and out of awareness. Her mother would present questions lightly, indirectly, and with hesitation as if to the air: "I wonder what to do about your sister; I get a sense she's improving at school, but I still wonder if that's the right school for her." She remained lightly presenting, drifting in direction and focus, never coming to any conclusion, never taking a position she held on to with strength. At such junctures, Abby felt compelled to take control of the action and move in abruptly with strength, either pressing her mother into action or by herself, taking a direction and deciding on what action should be taken. They formed a unit of Abby/mother, with Abby making decisions that mother could carry out since she was ostensibly in charge.

At the same time, her mother criticized her and was unappreciative of Abby's role and how much she depended on it. She called Abby's behavior "unladylike" although she did not offer any option in herself or in others as a better model. She would criticize, then sigh, again lightly, "Oh, but, I suppose I don't do any better." So both she and Abby were out in the cold of her mother's contempt.

Clearly Abby's pressing me to "getting her going" derived from this adaptation to her mother. Through our explorations, Abby became aware of panic behind her attacks on me that was tied to her yearning for me to take over the role she had played with her mother, the decision-making and impelling role. But even when she felt uncertain herself and wanted to relax her control, she was afraid of the exploratory, open-ended quality of the analytic engagement as it felt like the frightening experience of parental absence.

There had been no adult taking appropriate action in her childhood, and so Abby thought that she must always take over. Her father's *manner*—"Let's go, take action"—had felt better than her mother's aimlessness. But his "solutions" were inappropriate and never really solved the problems in front of him. His reaction to Abby's mother was to lose patience with her endless wondering and wandering. He pronounced that he "didn't give a damn" what happened. His abandonment of her mother—and indirectly of her—was frightening to Abby.

In trying to understand our actual interactive behavioral repertoire, I looked at two levels: (1) temperamental indicators in movement, how our movements were performed, and our favored posture gesture mergings (Lamb, 1965; Kestenberg and Sossin, 1979), and (2) kinemorphic constructions, the interactive habits that were continually replayed (Scheflen, 1964, 1965; Birdwhistell, 1970). Besides expressing her adaptation to parental inaction (kinemorphic construction), Abby's temperamental similarity to her father (innate temperamental patterns) predisposed her to attempt to solve problems by taking action. It was not easy for her to take time to think or, once she had taken an action, to invoke a different repertoire of behaviors that might be needed to continue or to assess where she was. Sustained, even attention, for example was hard for her. She could not see the usefulness of my lightness and evenness in exploration, for they triggered only a panicky assumption that I was like her mother. She could not appreciate my wish to sustain the *action of understanding* before anything new was attempted. Abby, replacing her father, who kept "dropping out" of the proceedings, held back from learning these other behavioral modes by maintaining her dual role as agent provocateur and decision maker with her mother.

As we struggled to formulate what was happening between us, subtle shifts in our interactions were occurring. There began to be room for a shift in Abby's feelings about herself and in her activities and relationships. These changes occurred as she stopped overattuning to me, which allowed me to attune to her. Let me note here that these words and this description lend a mistaken linearity to the process, which was in fits and starts. That said, a process of behavioral change got underway. Although the verbal content of the dialogue between Abby and me stayed the same for a time, still often involving her complaint and apology, the rhythms of our words and our bodies started to change, and our interactions felt better.

Early in the treatment, in moments of remorse and fear, when her passionate outbursts threatened to disrupt our connection permanently, Abby silently and without identifying to herself what had happened, would return to her unconscious rhythmic and intensity-matching accommodation to me. In this general context of her overattunement to me, I did manage to attune to her in her outbursts. First of all, I registered alarm, an abrupt rise in intensity. When she flew into a rage, I would move forward in my chair, at first defensively, concerned to calm her down so we could get to understanding what she was feeling. Once, in a moment of frustration, I said, rather abruptly and vehemently, "I think you imagine that I have to know, be certain of everything for you to feel safe. But I *don't* and *I can't*. But *what* I know is that it's *okay* not to know." She replied, "Somehow I feel helped." But then, backing up, not quite sure, she said, weeping, "Oh, god, this is so dumb—you have no position, and you are pushing me with it. Great. And I like it. How crazy is that."

Later, as I felt more confidence in our connection, I would respond to her outbursts with intensity closer to hers, sit up abruptly, and say, "Okay, something's gotten to you, so let's figure it out!" This actual experience of my meeting her with strength relieved fear, which no amount of "just talking about it" was doing, and then she could settle down in her own way and time to talk about it all over again. But, subtly, we were acquiring new data with which she could begin to get hold of what had been missing and why it felt so important.

As I caught on to the mismatching, and we began to use movement-descriptive language to identify the problem, she could express her fear of being "alone" when she moved away from her attunement to me. She had trouble allowing even a short gap in attuned behavior and felt sure that I would not come halfway with my body. I pointed out that she imagined me to have only the very limited range of behavior of her mother and that I could not change my body rhythms to meet hers. We spoke about her experiences of my attunement to her humor and her anger as evidence that I have a wider range than was immediately apparent in my working, listening, analytic stance. She could not imagine that I might enjoy following her rhythms.

Our efforts to verbalize these experiences and then the eventual, more detailed formulations that followed came from our struggle to tolerate and endure her anger, a struggle that helped her develop a more comfortable physical state with me. The work on the verbal level, my asking her to talk about her discomfort in descriptive terms, entwined around the nonverbal behavioral changes that occurred from session to session, as we both unconsciously shifted our rhythms, phrasings, and intensities while talking about these difficulties. For example:

"I mean, I *don't* feel like you are *in* it and if you aren't *in* it, then *how* can I be?" Abby begins.

In my response, I at first use my own phrasings: "How am I that you experience my not being *in* it?"

She goes on, but keeps her own phrasing: "Oh, *god*, I find this so *hard*— I don't know if you *know* enough to *help* me at moments like this. You *don't* have an opinion, and so I can't get *into* it myself. I don't *want* to tell my*self* I'm doing okay—and if you don't have an *opinion*, I could be getting away with *mur*der or something or be *way* off the track. You are too *easy*—You just *sit* there so still—"

Now my response reflects more of her rhythm: "It *sounds* like you're *afraid* I won't hold *on to* you, or *point out* when I think you might be going *astray*. I remember last week, when you were giving me the details of *A and B*, and *some*time into the *session*, I pointed out that I *thought* you might be *racing*, going too *fast* over details that were important to touch on. But you wished I'd said it *ear*lier, so you could have focused more deeply *sooner*."

Now she makes her phrasing more gradual, less abrupt: "Yeah. . . Actually you were *good* in that other session. . . . You know, it's, I want *more* of you somehow. Maybe it's not what you say or not. [Out of character, she stops and thinks.] I am criticizing out of *habit* here, or something. I'm not really sure though. But it *does* seem like something is different—I feel like you stay *with* me now. [Another pause.] I think I don't like it totally. Oh, god, I really am *hopeless*."

Better attunement created new complications. No sooner had she accepted that I was comfortable attuning to her rhythm than she grew frightened of the feeling of flow back and forth between us. She later recognized that she was afraid of the loss of control that it entailed. She objected if she thought I showed "too much caring" somehow and was afraid it was "just seductive." The benefit for Abby of her adaptation to her mother and father had been that she could control the action: she never experienced the uncertainty that comes with having multiple considerations introduced by another perspective or the feeling that another could control her, oddly by attuning to her. Nor did she ever have to function outside of her most comfortable area of "doing." She yearned for, but also dreaded, someone else taking over.

As we worked beyond this, my nonverbal attunement to her rhythms occurred more. Abby noticed that she experienced more physical sensation. This was new experience, which brought with it fears that I would control her and abuse her feelings. She related a long dream that involved me and my imagined husband and child. At one point in the dream, she watched my child, whose facial expression, like mine, she described with sarcasm: "Very therapisty—you know 'concern, care'—And I thought, 'Well, of course, if she's your kid. She's gonna be like you.'" In talking about the dream, she acknowledged that in her yearning for the attachment to me she was afraid she would actually lose herself in an identification with me. Needless to say, in creating a caricature of my "expressions" in my "child," she also expressed her lack of trust in my feelings toward her.

In those moments when she could get past her fears, she felt "undistracted," able to feel "herself," as she allowed herself to be "held" by me through attunement, kinesthetically, and through my watchfulness over her. But this experience also increased her painful yearnings and fears of her unmet cravings for care and physical contact. During this phase, she asked to use the couch, not to evade our engagement, which felt very intense to her, but to find the right distance at which to experience her new feelings.

Despite her awareness that I was able to be attuned to her, her most comfortable "action" mode would often still take over. Once, she stormed out of a session in which she felt acutely her wish for physical holding. Another time, in a similarly intense moment, she collapsed at my feet, and put her head down on my lap. My suggestion that we also talk about her feelings was met by her criticism of me for my lack of "passion."

The meaning of her "action" here was layered. She wanted her painful longings to go away. She had never experienced such longings as having been adequately met physically or verbally by her parents. Her mother had always rejected them and seemed incapable of meeting them. Her father's quick, action-oriented approach did not contain them, but made them vanish for a time with a manic solution. In the present, her longings made her feel like a child—helpless, humiliated, and "one down"—for she wanted something from me that I controlled and, she believed, would withhold. She did not want these feelings to *shape* her.

Abby's experience of words and action had been split. Words to her meant the avoidance of action and engagement. When we became more mutually attuned, we began to correct the split and create a more flexible set of verbal and nonverbal structures that could grasp that understanding and exploring are actions. She had typically used action in the service of ridding herself of fear and uncertainty by eliminating painful experiential data. To balance this tendency, she did not need to inhibit her action as much as to alert herself more to what propelled it, and augment it with additional actions. When she did allow herself to hold on to the experience of her longings, she found her new feelings much more difficult to bear than her feelings of anger and disappointment in me, but also richer in layers of sensation, image, and feeling. These had been shunted aside in all the frenzy of trying to keep doing, of staying in control and complaining about being in control simultaneously. She became quite shy with her feelings, at this point, as she explored areas of experience that she had always raced over.

In the process of our struggling with these difficulties through the course of our work, the feel of our interactions changed. By allowing her own rhythmic qualities full play, she made it possible for me to move more into her phrasings and movement qualities. The ordinarily unconscious process of mutual attunement (Condon and Ogston, 1971; Condon and Sander, 1974; Kestenberg et al., 1975; Byers, 1976; Kestenberg and Sossin, 1979; Condon, 1982; Stern, 1982b, 1985) could begin to occur in our interaction instead of her one-sided attunement to me and also instead of our mutually self-conscious examination of our behaviors. I understood her states and moods better and more quickly than I had because more of her own experience was presented in her body and speech. Sessions went more smoothly. She no longer raged and said, "I feel alone" but showed a range of emotion and attitude in her face and body attitude, rhythms, and varied movement qualities. As she lingered longer in her sadness, she made room for me to feel a reciprocal experience, and then she received more of what was available in our interactions now through the sound, rhythm, and content of my verbal reflections about her experience. She began to notice my wider range of intensity, as it had expanded naturally without effort in relation to her changed behavioral range.

At this point, she began to speak about the fact that she felt afraid that she wasn't "the right kind of girl"—that is, she had long felt thwarted because her mother's self-criticism and criticism of Abby had made her feel that she was an "ugly" or "freakish" girl. Her father's love for her was as a "pal"—also not affirming her sense of herself as a woman. And she did not quite know what sort of woman she was. She knew also that she was not like me, a knowledge that again aroused her despair, although she could be more clear about it at this point and did not need to project blame or scream at me to fix it. We began to talk about there being different kinds of "girls" and "women." It was amazing, she said, that it just had not occurred to her, although, when I said it, she could of course think of examples. She thought of herself as the "Annie Oakley" type. Abby left treatment feeling, "It has given me my *self*."

Beth: Too Good a Match

Beth and I maintained an easy attunement to each other. We were well matched temperamentally. But at times in the work with her I felt an uneasiness that I found difficult to explain. Examination of nonverbal behaviors understood in a variety of frames allowed us to see details of what was happening to create my uneasiness and opened ways of understanding her difficulties that might otherwise have remained closed.

A 30-year-old single woman, Beth entered treatment because of her lack of resolution about marrying her fiancé. Her conscious hesitations revolved around their joint financial insecurity—he had a large debt from a failed business transaction and years of graduate school, and Beth felt that she earned too little to make up for this burden. Probably more significant, she thought, was a recently developed sexual problem between them. She was worried that her fiancé no longer initiated sex between them. Their sexual relationship prior to their engagement had been good. Also, Beth had had numerous lovers and a serious relationship before him which had been rewarding sexually and in which she and her partner had been equally engaged. Although she and her fiancé talked about their financial and sexual problems quite openly, nothing was changing.

Beth came to sessions, spoke easily, and felt helped. She appeared to have no hesitation telling me what she was bothered by in her work life and with her fiancé. She struggled to put her experience into words and made use of my comments, questions, and interpretations. Moreover, she showed a wide range of affect and seemed quite engaged with me and the work. She gave me no reason to suspect any inauthenticity, emptiness, or shallowness. Nonetheless, I experienced an uneasiness that, as I discovered, centered on a physical attunement between us that was too easy and unvarying. There was something about our ease that bothered and puzzled me despite the apparent richness of conversation and my sense of the fullness of the sessions.

I found the relationship puzzling. I could not feel myself in action; perhaps, I thought, because I am accustomed to some subtext defensiveness against engagement in the beginning of treatment. I alternately wondered if I simply mistrusted ease and was too suspicious or that I was missing something and the ease must be false. When, in my effort to understand my misgivings, I asked Beth about how she felt working with me, she was surprised by my question. Nevertheless, she was able to give a detailed description of the difference in her reactions to me, to her mother, and to her former therapist. At the time the description seemed more a help to me than to herself. I was surprised at her awareness and easy formulation of what she had been experiencing through our interaction. She explained that she experienced working with me as a great relief and as enabling her to "feel her 'self'." She had felt her mother and former therapist to be intrusive and overwhelming, and she found herself withdrawing and closing up or intolerably anxious in her interactions with them. Before working with me, Beth had not been able to identify what had been a problem with her former therapist or with her mother, and so she had been unable to address this with either of them.

As she identified what was different in her experience with me, we came to think that both her mother's and her former therapist's high intensity and abruptness jarred her, for Beth functioned most comfortably with moderate and low intensity. Their insensitivity to her experience—and the lack of a frame in which to understand it—and their consequent inability to modify their behaviors to attune to her had interfered with her capacity to experience her own sensations with them, disrupting her rhythms because of the need to cope with what they introduced into her experience. Perhaps, I wondered with her, she had been overattuning to her therapist. Beth thought not.

From Beth's descriptions of their interactions, we understood that her former therapist's demeanor, which came through to her in speech patterns as well as in her movement, was inclined toward abruptness and high intensity, in itself startling to Beth—and evocative, she realized, of her mother's behavior. Beth said she felt uncomfortable, and in pain, and always ended up helplessly crying in her sessions. Although Beth could discern important differences between her therapist and her mother, like her mother, her therapist was abrupt and intense. Unlike her mother, who was always anxious, the therapist was quite relaxed in this mode, just very forthright. But Beth could not relax with her and did not understand why. When she tried to speak about what upset her, she felt ashamed of herself. Because the therapist often "backed off" and asked Beth to explain, or made interpretations that often seemed correct, Beth felt unreasonable and wrong, guilty and confused. Sessions felt like "arguments" to Beth even though she was aware that her therapist was making an effort.

Beth's former therapist's manner of abrupt, high-intensity behavior had not suited Beth's needs, unformulated at that time, for an undisturbed state in which she could "get hold of herself." Without being able to address and possibly change such a basic clash—not of thoughts, but of rhythmicity and intensity factors—Beth and this particular therapist could not connect.

It was interesting to me that, despite a long-term lack of attunement with her mother, Beth to some extent had her "self" in hand. She had a clear sense of what felt good or bad to her. She had not given in to her mother's behavior by overattuning to her, probably because her father had been a primary caregiver, along with baby-sitters. Both parents had acknowledged that mother had been "an anxious mess" when Beth was a baby and young child. Beth had experienced her father as much more like herself, "more relaxed," and able in her early life to understand and guide her.

Although this initial exploration eased some of my misgivings, I still felt a bit unsettled in relation to her presenting problem. We made very little progress in my inquiry about it. I did not sense that anything in our relationship was being addressed or enacted that might connect to her experience with her fiancé or to any other issue in her life that came to light from time to time. Instead, our relationship seemed a comfortable, safe place in which Beth explored her worries and confusions.

The details of her difficulty with her fiancé as she described them were elusive. She stated that, while she loved her fiancé very much and felt easy and comfortable with him, she often felt like leaving him. She often met men who tempted her away from him. She could not understand this feeling, and it paralleled the long-term dwindling of sexual engagement between them that she also found difficult to explain. While Beth wanted more love-making than her fiancé seemed to want, she did not see this as the primary problem. Rather, she felt something more was involved. We tried to approach this problem from a number of different angles. Although I continued at times to feel disquieted by things going too smoothly or by the lack of interactive "electricity" between us, I did not immediately connect this feeling with her difficulties with her fiancé.

In what seemed to me at the time an inquiry independent of concern about her problems with her fiancé, I raised more questions about the genesis and significance of the ease of behavioral attunement with me. These questions provoked explorations of her childhood relationship with her parents and further definition of her early and adult experience. Beth had not "known" she needed our attunement—it was just a happy discovery. Having found it, she could then define her problems with her mother's ongoing "intrusion" of strong, physical abruptness, agitation, and inappropriate anxiety about Beth's safety, which had varying manifestations in different phases of her life.

Beth remembered and had been told that as an infant and toddler she preferred her father because her mother was tense and explosively reactive to her early explorations. She was easily frightened and angered by Beth's ordinary baby explorations because she was overly fearful for her safety. Beth developed a precocious "independence" from her mother to the extent that her mother even mentioned to Beth that she had always refused to cuddle or stay in her mother's arms. Her mother expressed a mixture of sadness and resentment about this. And Beth felt guilty and sad about it now. This pushing away continued and increased in her youth and adolescence.

Her parents were divorced when she was 10 years old. Beth had continued regular contact with her father in her parents' shared custody, but she felt angry at his abandonment and worried for her mother. Complicating the divorce, her father's character and life style altered drastically when he became a "hippy." Previously he had been rather strict and orderly in his own behavior and in what he required of Beth. But he became, at least on the surface, a libertine, adopting a "laissez faire" attitude, and no longer assumed any authority over Beth's behavior. She was suddenly thrust into a "peer" relationship with him in which she was treated as his equal in decisions about her behavior. Also she was aware of his many romances of very short or long duration for several years before he remarried when she was in college.

As a result, from age 13, emboldened by her father's permissiveness and not aware of her fear resulting from his abandonment of his authority, Beth engaged in intense, precocious sexual behavior. Father raised weak questions about her behavior but did not prohibit her activity, since he no longer believed in "imposing external structures" on behavior. Her mother's furious condemnation of him and her daughter fueled Beth's defiant independence, as it had early on, so that what had been appropriate in her mother's concerns was rejected because it was presented in a way that overwhelmed her or seemed based, as it had during Beth's infant and toddler years, on exaggerated fear. Beth moved in with her father because she and her mother could not agree about her behavior. Her mother's "giving her up" felt like a second abandonment. Beth grew sad when recalling how her mother's concern was quite appropriate, but how their inability to communicate physically since infancy led Beth to reject her.

Currently Beth was less bothered by her mother's anxieties and could allay them through their conversations. She could now enjoy her mother more, and her mother could be supportive of her. Her mother approved of her work and encouraged her professional development. Beth could understand and appreciate her mother's concerns about her and accept some of her suggestions, for example, her urging Beth to pay attention to the need to earn a good living or to be conscientious in her work life. But Beth remained wary of her mother. They remained physically distant and restrained with each other. From Beth's descriptions, her mother seemed to have a rigidly bound *body attitude*, with *movement of high intensity* and *abruptness*. She could still be aroused easily to anxious vehemence and was unable to soften and mold to Beth or to accommodate to her low to moderate intensity, lightness, and graduality.

Her father more recently had become a problem to her. On one hand, they could still communicate easily, see eye-to-eye about many things—theater, movies, books, for example. But she felt he had disappointed her somehow. The picture on the surface offered little clue to a more intense disturbance connected to her father. While she had "grown into" her peerdom with her father, she was aware of some resentment about it. In addition, he had become obviously more self-centered with age, making demands on Beth for care and comfort. She was more sensitive to how he still violated the father–daughter boundary. He became too much a friend when she still wanted and needed someone to lean on. Our relationship was allowing her to take more distance from her father, a distance from which she could be critical, fostering a clearer separation from him. Beyond this, her problems with her father did not seem immediately to have a place in our relationship. It was unclear how or whether they were alive in connection with me or with her fiancé.

Thus we arrived at some initial formulations about the nature of the problem with her mother that underlay Beth's comfort and relief in our way of being together. Although she had had her father's early attunement, it had not satisfied her need to "heal" a connection to a mother. This lack was complicated by the divorce and furor over control in her mother. Beth discovered what she needed when she found me. My normal listening posture, my few interpretations, reflections, and questions to her had things running quite smoothly and were in themselves "interactive food." For Beth, this process was an essential ingredient in making our work possible.

After my initial lack of trust of our rapport, I relaxed as Beth began to use my rightness for her in visualized images of me and in kinesthetically experienced interactions with me actually during sessions to "make a new mother" internally for herself—using me as "new mother" to allow herself to reconnect to a baby and mother experience that had been fraught with pain and fear. Her experience of me was quite physical despite our not touching. It was clear to her that I was providing containment for her thoughts and also for her body. She pictured herself as a young child and baby interacting with me as her mother. For example, she would curl up on the couch and visualize herself on my lap, cuddling quietly with me. In other sessions as she spoke of various things, not always related directly to her yearnings, she altered her position in the room. Sometimes she sat in the chair, sometimes lay on the floor because her "back hurt," or she lay on the couch, on her back or on her stomach. In these sessions, her use of the room seemed to make it into an extension of my body. When talking about her own mother's typical reactions to her in infancy, Beth, seeking comfort, would imagine how in contrast my lap would have been to climb into, and she visibly experienced and reported a new physical ease. Her spastic colitis stopped during our work. She spoke of the importance of the way I moved and spoke to her and my tone of voice, which, she said, allowed her to find her own feelings and be at ease with them. Although her exploration was accompanied sometimes by intense and disturbing feelings—coy, loving feelings, grief, and confusion—she returned repeatedly to the safety of "us."

She was nearly silent at times, as she went through varying states, my impression of which I would try to describe to her, to express my recognition that she felt like a very small baby with me. She felt the need for "mother" very strongly, to undo a kind of traumatic experience about which she did not "know" until she began our work.

While very positive behavioral changes were occurring within Beth, her problems with her fiancé remained. She had brushed them aside, but, as her self-experience improved through her regressed reworking of her early experience, she emerged from her immersion in our relationship, and her problems with him returned to central focus. As they returned, I found that my earlier, uneasy questioning of our rapport returned. I broached this turn of events with her. Our feelings and words for them were quite vague at this time. But it was our discussions about our nonverbal process that allowed us to identify a kinesthetic "something" we both felt as problematic and "in the way" of some sort of different or fuller connection.

The order of succeeding events is difficult to pin down. Beth began to feel, but did not immediately report, that at times she wanted to rage and scream. When she was clear that she did not want to be "patient, or wait, and be understanding," she felt frustrated at her continued lack of satisfaction in her sexual relationship with her fiancé. Her clarity it seems, followed what with hindsight was a pivotal discovery about her nonverbal behavior in relation to me. I noticed what I called "a little no" that she began to insert at times after I spoke. For example, it occurred in the following interaction. She began:

"I don't know what to say today."

"You seem out of sorts, maybe annoyed?"

"Oh, I just don't know where I am. Nothing has changed with Bob—Well, he's doing a project so he has to work some nights late. So, of course, that doesn't help. Then, we have the excuse that he is too tired for sex."

"You think it's an excuse—what keeps you from doing something about it?"

And then came a "little no"—a gestural looking away, a shake of the head so tiny that it could be easily missed, as she said, "I don't know, I suppose you are right, I could do something about it."

Her gesture was so fleeting that she herself was able not to notice it. It was manifest in a "micromomentary" shift in expression or position (Ekman and Friesan, 1974b; Ekman, 1985; Stern, 1985). I began to notice its occurrence more frequently. She might shift her head away from my direction just slightly, or move her hand ever so slightly as in a "no" gesture of the head. There was even a parallel in her verbalization; as she said, "I don't know," she might as well have stated, "I don't 'no'." As we explored her gestures with the play on words, we discovered that the minuteness of her "no" was related to her wish not to disturb our harmony, which she found so comforting, safe, and helpful. She was afraid of her negative reactions to me, she discovered, because she valued my "patience" toward her so highly that she thought she *should be like* my analytic persona all the time. In addition, she recalled that her family was full of loud, unrestrained people screaming at each other, which increased her reluctance to give vent to her own angry, frustrated, or aggressive feelings. Her awareness of her pressured maintenance of "calm" allowed her to acknowledge the value of a modified version of her family's behavior—which, in its extreme, had intimidated her.

I asked why she could not sometimes push harder to get the attention her problems needed. Was it a fear of being "aggressive," or anxious like her mother? It turned out that this angle was a minor theme. The major factor was her fear of becoming a sexual person. Although she had precociously engaged in sexual relationships, Beth discovered that she was really quite frightened of the "transformation" of a person in sexual passion, and she was afraid of something else, elusive as yet.

Her reactions to her father's leaving and changing reemerged here. She feared that differentiation meant destruction. In her inner world, her father's change from a maternal/paternal figure to an "in your face sexual guy" had felt like a destruction of his "old self." In her childhood experience he had died or transformed horribly. This formulation came from her reports of "bad dreams" during this time. Her dreams were of monsters growing out of, or taking over, people or of the transformation of ordinary, domesticated animals into horrifying and unrecognizable beings. That her father's transformation had been extreme was significant, as was the fact that it involved the breakup of the family. She had translated her experiences of her father into a fear that she too would become "horrible." She had evidence to confirm her fear about herself, she thought, in her temptation to leave her fiancé. But, paradoxically, she was tempted to leave her fiancé also out of fear of the transformation itself.

Working from her awareness that she was protecting our sameness, we connected her restraint with me directly to her difficulties with her fiancé. Now she could feel how with him, too, she protected the comfort and security provided by his low intensity and graduality of change but suffered from his lack of initiative and passion. She had not only dampened her sexual urges toward him but also her annoyance and frustration as she had with me, in favor of their comfortable calm. She had taken issue with him about the frequency and quality of their lovemaking but left initiative and the "exciting" role to him. She tended instead to drop the question and lose track of her own desires because she was afraid to threaten the security and calm of their relationship. In lovemaking, she thought, she did not want to be the initiator, the one to make change happen, because she was frightened of the change accompanying sexual passion. Despite her overt wish that he initiate, she gave up pressing him for more engagement as soon as he offered reassurance of his love. She recognized in our dynamic around her "little no" a similarity between her interactions with me and with her fiancé: she would grow quietly withdrawn, not even herself aware of her frustration. She resisted his small initiatives, which resulted in cyclically increasing distance between them.

She began to allow her "no/know" to be larger between us. She also pressed her fiancé to look into his side of their problem, which became more apparent as she became clearer about her own. She had chosen him, without recognizing it, in part to meet her need for a soothing mother or an unchanging, maternal/not sexual father. Further, she participated in keeping their connection on that level. She had been unable to use the relationship with him to establish an independently stable experience of a calm and centered self because she could not let go of the effort to control his state. She was "on guard" to maintain his calm body state. Always watchful of him and attentive to their behavioral nuances, she could not really reach the calm state in herself she sought. Through the course of analytic work, our actual behavior, and her extension of it in fantasy, she had been able to establish this body state in relationship to me and she could relinquish control over it with me because it was just *there* in my ordinary way of being as an analyst. The additional, and potentially disturbing, issue of sexual experience could be set aside for a time. She was watchful and controlling of her fiancé because she was warding off in herself and in him the frightening, excited, split-off libidinal father who had in a disturbing way become "libertine" in her sexually formative years. She had felt forced to be aware of a sexual aspect of his experience in a way that was traumatic, although at the time she had made it seem "cool."

So, in the course of our analytic work, Beth found in relationship to me a reliable reciprocal to her calm state, in which she could feel "herself" because she did not need to control me. But, as she moved out of that need and into areas that required her to disagree with me or to be assertive, she reverted inappropriately to her calm, easily attuned relationship with me.

After we had discovered her "little no" and made strides to understand it in relation to her sexual experience, I observed that Beth went through periods of intense upset. She arrived, at two or three sessions in a row, distraught and completely unclear about what was bothering her. Sometimes we would discover an external "reason" for her upset that we thought about explicitly. Often, though, we could not pin it down. But, whatever the cause, Beth felt that the cure seemed to be simply my presence and calm, *same* state rather than the analysis of the situations that might be the topic of our dialogue. She was calmed most, it seemed, by knowing that she could find her own calm state with me. At a later point she reported calming herself after a "bad" time by thinking of me. Thus she began to "lose her calm" and find it again with me when she needed it.

The meaning of this repeating interactive set (kinemorphic construction [Birdwhistell, 1970]) was overdetermined, it seems. On one level, Beth was living out a separation process with/from me that related back to her disturbed early relationship with her mother. It was perhaps I, as good-enough mother and as the good, well-attuned, stable father of her early childhood, from whom she was forging a separation. But, at the same time, the terrifyingly changing, sexual father emerged in a global way—he was everywhere—and she retreated to her image of me as the same, unchanging, soothing, well-attuned mother she never had before. It was at this point that fears difficult to fathom appeared in her dreams. One was about the murder of a mother and baby, and another involved animals and their babies whose genitals were mutilated by a nameless, genderless person. She thought she was dreaming of attacks on sexuality and attachment that had no identifiable perpetrator. It was as though she herself were attacking and being attacked all at once—attacking her attachment to her mother (in her mother/baby state) with her emerging sexual feelings and then retaliating against her own emerging sexuality (in her early childhood and teen-aged state). The dreams of transformation into monsters seemed to refer to her father's transformation and her subsequent counterphobic behavior, as well as to present fears of her own impulses to "be different"—to transform into an assertively sexual person physically and psychologically. She was surprised to realize that she felt such change would involve the death of other aspects of herself not incorporated easily into her image of sexual assertion.

Beth needed to get hold of her ability to calm herself and to permit feared aspects of herself more play. She had been comfortable enough with herself to leave a therapist who was not well attuned to her and unable to recognize that problem. But, in meeting and separating from a calming and separate other, Beth needed to form her own calm and differentiated body/self. She found these aspects of herself by establishing, disrupting, and finding again attuned states with me. Later she fearfully showed her need to risk letting go of the calm to reach her sexual and aggressive feelings. She could not fully "have" the calmness as her own until it was lost and found repeatedly.

Often it may seem as if words alone convey meaning and create understanding. Two people talking glide along most of the time without conscious awareness of the physical dimensions of conversation. In the cases of Abby and Beth, we see how crucial to understanding the nonverbal patterning of conversation can be, how the evidence of attunement fault lines was available to me through my attention to nonverbal behavior. And, by paying attention to that behavior, we were able to change the rigid interactive patterns that were the previously unnoticed bases of verbal and nonverbal interaction that was going awry.

CHAPTER 13

"Drive" as an Aspect of Interaction

⚛

Carl

The nonverbal depiction of drive (Kestenberg and Sossin, 1979) was especially useful in working with Carl. As I noted in chapter 10, the Kestenberg Movement Profile (Kestenberg and Sossin, 1979) refigured drive theory. As seen in the KMP, drive is a physically manifest vector of psyche–soma functioning that visibly and kinesthetically shapes individuals' behaviors. The tension-flow rhythms can be seen as mixtures of rhythms typical of drive phases—oral, anal, urethral, inner genital (uterine or scrotal), and outer genital (clitoral or phallic). These mixtures give characteristic shape to an individual's behavior, which evokes responsive behavior from others, and such action–reaction reshapes the drive behavior itself. In this way interactive sets forms particular to the drive configurations of the participants. The motoric manifestation of drive unfolds developmentally as in Freud's (1905a) conception, but each drive phase's intensity and clarity are also influenced by the individual's temperament. Aspects of drive development are enhanced or muted, depending on the existing basic repertoire of rhythms and temperamental characteristics. For example, a person may be born with urethral tension-flow inclinations. In that case, movement attributes required in the urethral phase will be pronounced and, depending on how they are met by parental handling, will be enhanced, reduced, or remain the same in the individual's repertoire as the person goes on to later stage development. Carl struggled with a cluster of problems that prompted his seeking treatment. His first concern was his difficulty reconciling earning a living with his aim to be an actor. He also wanted to work on problems he experienced with women. He could easily and quickly become involved with a woman but found he wanted to be on his own as soon as he secured a relationship.

Early in treatment, I felt myself making unusually abrupt verbal interventions—questions, clarifications, interpretations—that seemed to have the quality and aim of stopping his speech or his aims. At first I thought my reaction was related to Carl's allowing very few natural breaks in his verbal flow, reflecting his obliviousness to turn-taking signals (Dittman, 1972). My inquiry about Carl's experience of me led to explore his awareness of his background worry that he "bullied" people. He expressed relief that he did not need to worry about this with me, since he had noticed that I seemed able to take care of myself in relation to his behavior. This discussion did not bring any shift in my often moving in to stop him.

I pressed further about Carl's initial concerns for me and for others who might not be able to interrupt him. He seemed to dismiss the concern too quickly. Was there anything more he thought about it or anything he could do about it? There was: he did not want to think about the other person since doing so interfered with his own process and aims, which he felt were actually too easily derailed by other people. He was "bullying" in order to avoid interference.

I continued to find that my words and my small movements were abrupt and strong, directed toward corralling and slowing down his rapid, jittery speech and gestures. I would find myself leaning forward, making sudden, emphatic statements. This behavior paralleled what I understood of his verbalized content, as when I felt alarmed listening to his proposed projects, which he launched into excitedly without any hesitation. I could think only that there were too many projects coming too fast. Yet I was also concerned about my reactions, and afraid of stifling him by questioning his aims and manner too much.

The feelings I experienced brought to mind one of Kestenberg's films, showing toddlers running and their mothers catching them and sweeping them up in their arms. The toddlers were delighted to be chased and caught but dismayed to stay caught for more than a second; yet they delightedly repeated the game of running away, getting caught, and wriggling to get free. The film captured much of what I felt with Carl: that he provoked my participation as restraint and then wanted to be let go.

I do not start out to think about a patient's tension-flow or any other particular aspect of his behavior. Rather, the tension-flow depiction of drive fit my countertransferential experience at this time. Carl's movement behavior and speech had a high loading of what Kestenberg (1975b) and Kestenberg et al. (1975) call urethral-libidinal and urethral-sadistic tension-flow rhythms. These are characterized by very rapid, small amplitude tension-flow fluctuations in intensity and by repeated, jittery stops and starts.

Figure 8: Carl's urethral rhythms.

The rhythms are also called the "running" rhythm and the "run-stop-go" rhythm, respectively (Kestenberg and Sossin, 1979). Traced from Carl's movement, they might look like Figure 8.

At the mother–toddler moment[1] that Carl's and my behavior brought to mind, mother and toddler are still appropriately a symbiotic behavioral unit. That is, the child's action is not yet independent of the mother. At this point, they form a "mobilizing-containing" system that incorporates the previous "holding–releasing" pattern of the anal phase in the mother's and child's behavior (Kestenberg, 1975b; Kestenberg et al., 1975). I was experiencing Carl, like the toddlers in Kestenberg's films, as having more ambition than capacity to see projects through, but, at the same time, a need to "be off" in order to develop. For him now as an adult without a mother/container to deal with the real world, this kind of behavior was problematic. A mother is in charge: she takes a toddler from place to place, makes him rest, and creates a time structure while he plays at ordering mother about. The toddler enjoys making mother and other things move and stop. All these activities contribute to the development of a sense of time and the anticipation of sequence. These crucial structures were lacking in Carl's behavior.

In movement terms, Carl did not use *stabilizing rhythms* and rhythms involving *the attributes of evenness of tension and sustained high intensity bound flow* (anal, straining sadistic) or *graduality* of tension change (inner-genital, swaying, rocking also called feminine) (Kestenberg, 1975b; Kestenberg et al., 1975). After an initial period in which I felt that there was something going on that I did not grasp yet, thinking about the combinations of behaviors we were involved in helped me grasp our behavior. I was using *containing and organizing attributes* even more than is my norm just to hold on to one experience with him long enough to keep it in focus. Carl could not think about or care about what might follow from an action; he could only careen along producing new ventures in action.

I drew on Lamb's (1965; Lamb and Watson, 1979) theory of action to understand further my reactions. I was serving to balance our interaction to enhance symbiosis in relation to action. I was compensating for what

---

[1] Since Carl's mother was his primary caregiver, I refer to mother and child in general as well as in specific.

was missing in Carl's behavior. This happened as we behaved in relation to the wholeness of action sequencing. Carl was all "operator," not an "explorer" or "planner."[2] Carl's behavior omitted elements of complete action sequence that I felt compelled to supply in order to balance our immediate conversation and his situation.

I described for Carl our interaction in movement terms: his running, my catching him, his wish to wriggle free, and then to provoke me to catch him again. What had perhaps been driven in early development, had become a stable pattern within himself that engaged others in a reciprocal process with him. From his own experience, Carl could identify what I was describing. He said this captured for him an overall feeling he had in interactions with his mother and father. He felt that his mother and father were always hovering over him, as if certain he would "fail." He linked my descriptions of my reactions to his ongoing sense of their lack of faith in him, which always made him angry. I wondered with him about the genesis of the problem. Did they hover because he was particularly at risk? Or were his extreme behaviors then and now a chronic reaction to some behavioral patterns of theirs? He could not know which came first, but he was aware that he had often felt compelled to do extreme things: once to his parents' horror, he climbed a mountain cliff with no ropes.

Now, as an adult, he felt that he was failing, but that feeling stimulated more action taking, not necessary consideration of action. He was "failing" in his effort to get a business off the ground and was living on small, dwindling savings. In his assessment of himself as a failure, he did not take into account that he had an extremely high ambition: he wanted to create a business that would free his time and provide a living so that he could pursue his work as an actor. It was as if he had defined his climbing capability entirely on the basis of the expectation that he scale Mt. Everest without training. And this consequently false sense of failure fueled even more his desperation to prove himself. These behaviors and feelings were an elaboration of his basic, physically manifest urethral pattern, unbalanced by other movement attributes.

As we noticed his compulsive rush to start an entirely new venture or to buy an expensive piece of equipment for his business, he became aware

[2] For contrast, consider another patient, Bob, who is extremely depressed. Bob omits the "operation" aspect of action. After a number of years of treatment, he understands the determinants of his lowered affect, including the tempermental, but this knowledge does not lead him to plan and to do. He tends to revert to further exploration. But this is not a solution at this point. He needs now to attend to what to change in his external circumstances, for example, call a friend, find something pleasurable to do, exercise and the like.

of his need to feel both hurried and "heroic" at all times. This was a familiar vicious cycle: he was on the edge, looking as if he needed containment, but angry at interventions that seemed to undermine his confidence. My containing behavior caused him to up the ante by becoming more ambitious, creating more alarm, even in himself.

His "heroic" ambition connected directly to his parents' lack of faith in him. He experienced himself as being under pressure because of their *unceasingly doubtful* attitudes expressed in their words and in their own rigidly maintained body attitudes: domineering anger or condescension in his father, and patronizing conciliation in his mother (Mehrabian and Ferris, 1967; Mehrabian, 1969; Birdwhistell, 1970). Moreover, he had the physical sense that if he could not accomplish his aims *effortlessly*, quickly and easily, something was wrong with him. "Straining preefforts," or the effort of strength and holding tight (Kestenberg and Sossin, 1979), all felt bad and made him want to run away. As we talked about and defined his motoric experience further, Carl reported that he felt these aspects of behavior belonged to me and to the parents who "wouldn't let him" do anything. He forcefully rejected such behavior as he dismissed caution and attempts to examine and think through what was involved in his decisions.

When Carl began to locate his behavior in relation to his images of me and his parents, he was better able to disaggregate the rejected behaviors from the old situation. He could also see a connection between his action patterns and his difficulty in holding on to thoughts and positions long enough for us to understand them. The significance of my body and movement repertoire became explicit. He noticed that I could move quickly from "holding," straining modes to "letting go." This is an adaptability that was foreign to his parents. Perhaps because of their frozenness in own pattern, he had polarized these two rhythms and kept them apart, as if only one position were possible in one person.

The importance of my body to him had other dimensions as well. He recurrently wished that I were a man because he felt strongly that he needed a man "to identify with." These yearnings could be seen as a demarcation of his struggle to develop beyond where he was motorically/psychologically. The psychosexual stages beyond urethral are the inner-genital (referring to internal genital organs in females and males) and the phallic (called outer genital by Kestenberg (1975b) and Kestenberg et al. (1975) to include both females and males). Carl's movement repertoire contained few of these rhythmic characteristics. Thus, Carl's movement behavior could fruitfully be seen as reworking a shakily established masculine identity and sexuality. Indeed, Carl reported that sexual engagement was often a struggle after his initial excitement. And, not surprisingly, he often felt trapped once a relationship became more than a flirtation.

The full exposure of Carl's worry that something was missing in him-self and his wish to find a man in me to identify with did not emerge in a straightforward way. In fact, this experience was intermixed with his feel-ings about and experience with me as a woman. Over time it appeared that his shifting view of me reflected shifting projections in his process of work-ing over his "masculine" and "feminine" dimensions. Movement-descrip-tive concepts offered the possibility of operationalizing these rather glo-bally experienced ideas of female and male. The question became what after all is male or female, and how did Carl define and live gender? I felt the questions in the experience of actions of my own in response to his behavior. Up until this point, I had been using the containing rhythms, anal-sadistic and inner genital. These are rhythm phrases of longer dura-tion that literally contain other rhythms (Kestenberg and Sossin, 1979). Figure 9 is a visual depiction:

Figure 9: Containing rhythms, anal-inner-genital-sadistic, "holding" anal-libidinal and urethral-libidinal units.

I could feel in myself (without any explicit decisions or preawareness) that in my interactions with him I was sometimes using behavior that he felt were "masculine" or "fatherly." Probably again in an unconscious "fill-ing in" of absent movement qualities, I found myself using more high in-tensity, abruptness, and strength and "phallic" movements. For example, if he was troubled, I found that, instead of experiencing leanings toward "coo-ing" and moving and speaking with much "flow adjustment" in my tension flow, I felt as if in my speech I were patting him briskly on the back, brush-ing him off (probably using a "phallic" rhythm, abrupt change from low to high intensity), and getting him on his feet (inner-genital sadistic, gradual change from low to high intensity). These rhythms may be depicted as in Figure 10:

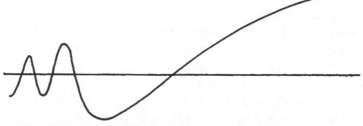

Figure 10: Phallic rhythms followed by inner-genital-sadistic.

My experience of myself also sometimes took on the character of sparring with him, involving phallic rhythms, jumping or leaping rhythms, quick returns, abrupt alterations of tension from bound to free to bound. I felt these rhythms regardless of the content I was conveying, whether interpretations actually related to "getting him on his feet" or were connected to feelings he was expressing in regard to issues in his history. When I was noticing this about myself, Carl made the observation that I was not "wimpy." At other times, however, he reacted powerfully against any sign of my femininity, which was there, too, as when I reverted to my more common gradual rising and falling intensity, generally "inner-genital" feminine rhythms with some flow adjustment or evenness added (anal rhythms).

The following material comes from one of a series of sessions that brought to light Carl's struggle to bring more of himself into action as well as his yearning that I could be a man he could identify with. It illustrates the entanglement of his desire to be caught/held and his desire to exchange roles and become the catcher/holder. In this sequence, our movement and rhythmic qualities were reflected in his visual imagery and came into our verbalized exchanges. He began:

"Your coffee cup with dogs dancing on it is different from the rest of the room, which is abstract. The books, designs on the rug and fabrics—especially the rug."

"How is that significant to you?"

"It feels like you are rubbing my nose in your emotional life with that cup. Like your wearing pink last time seemed to me as if you were with a baby all day. This is like you're spending the afternoon in the park with kids. You're overeducated for it—maybe you even hate it—but you do it anyway."

"That bothers you."

"I'm excluded and you're making me aware of it. Actually I don't even feel that way about spending time with children. But I'm afraid you'll evaporate like cotton candy. You're too pink. I thought after last session that I didn't like your pinkness because I don't like mine. I saw photos of me as a child—there is a sweetness covering over me—I hate it. Even when I'm out helping to cut down a tree—doing something that requires a lot of strength. I'm there with this crew cut and a kind of leer."

"Does it feel like you are covering up some other feelings?"

"Yeah. How did you know? It's as if I can't be all in one feeling. In one home movie I'm playing baseball. At first I hated it because I was taking the game so seriously. I really got upset if someone got a hit or missed a catch. I'm not supposed to show so much intensity."

"Is there a connection with me there?"

"I guess you'd say I should calm down."

"What would make me say that?"

"Hm. My roles [in theater] that I enjoy playing are jagged and tough like the pattern on your rug. There are soft curves sometimes too—that's the part of my hatred of your pink last time. I'm afraid of it in me. I can feel very pink and if you are, then who will be the one to take care of things. You're there with a baby and I have to be in charge to help you. The other piece is that I can't be this jagged, attacking, direct thing. It feels like (makes a gesture in the air above him showing sharp angles, using high intensity and quickness to "draw" them). I am lying here and there is this saw tooth shape coming over my head and arm and down." [He describes the feelings that occur when he plays various roles—the difference between this and soft curves of other roles or of himself in other moods.]

"It sounds like you might think I can't take your jagged intensity."

We went on to talk about how he seemed to be saying, "I can't be pink and female and with the babies anymore, so I am separated from you, but would like to be with you, and yet I'm afraid I might harm you with the other jagged, sharp feelings and movements. But I also disdain pink activity, and I am afraid of feeling that way." And, so, perhaps he was indicating his experience of his lack of a strong father who, he imagined, might more easily than a woman withstand his attacking jaggedness and help him find a safe, useful place for it. The notion that both genders might contain all elements is an advanced discrimination that he was beginning to think about. He was also struggling with the seeming impossibility that he would be the strong one, helping me without the benefit of a father intermediary. In making do without the father, he had a difficult time with his fear of my femininity and felt pushed to want, in a confused way, a sexualized relationship with me that he felt unprepared for. The need to polarize masculine and feminine was a step in the development of these concepts.

The history of his feelings about my femininity and sexuality (and his own) seemed connected to his having had a better relationship with his mother than with his father. He was still very angry, however, at his mother's "overmothering" as well as at the more than hints he had had of that in me. Closeness with his mother had overwhelmed him because he could not get away from it without completely leaving her and the strained, but at times necessary relationship to her functioning as container. Carl felt that she had not changed her relationship to him at all since his early childhood. Her sameness reinforced his sameness and evoked behavior in me that was similar to his mother's. But also the absent, "good-enough" father kept him from moving into other ways of being.

Exploring his parents' rhythms allowed room to differentiate those attributes of movement of mine, mother's, and father's that he might want to claim as his own. Also, I think that the definition of movement patterns made him more alert to his physical functioning and this awareness helped him to expand gradually. That is, the mechanism of change was not only an intellectual one of identifying missing attributes, but also operated by reminding him to allow more expressiveness with his body. In our explorations, Carl imitated each parent's problematic style in the ways each spoke to him. Mother was overly, falsely praising, full of flow fluctuations (anal-libidinal) and graduality (inner genital):

"Oh, now, isn't that just lovely, you've done such a good job."

"Now Carl, I want you to be sure to clean your room before you go out."

FIgure 11: Mother's speech intensity-tonal changes showing anal-libidinal and inner-genital-libidinal rhythms.

He abhorred his father's angry bullying and evident anxiety in Carl's presence, which had also not changed since his childhood. He remembered that his father always reacted to any of his ideas with extreme anxiety:

"Oh, no, you can't. How can you even think of that?"

Figure 12: Father's speech intensity-tonal changes showing phallic-sadistic and anal-sadistic rhythms.

When Carl reported this statement, he used bound flow and abrupt high intensity (anal sadistic and phallic sadistic) to show his father's manner of opposing him. Carl also described his expressive manner in responding, at first forcing his father to listen: "I have to *steel* myself [bound flow], then I *go* to him [abrupt], but very quickly I get agitated [urethral sadistic, loss of sustainment] and go do whatever it was I wanted [urethral libidinal and sadistic]."

His inability to identify with either parent left him unable to use, for example, inner genital libidinal or sadistic rhythms like his mother's, or anal sadistic rhythms like his father's. Both parents' rigid drive structures—their unyielding and unchanging body attitudes and movement attribute ranges—remained unattuned and unresponsive to his growth and changing needs and forced him to hold on to his urethral running away. There was no opportunity with them to locate other kinds of behavioral modes.

We came to think that Carl rejected his parents' repertoire of movement because it was rendered useless to him by being always unhelpfully applied. Both inner genital and anal sadistic are integrative rhythms helpful in coordinating oral, urethral, and phallic rhythms, if they are appropriately applied. But Carl's father used the sustained bound flow of the anal-sadistic rhythm to oppose, rather than to foster, his son's youthful and developing ambitions. Phallic rhythm can get things moving or it can be threatening. Carl's father's obviously had been mostly threatening. Carl had not been able to appreciate his father's appropriate use of these aspects of behavior in his own work. He rejected his father's approach across the board, but through our examination, he began to see that it might be useful under certain circumstances. His mother's inner genital sadistic rhythms, which could have been helpful, were infantilizing and excessively controlling, applied rigidly rather than in harmony with his needs.

On what might at first seem a completely different level, Carl found himself speaking about what he thought were unrelated, physical issues. On examination, however, these issues were seen to be of the essence of urethrality. I bring this matter up at this point to emphasize both the utility of *tension-flow* rendering of drive concepts for focusing bodily experience and its interconnection with social and psychological dynamics. Carl complained that he often had difficulty peeing, and that he was especially worried in public men's rooms lest another man come in while he was using the urinal. He felt afraid of the "suddenness" of a man's entrance, which could make him "jumpy" and unable to pee. Exploration brought to mind his father's sudden, intense, anxious reactions to his ambitions. In the action of peeing, Carl perhaps still sensed his ambition and pride as a somatic memory of the earliest, body-based experiences of ambition, peeing like father. His ambition and pride carried, too, Carl's fear of his parents' responses, again expressed at the bodily level.

Similarly, Carl made reference to experiencing feelings of "aridity" both with me at times and with a woman he was seeing. He connected this feeling of aridity to a fear of "letting go, letting things come," again linked, *symbolically* by likeness of structure and also through somatic memory, to early urethral experience of wetness and dryness, releasing and holding urine. In this context also, he felt he could not tolerate any external control but feared, as well, that he might not control himself. He was troubled, as a result, by sexual difficulties and related problems in sustaining contact with a new woman friend.

He was struck now with his repeated, abrupt entrance into very intense involvement and his equally abrupt disengagement. He observed that it was as if, having secured his woman friend's interest in him, he needed to be off "on his own," performing solitary activities until he was again in need of attention. He did not understand what made him react this way, and he could not imagine other styles of relating, which might involve, for example, sequences of gradual buildup of engagement and resolution, interspersed with stretches of high intensity connection, and solitude. There were only two notes in his theme song. He found my inquiry about whether he could imagine different approaches to and kinds of flow of engagement to be intriguing, but difficult to feel. He recalled uncomfortably that usually no hint of sexuality was present between his mother and father, and, when it was sensed at all, it alarmed him. Carl also noticed the importance in this context of the long-standing lack of physical affection between himself and his mother. His mother reacted with fear even to his hugs. He felt extremely sad at this point in our work. He had only felt puzzled before when he withdrew from women. In discovering how this dynamic was mixed into the pattern of being "off and running" into his own projects, he could separate out an aspect of his own desire to remain. He began to distinguish his mother's overcontrolling holding from affectionate holding, which he wanted.

Undertaking now to incorporate a wide range of behavior, he reluctantly raised feelings about me to the surface. He spoke of wanting me to hold him against me, very definitely *not comforting* him, with a "sexual but not sexual" aspect that he felt came from his needing "just my physical presence." He felt that, while his wish might be understood to be symbolic of something else, to him it was something in itself, which he felt he needed to allow him to "expand." He said that he seemed to need an image of me as "allowing and having sexuality" but not imposing it on him. This image gave him room to find his own sexual experience in relation to me through my openness to his developing images and fantasies about how we might interact together in satisfying ways for him. These included images of quiet holding or more excited embraces, which sometimes included his imagining or dreaming of full sexual encounters.

Inclusion of our action and our descriptions of actual and imagined body-based, nonverbal behavior was thus central in our approach to his difficulties. Because body behavior had been so rigid in his family, he could not use or find additional behaviors he needed. His parents rigidly reacted to him, reinforcing and trapping him in one pattern. Also, he could not admire their behavior enough to emulate them, since their behavior was used most in inappropriate control. Our work on the body level exposed his avoidance of behaviors that were like his parents' rigid behavioral repertoires. Talking in a very detailed, descriptive way about body behavior provoked his awareness of his body and how he operated, which then stimulated change.

Temperament was, again, highly significant in this relationship, but in this case I found that the descriptive drive concepts, as well as their more abstract attributes, to be very useful. The stage model of development seemed more relevant in this case than in some others. To be noted here is that Kestenberg's (1975a) drive model clusters interactive experiences and individual body experiences. That is, the growing individual's drive/body stage is seen in relation to the needed reciprocal parental behaviors, so that neither is defined in an isolated way.

Thus, drive theory's reference is broadened from the intrapsychic to include its integral place in relationship. In addition, the frozen interactive pattern (Scheflen, 1963, 1973; Birdwhistell, 1970), which came into use "between" him and his parents and then between him and me, was equally significant. That is, his temperament and his parents' responses "froze" a set of rules of play—behaviors that kept being repeated. In optimal circumstances, their more flexible repertoires of behavior would have loosened and expanded his range or allowed him to take more responsibility for his behavior. In our work, this frozen aspect of his ongoing functioning met with my behavior, which could resist the repetition and offer alternatives.

CHAPTER 14

Body Attitude and Countertransferential Experience

⋙

D onna and Ellen appeared quite open in their verbal dialogue with me and unaware of any distrust of me. I first experienced blocks in our communication as negative countertransferential feelings that were at odds with my generally positive feelings towards them. I traced these negative feelings to particular body-attitude rigidities. Body attitude is defined by how the body is shaped and aligned in space and how body parts are positioned in relation to one another, as well as by favored positions of the whole body. The body attitude carries readiness for certain patterns and qualities of movement (Kestenberg, 1975a). Body attitude may convey an emotional "position" (Scheflen, 1963, 1964), such as lamenting or questioning, or it may constitute an "interpersonal attitude" (Mehrabian and Williams, 1969). In Donna, the specific details of body attitude were obvious visually, but in Ellen they were much more difficult to detect.

Donna

Right away I had difficulty listening to Donna despite my interest in what she was saying. The content was always germane, but, even so, I found myself drifting sleepily—or else literally feeling physical pain. I began to notice my posture in response to my pain and exhaustion, for I was uncharacteristically slumping in my chair. Then I noticed Donna's posture. She invariably worked her way into a position in the easy chair, with her feet drawn up into the seat and her back to one side, her left shoulder in front. Also, she held her chest in an extremely concave shape, with her shoulders pressed forward, a posture that suggested fear, withdrawal, hiding, or lack of assertion of her feelings. This posture was in keeping with her ongoing body attitude. Whether standing or sitting, she tended to drop her chest and round her lower back. Everyone has a particular body attitude, but it does not always unduly limit adaptability to differing emotions, tasks, and interactions. Donna, though, was presenting herself with a frozen body attitude, which I was mirroring in the ordinary give-and-take of our dialogue.

Donna had entered treatment to deal with feelings of self-doubt that lingered despite several prior years of therapy that she had otherwise found helpful. Since her therapy, she had entered a new relationship and was now living with a man whom she found both supportive and constructively provocative. Nevertheless, she remained unsure of his love and unable to feel herself to be his equal. The same feeling of being unequal also pervaded her sense of herself in work, where she thought she had not realized her potential. She was unsure about how to develop herself further.

In my effort to understand my physical state, I asked her to think about her physical experience: what did she feel physically, was she comfortable, tense? She found my questions irrelevant at best and irritating at worst. I felt concerned about how to comment without making Donna feel self-conscious and criticized. Thinking that I would find other ways to bring its operation into our shared awareness, I chose not to remark on our nonverbal behavior.

During one session that had become very uncomfortable for me, without thinking about it I stretched in my seat so that my chest moved in a circle, up to the right, forward, then left, then back, as I shifted from the position I had assumed while listening to her. I am sure I had stretched in this way many times before, but this time the movement elicited something different in Donna, and so it came to my attention. A few moments after my movement, Donna also stretched her chest forward, without commenting on or seeming to notice our movement interaction. This kind of postural mirroring occurs frequently in most interactions, so it is not in itself unusual. It was unusual, however, for Donna to mirror me. I had always found myself pulled toward mirroring her.

After a short silence, she began to wonder aloud if she would ever feel herself to be my "equal." It was clear to me that our movement interaction had affected her thoughts. I asked her if there was anything specific about me that made her feel that she wasn't. She said "no," and, without seeming to notice the movements that had preceded this sequence, she remarked on a feeling she was having in her chest and connected it to a kinesthetic memory of having ached in the chest when she spoke to her mother, who was extremely controlling and infantilizing toward all the children in the family. I interpreted that she might have felt that I was in some way doing that to her. She could not identify how I might, but she did feel as if I had. She could not understand why this would be so, but she expressed eagerness to understand the phenomenon since she could recognize it in feelings she had had toward most important people in her life.

Her beginning awareness of this problem seemed to come out of my shifting from mirroring her posturally to returning to my own posture, which perhaps had made her feel (without recognizing the source) as if I were antagonistic to her, or in need of her being "lower" than I. I asked if she had noticed that our physical interactions just then had included movements of the chest. She said that she had not and found it somewhat interesting. We spoke a bit about how she might have felt pushed down and held back by my movements, as she had by her mother. She brightened at this thought but did not refer to it in subsequent sessions.

Over the next few months, I was alerted to a repeating interaction that developed. She would appeal to me for instruction about interpersonal matters in her currently complicated work relationships. As she did so, I felt physically drawn forward by her and by the situations she described. I was stimulated toward an assertive/aggressive body attitude, manifested particularly in a lengthening of my torso and forward movements in my chest. All this while she stayed frozen, curled up in her chair. We were doing a dance of body attitudes. It was as though my movement patterns were manifesting what was needed but missing in her own responses to her life situation. That is, she would sink, physically and interactively, shortening and caving in her torso, and she felt unable to assert herself. Her lack of assertive behavior in herself as she described her situation aroused it in me. She seemed unable to tolerate or to find such experience in herself.

I raised questions about how she felt about being assertive in the situations she described and inquired about her feelings toward me as we spoke. But no sooner had I done so, than I felt as though I were dominating her by ostensibly being "helpful." Thus, there were two layers of context determining the meaning of her behavior and my response: first, her life situation, about which she felt uncertain; and, second, our relationship. The dynamics of our relationship were apparent both in the content of my interventions and in my behavior. I was using more "strength" than necessary for conveying my thoughts. I was displaying the missing assertiveness in her interaction with others. She was aware that she felt unequal to others but not aware that I behaved in a dominating way toward her. She was puzzled when I raised the possibility. She noted instead her needy feelings, and her confusion in deciding when it was all right to be assertive of her own needs and when to "give" (which, for her really meant "give in" to others).

She said she experienced assertion and giving as polarized and linked to being bad or good. If asserting herself was bad, I wondered, did she think I was bad when I was assertive in relation to her situation? She thought that what was all right for me did not feel the same for her—somehow other people could be assertive and good, but not she. But then, I said, perhaps I was being a bit "bad," for I might be helpful, but at the same time I was getting in the way of the development of her own point of view. She could not relate to my being anything other than helpful to her. She repeatedly found ways to place me above her. For example, she believed her anxiety centered on "not knowing," and so it was logical that my particular knowledge was essential, for example, when she needed a referral for a colleague. The problem in her emotional attitude toward me became more obvious because of its connection to her body attitude and its physical impact on me.

While none of the issues in themselves were unusual to raise, their continuous stream in the context of her posture and the sensations it provoked in me created the feeling that she was hostile toward me in a silent way. I often had a hard time believing my experience because we had also genuinely warm feelings toward one another, and she seemed completely unaware of her defensive–offensive postural behavior. She was discouraged at times by her inability to be more assertive, but such a feeling was only further undermining.

My physical state was unabated and unequivocal. I minimized further content interpretation, since she only assimilated this as my "helpfulness." But at the same time I did not allow myself either to be drawn forward into a "helpful" attitude or to mirror her slouch. When she asked direct questions with a "how to" format, I suggested that the answers might best come from the development of her own feelings and thoughts. This statement too was taken in the usual way—experienced as my great helpfulness. But she agreed and for the moment shifted to her own strategies, her thoughts and fantasies involved in her overtly compliant behavior. But, in the next session, she would begin again in the usual way. Thus, an interactive set was repeated.

I offered an observation to the effect that she seemed more involved in her feelings about how helpful I was than with her own needs and aims. And I wondered if there was some reason she felt I needed extolling in this way. With deep sighing and tears, she expressed relief and said that she had despaired of ever being able to have attention directed at herself; she linked this feeling with being overshadowed by her more troubled siblings. But, again, no change occurred. I withheld interpretation and stuck to questions which might expand her thinking while trying to maintain my own body attitude, not mirroring her shaping and shape flow and encouraging her to talk about her own experience.

Over several subsequent sessions, it seemed almost miraculously Donna began to talk about her fear of envy from others and her consequent need to diminish herself. She began to talk about this feeling in relation to me: she said that she felt challenged by me, that asked herself why she didn't dress up more, wear brighter colors, or stand straighter, as she noticed me doing. She admired these attributes in me but she was afraid to try anything like them. She thought that such changes in herself would be false and inauthentic, as if her behavior and my own were "natural" and any change would be forced. As she put it, no one would "believe" her because slouching and her own relaxed, unconscious way of dressing were "believable" in herself. It was all right for me to be the way I was—she did not think of me as vain or self-consciously creating an image (or as being a "bad" assertive person). Rather, in her view my appearance and the person she thought me to be were seamless and seem-less.

This was a complicated problem. In part, her feeling was due to overidealization of me to avoid any awareness of antagonism, envy, or condemnation that she might feel toward me and my behavior. Also, she discovered that, most important, she feared that people would know that she cared about her appearance, that she wanted recognition and admiration. If she went through some visible change in her appearance, she would invite attack, as my own behavior had invited her unconscious attack and lack of mirroring. This behavior stemmed from her relationship to her parents, who had been extremely overbearing and invasive as well as physically abusive. But her defensive posture was also in line with her comfortable body attitude and felt like her real self. Thus, she did not easily feel that she could alter it without becoming false.

As our exploration in these directions continued with expanding awareness, I found that my physical pain during our interactions had stopped. Also, I saw that she was moving around much more, sitting up, and stretching up and forward frequently. This behavior became standard for her, and she began to wear clothing that reflected a new delight in "showing off," as she happily called it. She then moved on to talking about the development of her creative pursuits, which had been stalled.

About one year after the period just described, Donna was speaking about her fear of an upcoming evening with the man she lived with and friends whom she experienced as "equals," or maybe "a little better" than herself, defined as more advanced toward their goals, not very "neurotic" or worried about themselves. As she related a remark of her partner's that she felt was critical of her, she was sitting forward in her chair. At that point, she placed her own hand on her chest and literally pushed herself back into the chair, assuming the former concave position of her chest and sunken position in her chair. At the same time, she began to describe her partner in terms that sounded more applicable to her father. She insisted that he was truly unreachable and belligerent, that he would never understand her, and that any assertiveness on her part would only cause an unresolvable blowup.

I questioned what I thought to be an exaggeration of her partner's likely reactions and its roots in her interactions with her father and brought to her attention her posture/gesture. Here I felt I could bring her body behavior to her attention without risking the interference of self-consciousness since the rigid body attitude had disappeared and returned now as a symbolic expression. She had developed alternative behavior, and so this posture/gesture did not constitute as much of her "self" as before. She commenced to sigh and to expand her chest as she spoke of her relief in her growing awareness that her partner was really not as difficult as her father had been. She also expressed awareness that she did have options that she generally did not use for fear her assertiveness would be received in the rigid and forcefully rejecting way that it had by both father and mother.

Donna's example shows how a specific rigidity of body attitude, with its concomitant self–other interactive patterning, affected me and for a time kept the analytic process static in repetitions of interaction sequences based first on my mirroring her frozen body attitude and then on my resistance to it. Our interaction involved her use of repeated action sequences that had a different meaning within the context of our present relationship than they might have had in a different context, taken at face value. Their meaning came from the behavioral difference they occasioned within our relationship. That is, they stimulated my "helpfulness" or "contentiousness" as reciprocals to her unworthy and helpless feelings.

Donna's physical and verbal behavior pulled me into enactments which preceded and also operated independently of our understanding. Unconscious and conscious body changes brought about a shift in her behavior and seemed to open up the room to speak about her experience. When Donna's former body attitude returned, she no longer felt it to be her only option. At this point, it was a symbolic behavior accompanying a lapse into an outgrown, narrow belief system.

Ellen

The impact of Ellen's body attitude took me longer to recognize than that of Donna's. Yet I felt it powerfully in my interactions with her, in which there was a great deal of body involvement for both of us.

Ellen could give only a sketchy description of her reasons for seeking treatment. She vaguely conveyed that she did not feel as well as she thought she could and that she wanted to develop herself more. I questioned her to see if she could give more detail. It appeared that she found it impossible to state her desires plainly or give account of events in her life, for her thoughts meandered, seldom following a logical path.

Ellen's marked indirectness fit with her body's overall dimensions, one an aspect of *body attitude*: slightly widened and flattened, giving more emphasis in the side-to-side direction. Also Ellen at first appeared to be unusually relaxed physically. These characteristics gave her an easygoing, indirect approach. Yet, despite her apparent relaxation, she mentioned painful tensions in her hamstrings, hips, and pelvic floor, as well as in her throat, jaw, and tongue. Her more obvious characteristics were whole-body movement attributes of flow fluctuation, lightness, indirectness, and graduality. These attributes are on the "indulging" or "yielding" end of the spectrum (Laban and Lawrence, 1947). Her "fighting" and "contending" (Laban and Lawrence, 1947) efforts were expressed only in her painful muscle tensions.

I was puzzled by my experience of Ellen. It was difficult for us to reach a focus for our conversation or for me to feel or think about what might be going on for her. I simply could not get a grip anywhere—I found her slippery. I began to feel quite negative toward her without any obvious reasons.

When I asked about her experience of me, she explained that she feared that I would attack her, because that was how she experienced everyone. And so, she explained, she "kept air in her joints" in order to cushion herself against (as opposed to "brace herself" for) attack. That is, she could keep herself a little extra loose and puffed out, so that she could afford to be deflated without damage. She believed that she did not feel afraid of me in particular, and she said she felt more easy with me than with others. But this exploration did not change my puzzling experience of the negative charge in the atmosphere between us.

Ellen was often "playful," light, quick, unserious. I experienced this behavior as a distraction, which made me feel impatient. I felt like being a "disciplinarian." It seemed to me that I often ended up making choices about what to focus on out of an array she presented and that she was avoiding making these choices herself. I wondered if she was simply childlike or was creating a deceptive cover. Was she, rather, watchful over me, perhaps hoping to control me by allowing me to seem to have control?

Beyond interpreting her fear of my attack, I could not find a way to bring any of my experience into our dialogue for quite some time. Although she denied feeling afraid of me, she did acknowledge that she felt intense shame at any hint from me that she might do something differently from how she was doing it. Her shame obliterated her capacity to engage with me at all. We connected her feelings to her experiences of her very harsh, critical mother, who had been physically intrusive and abusive. Ellen described her as having a "hard body, not someone to curl up with."

Despite recognition of her defensiveness and her belief that I was not, at least on the surface, like her mother, Ellen and I were unable to move through her shame with me. Rather than confront it, she seemed to increase her slippery behavior. At any hint of a question about her present feelings toward me, she became suspicious and skillfully changed the direction of what we were speaking about by adding asides, associations linked to a main thread but leading us astray. She could do this with such a playful and light demeanor that I would not always notice the shift until we were very far from where we began, logic and connections unhinged.

In a characteristic session she spoke in the manner I have just described about a number of things: she was advertising some clothes she wanted to sell; she was anxious about contacting a man who interested her; she reported some antics of her nephew who visited her one day. As I formulated an interpretation that might locate her in all this, I found myself growing annoyed and concerned about her lack of direction in the session and in her life. I asked if she felt she preferred to be playful and if none of the subjects she spoke about were especially important to her. She said she did not know and wondered why I asked. I told her that the way she spoke about her experience gave little emphasis anywhere—she treated all subjects equally. I noted that her tone and movement qualities paralleled her lack of emphasis. I wondered if she needed *not to know* that anything might be important to her. She did not seem to grasp this comment and went on in the same way as before. But she noticed my impassivity, which I was feeling and which was evident to her in my body-movement attributes. I was quite even in moderate-intensity bound flow, just the opposite of her fluctuation in low-intensity free and bound flow. She said, "I'm feeling something about you. I don't know if it's you or me, but I feel as if you are not with me."

She was right. I felt I simply could not or would not follow her meandering route. And I did feel annoyed. Meanwhile, I had been wondering about the source of my feelings: did I just not feel like going with her state at the moment, did she really not want me with her, or was I just so concerned about her lack of direction that I could not allow it to continue? If she really needed me to be with her and was unconflicted about it, would I be able to allow it, or was there some block in me that prevented my acceptance of her manner?

I asked how she wanted me to be with her and to say more about how she felt I was not. She said that she could not explain it; it was just a feeling, and she began to veer off to something else. I brought her back and asked if she were avoiding a more forceful approach with me out of fear or for some other reason. She acknowledged, as she had on other occasions, that she was afraid of, or did not like, aggression. I asked if she felt she would have to be aggressive with me to get me to be with her. (Of course,

I was being somewhat aggressive to keep her with me.) She moved over to talking about her fear of contacting the man she was interested in. She was afraid of trying to shape his behavior toward her just as she was afraid to shape mine. She said, "I hate it, it's true. I feel he should come to me without my really saying I want anything. I feel I can only call from a distance, but not close." I asked if she could identify what she was afraid of "up close"— was she, for instance, afraid of pushing me too hard? She said she could not answer because even that was too close.

This kind of exploration continued, when I could get hold of it, mixed in with other themes. I continued to feel frustrated about the lack of connection or change and by my own intermittently negative feelings. Nevertheless, Ellen reported that her interactions with others felt to her improved because she was more aware of hostility in other people and dealt with it more directly. In the past she had gone to great lengths to disarm people, and left herself with much less than she deserved. She was able to see this behavior outside our relationship and act on her awareness to some extent, but not yet to get at her continuing fear.

Despite her expressed optimism and good feelings toward me, she felt my frustration in my nonverbal expression and the movement between us. Ellen began to think of herself as "Helen Keller," perceptually closed and in need of strong intervention and active teaching. She wondered if I could be her teacher, "Annie Sullivan." She remembered a scene from the film in which Helen fights with Annie and Annie both restrains Helen and breaks through communicatively. She was beginning to recognize that she felt so closed that she only barely knew she was closed. She wept about her inability to see what she was doing to interfere with the communication between us. I felt hopeful for the first time.

While I had felt like being firmer before, I was held back by my own uncertainty and her powerful recoiling at my slightest move in that direction. She could experience it only as like her mother's intrusive, controlling, torturing criticism and physical abuse. Hence we were in a bind: she yearned for an Annie Sullivan to break through despite her protests, but she felt she had to protest nonetheless. During this period, Ellen and I had real difficulty discriminating my intention to be helpful in these instances from my anger at how she closed off communication. She was encouraged, but also frightened, by my insistence. Although I was pushing her to understand her needs better, she was afraid I was only "tricking" her as she had been "tricked" before by her mother, who had sometimes seemed to be helpful only to gain a better vantage from which to torment her. Ellen went through a period of thinking that I did not really believe that she had suffered at her mother's hands. When I expressed my understanding of the source of her distrust, she repeatedly asked, "Do you really mean that?

Or are you just teasing?" When I became firmer in holding her to one point, she voiced objections and felt pained and afraid that I was "attacking" and criticizing her as her mother had done. I reflected on how painful it must be to stop the ways she had kept in contact with me previously, before she found new ways.

As she complained about my interventions and I wavered in my own resolve, Ellen indicated that I should be persistent, not give in to her objections but allow and hear them. She said that she needed to react angrily to me, but that I should not let her anger stop me. But now, I wondered, was she getting me involved in some sadistic game with her? Shortly after she said this, something happened between us that signaled a clear shift of direction. Near the beginning of a session, I began, in an unconscious, incidental way, to rock my chair very slightly as Ellen was talking. She suddenly stopped talking and said that she felt rocked and cuddled by me. She had often said she yearned to be held and cuddled, but right now she felt disturbed that she both liked it and did not like it.

She reported that she felt instantly "competitive," that she wanted to do everything herself rather than depend on me, and she then stretched up through her back. I commented on her movement and said it suggested to me that she wanted to prevent softening or feeling as if she were molding into me. She agreed and said further that she was afraid I would hurt and disturb her either by dropping her too soon or by actively intruding and interfering with her good feelings. In spite of her recoiling reaction, I thought that my unconscious rocking at that moment had occurred in response to a physical change in her that I had reacted to but not noticed.

Over the next phase of treatment, Ellen oscillated between wanting and allowing melting closeness and "straightening away" from it. Her physical response was accompanied by her halting but increasing attempts to tell me more about her fears of vulnerability if she relaxed or if she became more active and assertive. Such behavior in herself reminded her of her mother's and sister's intrusive and sadistic behaviors toward her. She was afraid of being like her mother—a very forceful, hard physical presence and a devious, cruel person.

As she noticed that she feared becoming like her mother, she understood her dislike of "pushing" anyone in any interaction hard enough to shape the interaction to her own ends. She could not discriminate the different levels of intensity needed to match different aims from the use of blind, intense, assertive force. She could not imagine that she might shape our relationship toward her needs without alienating me as she herself had been alienated by her mother. Instead, she retained a kind of control by remaining at a slight distance—like "keeping air in her joints," a chronic body attitude rigidity. Here she could avoid making the other's goals her own but in the process lost her own focus.

As changes between us occurred, Ellen went through a period of envious anger toward me and toward the circumstances of her own life that felt very difficult in comparison with her image of my life. She was furious that she had to support herself when she so much wanted support from someone else. Then she felt ashamed of being "such a baby." Her earlier avoidance of anger with me, by minimizing her perception of differences between us was thus clearer. She gradually accepted her feelings, but she did not know what to "do" with them.

Throughout this period of anger and frustration, she felt frightened and awakened early in the morning, yearning to see me. She called occasionally between sessions, panicked that she had lost me or that I was angry at her. She reported on one occasion having awakened with the feeling that she had "shit" in bed. She could "smell it" and felt scared and dirty. She reassured herself that she was clean and remembered having washed the night before. She even realized that lately she had been washing herself after defecating, she was so frightened of being dirty. We thought that this behavior related to her fear that she herself was "a shit" for having angry, grasping feelings. Her "slippery" quality and my earlier dislike for her came to mind for me. We then talked about her fear of letting go with all her feelings toward me and others, her own worry that her feelings of anger, envy, vengefulness were shitty and shameful. She remembered now her mother's very extreme fixation on cleanliness and toilet training.[1] Her mother would polish the floors of the house and forbid the children to walk on them, checked the children frequently for worms, and accepted no deviation from her schedule or rules.

As we spoke, Ellen stretched for a moment in her chair and moved herself very briefly into a "toddler" posture: arms bent and hands up, her belly bulging forward. Then she sat back and reported, without being aware of her posture, that she had felt "weirdly" like putting her fingers in her

---

[1]It is also useful to consider the anal-sadistic and anal-libidinal rhythms (Kestenberg and Sossin, 1979) that Ellen favored and the anal themes in her behavior and history. Her mother had been pathologically interested in her toilet behavior. Ellen remembered having defecated on the floor on her second birthday, and her feelings of pride, followed by intense shame. Most of her problems came from her lack of "standing," "presentation," and the effort quality of strength, all associated with the anal-sadistic rhythms. These were manifest particularly in her mother and thus were avoided by Ellen, who maintained anal libidinal rhythms (twisting, light, indirect), except in her hidden tensions. I became aware of this aspect as problematic in our interactions. Her overt softness and hidden rigidities and her unchanging, yielding body attitude, along with the interactive block that it created, seemed pivotal for us. As her body attitude rigidity was opened up, the anal themes became more apparent and were worked on more directly.

mouth just then and lately when she thought about me. She connected with wanting to be my baby, to be cared for so that she could expand physically and emotionally safely away from her mother's taunting and control. She was afraid of her yearnings to start over, to be my cherished baby, not "a shit," as she put it. For a time, her feelings ranged between grief at what she had missed and more pleasant and relaxed exchanges about many topics. I was at ease with her stylistic indirectness now, which at this point had the characteristic of true play, not avoidance. She grew aware that our exchanges were easy and fun and not possible for her before.

Trends fade and others begin, and it is difficult to pinpoint exactly when change happens. Ellen began to work on her career. She had business cards printed and bought some new equipment. She was very happy, but she felt guilty and afraid to tell me because she felt that any added income she had should go to me; or that, alternatively, if I knew she had any money, I would raise her fee and claim everything as mine. Again, she would be unable to be tight, strong, demanding, or assertive. Her concern with money was tied in with her anal themes and also with her experience of her mother's claims to own everything. For the first time, Ellen could claim her home as her own. She was moving toward a sense of legitimacy and freedom from fear in separateness. This progress reflected her feeling that her body was her own, no longer used entirely defensively in fear of attacks on her or by her. But she could also accept in herself the aggression needed to be forceful and claim some ownership.

It is difficult to say exactly which factors created the gradual shift in our way of being together, but a few elements stand out. Ellen became aware of her distrust and her wish to change it in part because I held on to my physical and emotional experience of negativity between us despite her disavowal. At the same time, I refrained from demanding too soon that she recognize her role in it. Later my nonverbal firmness, not going along with her light, indirect indecisiveness, allowed her time to take on a new experience as her own through the nonverbal interaction that gradually made changes in our behaviors, which could then be expressed in verbal exchanges that had initially been so full of evasion.

My physical involvement—being "moved" by Donna and Ellen and "moving" both of them in turn—was crucial for understanding and changes to occur. Although the moving involved behavior beyond verbal interpretation, it required little of the kind of action that involves large displacement in space, beyond speech. A little went a long way. But, that said, it is still vital not to deny the reality of the reach of the action that takes place. As we have seen, the action of speech and its body accompaniments is a powerful sample of the analyst's reach and range of movement.

CHAPTER 15

The Interactive Effect and Meaning of Speech Rhythms

≫≪

Both Flora's and Geoffrey's speaking rhythms became the focus of my work with them at various points in treatment. The rhythmic nonverbal component of speech, rather than the content, had a powerful effect on our attunement and mutual understanding. As we came to understand, the problems that their speech rhythms created for me were also highly significant in their present and past lives.

Flora

Initially, I found interactions with Flora very stressful. I continually faltered, stumbled over words, and felt unusually clumsy. I could not find words and phrases to fit my thoughts and keep within a mutually established rhythm. I noticed the extremely rapid rhythm of her speech, which did not let up or change. As I came to understand it, my close mirroring of her, which she needed but did not recognize, seriously interfered with my own thought and speech rhythms. As I tried to keep up with her rhythms, I simply could not say what I wanted to say and use the rhythm I needed to use to stay with her. Flora drew me into a rhythmic time frame that was too far beyond my own range of functioning: I did not have enough time to think and express myself while making sure that she felt that I was in touch with her.

Here is a sample of her speech filled with abrupt starts and stops, and very rapid, small intensity fluctuations in moderate range:

"I shouldn't be this nervous—do you think I'm crazy? I guess I think I'll get the job. But what if I don't do well? Maybe it's not the right one. How do I know if it is or not? I had jobs before I got off drugs. But everything is different. My brother always worked. He never had trouble. So I went to see this guy about a job, and I felt so bad about myself. I was positive he hated me. I feel fat and ugly. I keep trying to exercise. I run—I ran here today. But I'll never be skinny enough to make me happy. Happy, I don't know what that is. Maybe I'll never be happy."

Her inability to take turns was also significant in my difficulty speaking. I felt as though I was trying to get into a very fast jump-rope game, and I had to watch for an opening, and jump in, ready to jump very quickly. I stammered out thoughts such as, "You seem to be wondering whether you are in the right place. Maybe yes, maybe no. You are not sure how to know whether you are or not. You are wondering if you will be accepted, and helped here. Can you feel better?" She was frightened of her feelings about me, and actively deflected discussion of our relationship by bringing us back to here and now concerns about job interviews, diet, exercise and her recent recovery from drug addiction.

My attunement was so close to Flora that I lost my own rhythm. I was reacting to her apparent inability to be on her own, to allow any difference or gap between us. When I did recognize what was happening to me, I did not think that Flora would be able to tolerate direct discussion or interpretation of this characteristic of our interactions so early in treatment. I asked questions about her experience of starting to work with me, thinking that perhaps her rapidity and lack of attunement to me was related to some namable anxiety. She spoke about her fear of being involved in therapy at all and her conviction that it meant that she was very "sick." She was unable to reflect on what was happening between us or in herself because she was too frightened of a devastating diagnosis or criticism. Although we did speak about her fears of me and of therapy, the rate of her speech did not change. Thus I was left to struggle with the discrepancy in our rates of speech.[1]

Clearly, it is not always necessary to make a conscious decision to attune to a patient. Attunement comes from an interactive, physical "pull" in communication and understanding. I had to try *not* to attune to maintain my ability to think, but that left Flora feeling too much alone. Another

[1]Notice that Flora's rapid speech did not strike me in the same way as had Carl's rapid rhythms, which included his speech rhythms (see chapter 12). I could speak with him in my own rhythms because his behavior drew me into a reciprocal containing rhythm, not close mirroring.

therapist, more quick-paced temperamentally, might not have experienced this particular difficulty. Still another, perhaps even more gradual than I am or less adaptive temperamentally, might have forced Flora to register more of the discomfort herself. I believe in this case she would have left therapy before the issue could be worked on.

Thus, in my struggle to think and speak with Flora, to locate phrasing and vocabulary, I found myself gesturing and moving in my seat more to fill in my part of the rhythm she set, and I was aware that I felt concerned about allowing lulls that panicked her. In my inevitable moments of mismatching, she experienced pauses or breaks in the flow as indications of my critical feelings toward her. When I addressed her reaction and explained that I simply needed to take a moment to think, she understood that there might be alternative ways to understand our pauses. This realization eased my concern a bit, but did not entirely allay my feeling of clumsiness when I did need to speak. Although the nonverbal aspects of her speech were still hard work for me, we did explore areas of experience that shed some light on her anxiety. Flora was a recently recovered drug addict. Although she felt securely in recovery after a year's sobriety, she still felt very ashamed of her prior condition, and her shame and other unknowns made even my short silences fill her with panic and dread of my disapproval and abandonment.

The power of her fear of my disapproval came also from her early and ongoing family experiences. Her disapproving and disapproved of mother had never been a nurturing figure. Also drug addicted, her mother was either entirely absent or abusively critical of her, taunting her for not being attractive or smart enough. Her parents had divorced, and her father moved to a distant city. The "pull" Flora exerted for extremely close attunement expressed her need for close attention mirroring, which she felt desperately but could not acknowledge. To stand at a distance and observe herself was itself terrifying or impossible. In this early stage of treatment she felt ashamed to think about any desires in the present that went beyond "normal." She forcefully kept discussion to current concerns about job, friends, her recovery strategies. I could use my hypothesis at this point only to help me silently understand my experience that her pace provoked me to create a rhythmic jiggling dance with her that disturbed me. That is, I felt that I was struggling to hold on to a panicky baby who was not yet ready to take me in or to recognize that help was available. Perhaps she was even pushing it away in what seemed a blind dash. We were not yet mutually "attuned" and truly communicating.

Despite my continued verbal stumbling and extra gestures in my efforts to keep up with Flora, we were able to get to some information about our nonverbal attributes that did begin to alleviate my difficulty. Whatever nurturance she had experienced had come from her older brother, whom she overidealized and likened to me through similarities in our temperaments, which she thought implied similarities in attitude. Her brother was much slower paced than Flora. He was intellectually inclined, whereas Flora was more action oriented and very athletic. Flora had associated my basic temperamental qualities with her brother's temperament and interests. Added to the list of my similarities to her brother was that her brother was in training as a psychologist, increasing Flora's overidealization of him and of me and arousing fear that she could not come up to her brother's standard as a patient. She felt unable to be like her quiet, introspective brother or like the assumed me and was ready to believe that she was therefore a failure. These transferential connections, based on the details of my temperament, opened us to considering Flora's extremely critical judgments of herself, which rested heavily on her differences from me and her brother. After we discussed her self-deprecation and loosened its comparison to me, her panic gradually abated and I could let go of my extremely close mirroring of her which was making my functioning so difficult. The reason for the change wasn't immediately clear, but I think it stemmed from our discussion of her own strengths and our corresponding recognition of her separate existence and experience.

One of the problems that came out of her upbringing was Flora's inability to recognize or appreciate her own strengths, her extraordinary buoyancy, and irrepressible capacity for fun, which had survived her mother's abuse. She also did not see that these characteristics were lacking in her serious, rather depressed brother. But when pushed, she remembered that it was she who came up with the games when they were kids. At first, Flora found it difficult to question her belief that her brother's approach to life was the only good option. Her brother had received the little praise available from her parents and was treated as the good child, and she as the bad one. And he seemed to her to be quite deserving of this praise. She had no appreciation of the fact that not only her difficulties but also her survival were attributable to her own approach to life.

An additional complicating factor was that her brother was in psychoanalytic treatment and seemed, from her descriptions, to be depressed. In fact, it appeared to her that he was so involved in reliving the past that he could not engage his current life very well. She believed that his state of mind was expected in psychoanalytic treatment. Her brother told her that she should be "suffering more" in her treatment, and she was afraid because he was sometimes incapacitated for days. She imagined that, if she were smart enough and good enough, I would somehow induce the mournful feelings necessary for her to "get better." Whatever might have touched on some truth in this statement, her conviction about it rested heavily on her belief in my close similarity to her brother, the all-knowing, good child. We talked about the possibility that she might herself discover her own feelings about her past, but that they might not look like her brother's.

As these issues were spelled out over the first six months to a year of treatment, I noticed that I was beginning to relax more into my own rhythms. I could think and speak more easily and allow more pauses in our dialogue, although not as many as there might be with other, differently paced people. My relaxing into being more myself circularly increased her awareness of the (real) differences between us and between me and her brother. This awareness raised the need to examine the meaning of the differences (as had occurred first with Abby). Through this process, Flora gradually, and not without continued doubts, came to believe that she could be her own person with me. She could carry more responsibility for our connection, because it was clearer that she had basic necessities for thinking and choosing for herself and that such necessities did not reside in me and her brother. As my comfort increased, the issue of the rapidity of her speech passed out of my central awareness. It was there, but not intrusively for we had found a way to "dance" together.

But, at a later point, her rapid speech became intrusive again in a different way. This change took place in the course of Flora's talking about her family history and the atmosphere of her home life. Flora mentioned that, after having begun to speak at two years old, she had stopped speaking entirely for a year, from age two and a half to three and a half. She also confessed that she often thought there was something wrong with her capacity to think—as if she were "brain damaged" or had a "learning disability or something." These revelations, in conjunction with my experience of the nonverbal aspects of our interaction, prompted me to connect my problem with speaking to her early problem with speech and the abuse she suffered. Her problem with speech reflected her difficulty in developing a "voice" or a "self" connected with others. She had first presented to me as a terrified baby who could only show the need for "mirroring" and "holding," but who did not know how to be held or even that she wanted to be held. In a parallel way, she could speak, but she retreated from *self-expression*, which requires from others holding and containing actions, experienced by her as either dangerous or missing. She spoke, but not to me or with me.

Though lacking in self-esteem and hesitant to accept herself, Flora nevertheless showed great strength and integrity. She had pulled herself away from drugs, despite her mother's continued use. I imagine that as a toddler she had shown her strength—and defiance—in refusing to speak. Currently, her strength appeared in maintaining her own speech rhythms with me when she felt threatened. Perhaps her refusal to speak as a toddler—like her refusal to converse with me now—was a way to hold on to herself and stay away from further frightening engagement with another she could not trust. In light of this awareness, I thought that her difficulty attuning to me was part inability and part defense: she did not know how to be held and also resisted being held, again trying to hold on to herself, this time in a less obvious way than not speaking at all. For were she to let herself attune to me (by permitting us to find a joint rhythm), or to be held (by allowing my longer rhythms to add phrasing to her non-stop jitters), she risked feeling she was losing herself (which as I described in chapter 12, Abby had felt). Although she expressed her fear of being different from her brother and from me, she also did not really want to become like us. Unconsciously refusing to attune to me, she exaggerated her personal characteristics and, because of my temperamental differences, forced me to be the one who could not speak, and to notice her (difference) very clearly. In this way, she maintained her difference despite fear of my criticism, just as when she had been silent as a child.

Yet Flora also did not know about or experience any choice in this defensive behavior with me, because it was experienced as negatively reactive; nor could she experience her innate resilience and buoyancy. She did not feel she had any alternatives in growing up, so she could not recognize her strength. And, now, what had been a show of strength—not talking, not expressing herself—became a real deficit. Her fear that she had "brain damage" reflected her belief that she did not know how to think and speak well. As a child she had located these abilities in her brother, to whom she then felt tied in an overdependent way that made her feel envious of him and ashamed of herself. And, of course, now she sometimes felt the same way about me. Her admission of concern about her "underdevelopment" intellectually was a step in finding that she could have more control over her thinking and speaking—really, her *self*—than she thought.

It seemed clear that there was a connection between Flora's toddler "speech stopping" and her college underachievement. She could only think of herself as dumb and lacking until we began to reconceive what happened. We began to think about her past and present attitude in terms of her out-of-awareness need to keep her mind, or self, back and away from others, even as she stayed and participated minimally. In addition, in treatment she made me be the one who could not think or speak by exaggerating her innately rapid speech in a way that interfered with mutual attunement. In this way, she had turned the tables—I had become the dumb one. Her self-assessment took in only the "dumbness," without recognizing her abilities, and her proud defiance in her "dumbness." She attributed her so-called underdevelopment to her drug use during her high school and college years. While it contained a piece of the truth, her version placed cause and effect backward, since the problems of drug use and underdevelopment stemmed from her inability to find another way to remain at a distance from the neglect and abuse she had experienced.

Seeing her defiance and anger helped Flora turn harsh self-criticism into a measured need for attention to her intellectual development. At the same time the intrusive rapidity of her speech again disappeared. The act of our speech—my struggle to find a way to speak *with* Flora—was as important to Flora's development as the content. My whole engagement and responsiveness to her were the only access to understanding the complex layering of her patterns of growth and defense, which so closely involved her communication structures. The disturbances in my ability to communicate were clues to disturbances in Flora.

Geoffrey

Geoffrey's speech rhythms were also central for a time and at first seemed to block our doing the analytic work. But as we focused on our interactive patterns based on his speech, the possibility of understanding again opened up.

Geoffrey stated that he was seeking treatment at his wife's insistence. She said she wanted him to be more successful financially. He would not have come without her pressure even though he recognized that he had difficulty taking initiative: he could not hold on to and develop his personal interests. Indeed, sometimes he lost all sense of having any desire of his own. This lack caused problems in his work and with his wife. His work was uninteresting to him, but he did not know what else he might want to do, or, he felt hopeless about developing those interests he could identify. His wife's pushing was hard on him, for she was very intense, strong, and combative. But he felt that he needed her: she was as forceful and emotionally volatile as Geoffrey was quiet and nonreactive.

Geoffrey spoke very softly and slowly. His rhythmic alterations of intensity were of low amplitude and very gradual. I found my thoughts drifting off if I was not careful to attend, despite my interest in the content of what he was conveying. Did he not want my attention? Did he really not want to engage in the therapeutic work at all? Was he presenting himself as a lost, wandering person, or projecting into me, creating my wandering thoughts? Did he assume that I did not want to hear him? Was he so fearful of criticism that he did not want me to pay attention? These were the early questions I asked directly and indirectly of him and myself.

Geoffrey's extreme quiet and rhythmically laid-back speech seemed to be, first of all, an aspect of his temperament rather than primarily a defensive strategy. I sensed over time that his tension-flow attributes did not vary from graduality (rather than abruptness) of change of intensity, low (rather than high) intensity, and adjustment of intensity rather than evenness. Though Geoffrey's speech behavior was quite "natural" to him, he had also used it defensively against his father, an angry (and, as we later understood, very frightened) man who blew up regularly at his wife and children. He flew into rages and humiliated and physically abused Geoffrey. Geoffrey thought that he both "hid" from his father with his quietness and quietly rejected him by refusing to attune to him. His hiding in his low intensity or limp behavior sometimes provoked attacks, because his father wanted "to make a man" out of Geoffrey. But Geoffrey hated the idea of fighting and never fought back.

Father's and son's temperaments could not have been more polarized. From Geoffrey's descriptions, his father was always abrupt, high intensity, and rapidly fluctuating in tension-flow, in extreme contrast with Geoffrey's gradually changing, low intensity. Through our discussion, Geoffrey became aware of his pride in his use of quiet "neutrality" as a reproach and criticism of his father, exaggerating their differences and his own superiority. The two heightened their clashing interactive patterns with Geoffrey's increasing refusal of his father's tyrannical demand that Geoffrey be different from what he was.

Geoffrey's mother's behavior was a contributing factor as well. She was extremely depressed, herself the object of her husband's rageful physical abuse. She was not blameless in their marital problems, for she left her husband alone to deal with their problematic life circumstances. Her engagement with Geoffrey, too, was deadened. He reported that she had had little capacity to respond with much affect and certainly no delight in him. She was devoted and caring but passive and downcast.

My efforts to connect his quiet behavior to his fear of his wrathful father or to his feelings about his deadened mother did not seem to open any avenues or alter his behavior at all. His behavior could not change suddenly or drastically, since it was temperamentally his own. It was behavior that felt "like himself" and had been heavily reinforced, perhaps exaggerated, by abuse and neglect and his reactions to these assaults. But he was not hiding another self that would begin to emerge from repression or inhibition. And he could not or would not attune to me for reasons I did not yet understand.

At this stage it was difficult for me to imagine how salutary change would occur in Geoffrey's situation. The world of work, and Geoffrey's situation with his wife, demanded behavior that seemed impossible for him to perform. He seemed only to want to find a quiet spot, and apart from this yearning could not identify any desire. I struggled with this problem more than Geoffrey did, it seemed. I puzzled about how, in his situation, he could find the room to be himself more. How was it possible to be more fully the quiet, undemanding, gracious person that he appeared to be? His situation seemed paradoxical. We ordinarily think that more assertiveness would require an enlarged repertoire of behavior. Indeed, in a better parent–child situation than Geoffrey had had, a child showing temperamental extremes in behavior might expand in repertoire through engagement with family members having a different range. But was there another, perhaps equally important dimension of assertiveness: to remain himself *more* in relation to others—finding ways not to hide but to remain as he chose. In effect, he would "demand," by staying in his own range, that others move in his direction more, rather than having to match others' intensities. (Such an act is like Flora's making it impossible for me to speak by not attuning to my slower rhythms.)

I did not have this possibility formulated at first. In fact, I sometimes wondered if treatment was completely bogged down. If I was attuned to Geoffrey, there were very long silences, and slow stretches of conversation that seemed difficult to follow or understand. Sometimes I pushed, and information emerged about Geoffrey's life—relationships with his wife, friends, and employer. His useful engagement with me about these issues expanded, despite my ongoing struggle to remain alert and in touch with the subtleties of Geoffrey's range of expression. He remained out of touch with feeling his own desire.

He could feel no initiative of his own and no desire. He was functioning with his wife as a symbiotic action team: his wife formulated intentions, made decisions that he followed for both of them. This was true in many areas of their lives together. Geoffrey realized that this situation was his central problem. My problem was that his lack of emotional investment in changing that situation, added to my reluctance to interpret or even question his quietness. I realized that he experienced any questions or interpretations as pressure interfering with the development of his own initiative, which seemed at times to both of us nonexistent. Verbalizing this did not help move anything.

As time passed, another dimension of our nonverbal interaction began to take clearer shape. When I asked him more about his reluctance to speak, he explained that he did not experience any particular reluctance but also did not have a desire to speak. He was aware that he did not talk much to anybody and connected this reluctance again to his fear of his father's abusive rage. He had preferred to remain quietly neutral in the background rather than risk his father's attacks; he went further and linked this behavior response to fears of me and fears of his own anger—but without change.

We had made some intellectual headway with this approach, but still no connection to Geoffrey's ability to experience his own desires or direction. We connected Geoffrey's hiding from and reproaching his father to his present-day hiding from all interactions by remaining in the background, extremely uncomfortable at being noticed at all. He also saw that his inability to find some satisfaction in work was part of his withdrawal from any wish to "be anything." He knew that his withdrawal was grounded in his hidden vengeful feeling toward his father, who had wanted him to be tough, like himself. Geoffrey's revenge took the form of being nothing. His father's inability to imagine and convey an idea of a man that Geoffrey could realistically grow to be added to his abuse. We also explored extensively Geoffrey's related feelings about his wife's emotional outbursts and abusive verbal attacks. Geoffrey could easily think about the connection between his reactions to his wife and his feelings toward his father and could see how his coping mechanisms did not alleviate the present situation. Silent reproach only fueled his wife's anger. Complicating his dilemma was that, in his "neutrality," he had relied on father and now his wife to make all decisions—as he did on me to choose direction in sessions.

Then, once again, when I questioned Geoffrey about his not speaking and his quiet voice, he explained that he wanted to hear me speak, for he "enjoyed" my interpretations and other interventions as a chance to watch me talk. He did not relate to what I said as a spur to his own thinking but as a form of interaction. Words here were for him part of physical relatedness. He could not say much more about his experience though.

I was not at all sure of what to make of his statement about the effect on him of my speaking. But I did later relate it to a pattern that he had begun: he began to initiate "chats" about light, social subjects. Our chats became a recurrent pattern, despite my continuing, and at times foolishly dogged, efforts to interpret content in relation to feelings about me and our work or to inquire about what was behind his chattiness. Unless a crisis had occurred at home or at work, he did not initiate discussion about himself but introduced a chatty topic—movies, an art exhibition, a book. These were interesting and engaging topics, which caught my attention, and sometimes more than half the session could go by before we got into recognizable analytic material that I might dutifully introduce in a forced interpretation of the topics discussed.

My efforts to explore this pattern with him sometimes brought us back to his aversion to talking about himself or me or his wish to remain in the background. But gradually he felt a stronger conviction that we first just talk together because he found it helpful in a way he could not define. I began to think about his behavior, completely initiated by him, in the context of the framework of the analysis. His behavior's quiet challenge to the analytic process could be important, but equally important was its initiating aspect. In addition, I thought his effort to fill in or repair the experiential deficits were as crucial as his defensiveness in preventing change. All of this was going on at once in his behavior. Geoffrey's social difficulties were due in part to lack of "practice," which stemmed jointly from his temperament, his withdrawal in defense against his father, his interaction with his depressed, deadened mother, and his lifelong social shyness and withdrawal.

I noticed more detail in his nonverbal reaction to my speaking, to which he was highly alert no matter what was being said. When he did speak, he used his hands gesturally, and he had begun to "catch" his hands in his gaze, and grasp them in front of his face, somehow reminiscent of the way a three- to four-month-old infant explores his own hands and begins to grasp at objects. Geoffrey also sometimes seemed to be taking special care to control his vision as he explored the room more with his eyes. There was an unusual quality in his looking around the room, as if the act of seeing, not what was seen, were the important part.

Geoffrey noted something of his hand behavior too but did not have any thoughts about it except that he was mildly embarrassed by it and curious. He used many hand gestures (both "body focused" and "object focused" [Freedman, 1977]). He felt embarrassed as he noticed this change with me soon after it began. He said such hand movements were characteristic when he allowed himself to speak, and he worried that he moved his hands more than most people did. It was not his gesturing, however, but only his hesitation in speaking that was at all problematic socially. I felt that his new freedom to use his hands indicated that he was beginning to feel more at ease with me. I certainly did not feel that it would be useful to interpret his new freedom to gesture, or question him too much about it. I thought that perhaps he had begun to feel that he could venture out—"take something into his own hands."

During the period when I noticed his use of his hands while speaking, I asked him about his experience with his mother. My associative move in this direction probably resulted from my linking his hand movements and his yearnings to watch me speak to the early period of infancy. Geoffrey evoked for me the image of a baby beginning to watch faces, reach, and grasp. My questions stemming from these associations brought up his memories of his mother's severe depression, her fear of his father, and her ineffectuality in protecting herself and her children. And they also brought into focus what he had missed, as well as a glimmer of feelings of sorrow and desire. It was difficult for him and for me to hold on to his fleeting feelings, but Geoffrey did acknowledge them. Early memories were replaced by the experience, as he got older, of his mother's leaning on him for support. He felt ineffectual in dealing with her depression, and this experience was still another source of his feeling that his efforts were useless.

Geoffrey still did his verbal work with me haltingly. He answered my questions, and allowed me at times to prod him, with my questions, into showing some small feeling about what he was describing. But, apart from our chats, he did not initiate verbal explorations of his own. Yet he continued to watch me intently when I spoke. I wondered how this behavior might be related to his use of his hands. Because I was uncertain about the meaning of his close attention to me, and I feared making him self-conscious, I did not bring this physical behavior to his attention.

I felt, nevertheless, that the ongoing nonverbal experience of our interaction was central, but at this point seemed to me unreachable verbally. When I interpreted or asked questions about Geoffrey's experience with me, he would engage my inquiry reluctantly but work hard to make a statement about his pleasure at just being with me. My own feelings about his nonverbal behavior varied—at times I experienced it as defensively and quietly obstructing our connection. At such times, I asked what he felt toward me—if he felt resentful, defiant, or needy toward me. He gave my question consideration and occasionally acknowledged an avoidance, mild resentment, or some yearning.

Gradually I grew to think that most often his "chats" with me were an essential component to his growth: an effort to find a new beginning, which I needed to treat very carefully. They were also in part a very quiet rebellion against the analytic "rules," but, paradoxically, this rebellion was essential for him to experience his own initiative. He needed conversation, direct engagement outside the anxiety-provoking analytic content, because he needed to be able to reconnect his conversation structures with his own control before he could really communicate anything of a more frightening nature—perhaps, in particular, his feelings about our relationship. Our connecting in the nonverbal aspects of speech seemed to be providing the new beginning he needed. This conversation was providing the nonverbal dance that lively mothers and fathers do with their infants and young children to help them find and feel the self-with-other and identify their desire.

Therefore I proceeded in my uncertainty to try to determine, from my experience and Geoffrey's view of the situation, when he was acting defensively and when we needed to go with the flow of what Geoffrey was initiating. Sometimes I felt that we were not engaged in appropriate analytic work but were merely allowing his defensive behavior to take over. My doubts arose from the realization that the experiential deficit and temperamentally extreme quiet were serving defensive purposes at times but not always. Thus I had to accept his temperament, his own way of being, but also try to differentiate when the same behavior was defensive and when it was constructive. He needed interpretive work on its use as a defense, but such interpretation was made difficult by his as yet being unable wholly to remove the behavioral defense. It did not hide another self. During one session, he might enter the analytic work, speak haltingly, and stop because of frustration with his verbalizing skills. At another time, he might avoid difficult engagement by obstructively using the same casual chatting or quiet behaviors that were, at other times, crucial to let be.

I could not always distinguish when my doubts about what was happening came from sensing his defensiveness or from my own reluctance to chat, from just not feeling like chatting that day. He began to articulate when he could feel me being doubtful or reluctant, and I acknowledged his ability to sense my shifts. He could then note that he had been using his assessment of my state as a gauge to determine what he could speak about. He became more aware of his strong feelings toward me, which interfered with his ability to speak, because he could not find words for them. Clearly, he needed time and very little interference from me to feel his way through his feelings.

Geoffrey made very definite, though gradual, shifts over the course of several years. Change was slow for him because such graduality is consistent with his temperament, which at this point had to be *undisturbed.* Our movements back and forth between levels of chat, defense interpretation, and our growing belief in learning through our trial and error resulted in improvement in his ability to communicate. Along with his increased ability to talk, he took more initiative in sessions to examine the difficulties in his life. When he began exploring questions on his own, he wondered why he had not done so before. This self-question alerted me to the silent elements of change. He was aware of a difference in himself but was unaware of how it had occurred. The question opened the way to examining, in retrospect, what he had been doing over the course of the work with me up to that point.

The ability to communicate in speech is thought to be fundamental to psychoanalysis. But Flora and Geoffrey had problems in precisely that area. Nevertheless their examples show that the vehicle of communication itself can be worked with in the transference and countertransference, first in terms of its present interactive impact, and next as a reflection of past experience. To facilitate this kind of work, the patient's and the analyst's behaviors must change; the analyst must make use of subtle aspects of nonverbal as well as verbal interaction.

Conclusion

❋

How can a more articulated vision of nonverbal behavior help us enhance our analytic work? I have argued that such a vision directly promotes the agility we need to move between a number of behavioral and theoretical frames of reference that are key in meeting the diversity we encounter. From research in the fields of anthropology, ethology, dance, psychoanalysis, psychotherapy, psychology, and sociology, I have drawn and compared behavioral details of theoretical and practical interest. Further, I have tried to show that these different bodies of observed behaviors can be usefully grouped according to shared philosophical positions, which can be designated under three general headings: the intrinsic-meaning position, the cultural school, and the school of practical analysis. As I see it, no single point of view, no single school, can claim to predominate; none is superior to the others. Rather, the theoretical and technical tools of each competing school of thought cull a different layer of the nonverbal stream.

Successive psychoanalytic schools of thought, including both innovators and critics examining the nonverbal realm, have focused on specific and different aspects of behavior. My view is that the theories relating to these behaviors are not mutually exclusive but complementary. There is a rich theoretical heritage to draw on. Particular theories go hand in hand with equally particular choreographies for analyst and patient. Thus, we can recognize the usefulness of their distinctions in particular circumstances. The goal should be, not one victorious argument, but an expanded therapeutic repertoire.

Ideally, analytic listening should be joined by analytic watching and feeling in the service of having a "whole" organismic experience of and with the patient. This experience necessarily includes attending to, and

letting oneself be influenced by, the full range of a patient's nonverbal behavior. One should let oneself "be moved" by the patient. Theory should
be only a part of the whole sensed experience against which one feels what
is "stressed" or "dis-stressed," exaggerated or missing, in a patient's interaction. But what does it mean to write about "a whole"? Isn't that just a glib
catchword? A metaphor? Personally, it makes me wary. The theorist in me
protests a little: to be sure, each analyst must choose an initial style of psychotherapeutic intervention. But the point is not to be limited by one style.
Indeed, I would go further and suggest that openness to the full range of
the nonverbal gives us better vantage for seeing the value of each of our
theories and the behaviors they derive from. A specific theory may train
our ears, eyes, and kinesthesia in useful and creative ways. But having access to a range of theories gives options for thinking about our engagements that do not leave us feeling as if we were leaving logic behind when
we must make leaps beyond our original conceptions.

Historically, when analysts encountered behaviors that did not fall into
the expected range encompassed by their theories, they either identified
their responses as "tactical" or regarded the patient as "exceptional." Now,
as then, when a patient's behaviors challenge the limits of an analyst's operating theory, treatment often breaks down or proceeds outside the realm
of theory. Challenges occur because the full range of behaviors may occur
despite the application of one theory. Thus, if we can operate from a broader
theoretical perspective and use nonverbal research to help observe behavior first, the more richly observed behavior can be the center of our
theoretical understanding, not an exception to it.

Although each theory tends to identify and foster specific behaviors,
all levels of behavior inevitably occur. Attention to the nonverbal has helped
me to see the particular duet each patient and I create out of the range of
possibilities and how I must stay open to rechoreograph it in each session.
Sometimes we bring into focus elements of our interactive repertoire, and
sometimes they operate without attention. The behaviors themselves are
both subtle and large scale. Behavioral involvement is always present and
influential—subtle behaviors are as fulcral as are the more imposing and
obvious. Analysis of nonverbal behavior shows that, even at the level of
speech itself, nonverbal interaction and influence remain. Speech action
alone carries emotion, attitude, state, and the rhythms of temperament
and character even if masked. The behaviors of listener and speaker must
be attuned to some extent if communication is to take place at all and to a
greater extent if communication is to go well.

In the realm of clinical application, the nonverbal dimension revolves
around mutual behavioral engagement. Behaviors will be attuned or will
clash to varying effect, depending upon constellations of nonverbal factors

in each individual. We need to be able to recognize how nonverbal behaviors operate in interactive behavior "normally," that is, at a level which does not ordinarily provoke special attention or problems. Against the ordinary, we form hypotheses about what is extraordinary in what occurs nonverbally between ourselves and our patients, creating as well as illuminating transferential and countertransferential interactions. Thus awareness of the nonverbal amplifies our capacity to make verbal formulations of what we experience in nonverbal symbol and/or nonverbal interactive behavior. This is an immediate enhancement of what we expect of psychoanalytic technique.

But my aim here goes beyond the enhancement of technique. Nonverbal research suggests that in psychoanalysis the struggle to come to verbal understanding and the achievement of new behavior must involve both nonverbal and verbal behavioral process for both participants. There is a level of nonverbal interaction which is concrete and specific to the participants, functioning in a sphere at once connected to, and interwoven with language, but not coextensive with the content of words used. As the analyst and patient create their particular shared meaning in spoken discourse, on-going nonverbal interaction contradicts, feeds, and modifies this construction in the structures of behavior.

In the consulting room, the generalizations of nonverbal research yield to a nonverbal dynamic specific to each particular analyst with each particular patient. In any dyad, only some nonverbal interactive issues will stand out at a time, even though all dimensions identified by nonverbal research operate continuously. This dynamic operates like a chemical reaction: potential reactants are present in each individual which are activated in specific ways by the presence of others. So the kinds of significant difficulties which I noted in my clinical examples might be very differently experienced and defined by another person.

Nonverbal behavioral structures both contribute to the participants' ability to speak and to the content of their discourse. The analyst's verbal *and* nonverbal behaviors are inextricably intertwined with those of the patient and must change as the patient changes, and in order for the patient to change. This process is not to be understood in a linear operational way (i.e., that analyst behavior change from A to B will produce patient behavior change from C to D). Rather, it is to be seen as an on-going modulation: understanding involves necessarily behavioral accommodation as the analyst's and patient's rhythms, body attitudes and positions shift. So my aim has been to show both how inevitably we do interact nonverbally (even when we only verbalize) and how we can go beyond relegating nonverbal behavior to exceptional tactical maneuvers.

On one hand, we need not, indeed should not, deliberately set out to attune in movement or speech rhythm. On the other hand, there is much to be gained by the analyst's nimbly working with knowledge of the fundamentals of attunement, recognizing how the meeting of minds corresponds with the meeting of bodies. The inevitable and poignant links between biology, history, memory, and repetition mean that sensitivity to nonverbal behavior, and awareness of its diverse layers, opens new ground for sustaining the recognition that change is not narrowly an internal process and that change in each partner is required for change in one. With the nonverbal in mind, the analyst's special capacity—to be able to wonder for a longer time and to hold on to the salience of more levels of experience than others in the patient's life—is enriched.

References

Abraham, K. (1924). A short study of the development of the libido, viewed in the light of mental disorders. *Selected Papers on Psychoanalysis*. London: Hogarth Press, 1953, pp. 418–501.

Alexander, F. (1930). Neurotic character. *Internat. J. Psycho-Anal.*, 14:183–196.

—— (1950). *Psychosomatic Medicine*. New York: W.W. Norton, 1987.

—— (1963). *Fundamentals of Psychoanalysis*. New York: W. W. Norton.

—— & French, T. M. (1946). *Psychoanalytic Therapy Principles and Applications*. Lincoln: University of Nebraska Press, 1980.

Argyle, M. (1988). *Bodily Communication*. London: Methuen.

Arnheim, R. (1949). The gestalt theory of expression. In: *Documents of Gestalt Psychology*, ed. M. Henle. Los Angeles: University of California Press, 1961, pp. 301–323.

Asch, S. E. (1958). The metaphor: A psychological inquiry. In: *Documents of Gestalt Pychology*, ed. M. Henle. Los Angeles: University of California Press, 1961, pp. 324–333.

Bacal, H. A. (1998). *Optimal Responsiveness*. Northvale: Jason Aronson.

Bartenieff, I. (with Lewis, D.) (1980). *Bodily Movement: Coping with the Environment*. New York: Gordon & Breach.

—— & Davis, M. (1965). *Effort-Shape Analysis of Movement: The Unity of Expression and Function*. Unpublished monograph, Albert Einstein College of Medicine. (Available from Laban Institute of Movement Studies, New York City)

Beebe, B., Gerstman, L., Carson, B., Dolmus, M., Zigman, A., Rosensweig, H., Faughey, K. & Korman, M. (1982). Rhythmic communication in the mother-infant dyad. In: *Interaction Rhythms: Periodicity in Communicative Behavior*, ed. M. Davis. New York: Human Sciences Press, pp. 77–100.

Bion, W. (1962). *Learning from Experience*. New York: Aronson, 1983.

—— (1967). *Second Thoughts: Selected Papers on Psychoanalysis*. New York: Aronson, 1984.

—— (1970). *Attention and Interpretation*. New York: Aronson, 1983.

Birdwhistell, R. (1952). *Introduction to Kinesics*. Louisville, KY: University of Louisville Press.

—— (1970). *Kinesics and Context*. Philadelphia: University of Pennsylvania Press.

—— (1973). Kinesics. In : *The Body Reader: Social Aspects of the Human Body*, ed. T. Polhemus. New York: Pantheon Books, pp. 284–293.

Bollas, C. (1983) Expressive uses of countertransference. *Contemp. Psychoanal.*, 19:1–34.

Breuer, J. & Freud, S. (1893–1895). Studies on hysteria. *Standard Edition*, 2:1–309. London: Hogarth Press, 1955.

Bromberg, P. (1994). "Speak! That I may see you." Some reflections on dissociation, reality, and psychoanalytic listening. *Psychoanal. Dial.*, 4:517–547.

Busch, F. (1995). Do actions speak louder than words? A query into an enigma in analytic theory and technique. *J. Amer. Psychoanal. Assn.*, 43:61–82.

Butler, J. (1993). *Bodies That Matter*. London: Routledge.

Byers, P. (1976). Biological rhythms as information channels in communication behavior. In: *Perspectives in Ethology*, Vol. II, ed. P. P. G. Bateson & P. H. Klopfer. New York: Plenum Press, pp. 135–164.

—— (1982). Discussion. In: *Interaction Rhythms: Periodicity in Communicative Behavior*, ed. M. Davis. New York: Human Sciences Press, pp. 133–145.

Chapple, E. (1970). *Culture and Biological Man*. New York: Holt, Rinehart, & Winston.

—— (1976). Movement and sound: The musical language of body rhythms and interaction. In: *Interaction Rhythms: Periodicity in Communicative Behavior*, ed. M. Davis. New York: Human Sciences Press, pp. 31–51.

Condon, W. S. (1967). A segmentation of behavior. *J. Psychiatric Research*, 5:359–365.

—— (1976). An analysis of the behavioral organization. *Sign Language Studies*, 13:285–318.

—— (1980). The relationship of interactional synchrony to cognitive and emotional processes. In: *The Relationship of Verbal and Non-Verbal Communication*, ed. M. R. Rey. The Hague: Mouton, pp. 55–77.

—— (1982). Cultural microrhythms. In: *Interaction Rhythms: Periodicity in Communicative Behavior*, ed. M. Davis. New York: Human Sciences Press, pp. 53–77.

—— & Ogston, W. D. (1971). Speech and body movement synchrony of the speaker-hearer. In: *Perception of Language*, ed. D. L. Horton & J. J. Jenkins. Columbus, OH: Charles Merrill, pp. 98–120.

—— & Sander, L. W. (1974). Neonate movement is synchronized with adult speech: Interactional participation and language acquisition. *Science*, 183:99–101.

Darwin, C. (1872). *The Expression of the Emotions in Man and Animals*. Chicago: University of Chicago Press, 1965.

Davis, M. (1970). Movement characteristics of hospitalized psychiatric patients. *Proceedings of the Fifth Annual Conference of the American Dance Therapy Association*. (Available from the American Dance Therapy Association, 5173 Phantom Court, Columbia, MD 21043)

Deutsch, F. (1933). Studies on pathogenesis: Biological and psychological aspects.

Psychoanal. Quart., 2:133–150.

—— (1947). Analysis of postural behavior. *Psychoanal. Quart.*, 16:193–213.

Dittman, A. T. (1972). The body movement-speech rhythm relationship as a cue to speech encoding. In: *Nonverbal Communication: Readings with Commentary*, ed. S. Weitz. New York: Oxford University Press, 1974, pp. 169–181.

Duncan, S. (1972). Some signals and rules for taking speaking turns in conversation. In: *Nonverbal Communication: Readings with Commentary*, ed. S. Weitz. New York: Oxford University Press, 1974, pp. 298–311.

Efron, D. (1941). *Gesture and Environment.* New York: King's Crown Press.

Ehrenberg, D. B. (1992). *The Intimate Edge.* New York: Norton.

Eibl-Eibesfeldt, I. (1970). *Ethology: The Biology of Behavior.* New York: Holt, Rinehart & Winston.

—— (1971). *Love and Hate: On the Natural History of Behavior Patterns.* London: Methuen.

—— (1974). Similarities and differences between cultures in expressive movements. In: *Non-Verbal Communication: Readings with Commentary*, ed. S. Weitz. New York: Oxford University Press, pp. 20–33.

—— (1975). *Ethology: The Biology of Behavior.* New York: Holt, Rinehart, & Winston.

Ekman, P. (1985). *Telling Lies.* New York: Berkeley Books.

—— & Friesan, W. (1974a). *The facial action coding system (FACS).* Palo Alto, CA: Consulting Psychologists Press.

—— & —— (1974b). Nonverbal leakage and clues to deception. In: *Non-Verbal Communication: Readings with Commentary*, ed. S. Weitz. New York: Oxford University Press, pp. 269–290.

—— & —— (1976). Measuring facial movement. *Environmental Psychology and Nonverbal Behavior*, 1:56–75.

—— & —— (1982). Felt, false, and miserable smiles. *J. of Non-verbal Behavior*, 6: 238–252.

—— —— & Ancoli, S. (1980). Facial signs of emotional experience. *J. Personality Soc. Psych.*, 39:125–134.

—— —— & Ellsworth, P. (1972). *Emotion in the human face: Guideline for research and an integration of findings.* New York: Pergamon Press.

—— —— O'Sullivan, M. & Scherer, L. (1980). Relative importance of face, body and speech in judgments of personality and affect. *J. Personality and Social Psych.*, 38:270–277.

—— —— & Tomkins, S. S. (1971). Facial affect scoring technique: First validity study. *Semiotica*, 3: 37–38.

—— & Oster, H. (1979). Facial expression of emotion. *Annual Review of Psychology* 30:527–554.

Ellman, S. J. & Moskowitz, M., eds. (1998). *Enactment: Toward a New Approach to the Therapeutic Relationship.* Northvale, NJ: Jason Aronson.

Fairbairn, W. R. D. (1940). Schizoid factors in the personality. In: *Psychoanalytic Studies of the Personality.* London: Routledge & Kegan Paul, 1978, pp. 3–27.

—— (1941). A revised psychopathology of psychoses and psychoneuroses. In: *Psy-*

choanalytic Studies of the Personality. London: Routledge & Kegan Paul, 1978, pp. 28–59.

—— (1943). The repression and return of bad objects (with special reference to the "war neuroses"). In: *Psychoanalytic Studies of the Personality*. London: Routledge & Kegan Paul, 1978, pp. 59–81.

—— (1951). A synopsis of the development of the author's views regarding the structure of the personality. In: *Psychoanalytic Studies of the Personality*. London: Routledge & Kegan Paul, 1978, pp. 162–182.

Fenichel, O. (1945). *The Psychoanalytic Theory of Neurosis*. New York: Norton, 1972.

Ferenczi, S. (1919). On the technique of psychoanalysis. In: *Further Contributions to the Theory and Technique of Psychoanalysis*. New York: Brunner/Mazel, 1980, pp. 177–188.

—— (1924). On forced fantasies. In: *Further Contributions to the Theory and Technique of Psychoanalysis*. New York: Brunner/Mazel, 1980, pp. 68–77.

—— (1925). Contra-indications to the "active" psychoanalytic technique. In *Further Contributions to the Theory and Technique of Psychoanalysis*. New York: Brunner/Mazel, 1980, pp. 217–229.

—— (1926). The further development of an active therapy in psychoanalysis. In: *Further Contributions to the Theory and Technique of Psychoanalysis*. New York: Brunner/Mazel, 1980, pp. 198–216.

—— (1931). Child analysis in the analysis of adults. In: *Further Contributions to the Theory and Technique of Psychoanalysis*. New York: Brunner/Mazel, 1980, pp. 126–142.

—— (1933). Confusion of tongues between adults and the child. In: *Further Contributions to the Theory and Technique of Psychoanalysis*. New York: Brunner/Mazel, 1980, pp. 156–167.

Firth, R. (1970). Postures and gestures of respect. In: *The Body Reader, Social Aspects of the Human Body*, ed. T. Polhemus. New York: Pantheon Books, 1978, pp. 88–108.

Freedman, N. (1977). Hands, words and mind: On the structuralization of body movements during discourse and the capacity for verbal representation. In: *Communicative Structures and Psychic Structures*, ed. N. Freedman & S. Grand. New York: Plenum Press, pp. 109–132.

—— O'Hanlon, J., Ottman, P. & Wilkin, H. (1972). The imprint of psychological differentiation on kinetic behavior in varying communicative contexts. *J. Abnormal Psych.*, 79:239–258.

Freud, A. (1926–1927). Four lectures on child analysis. In: *The Writings of Anna Freud, Vol. I, 1922–1935*. New York: International Universities Press, pp. 3–73.

—— (1965). *Normality and Pathology in Childhood: Assessment of Development*. New York: International Universities Press, 1978.

Freud, S. (1895). On the grounds for detaching a particular syndrome from neurasthenia under the description "anxiety neurosis." *Standard Edition*, 3:87–117. London: Hogarth Press, 1962.

—— (1905a). Three essays on the theory of sexuality. *Standard Edition*, 7:125–245. London: Hogarth Press, 1961.

—— (1905b). Fragment of an analysis of a case of hysteria. *Standard Edition*, 7:7–122. London: Hogarth Press, 1953.

—— (1909). Notes upon a case of obsessional neurosis. *Standard Edition*, 10:155–318. London: Hogarth Press, 1955.

—— (1911). Formulations on the two principles of mental functioning. *Standard Edition*, 12:215–226. London: Hogarth Press, 1961.

—— (1912a). The dynamics of transference. *Standard Edition*,12:99–109. London: Hogarth Press, 1961.

—— (1912b). Recommendations for physicians. *Standard Edition*, 12:111–120. London: Hogarth Press, 1961.

—— (1913). On beginning the treatment (Further recommendations on the technique of psycho-analysis: I). *Standard Edition*, 12:121–144. London: Hogarth Press, 1958.

—— (1914). Recollection, repetition and working through. *Standard Edition*, 12:147–157. London: Hogarth Press, 1961.

—— (1915a). Further recommendations in the technique of psychoanalysis: Observations on transference-love. *Standard Edition*, 12:149–161. London: Hogarth Press, 1961.

—— (1915b). Instincts and their viscissitudes. *Standard Edition*, 14:117–140. London: Hogarth Press, 1957.

—— (1920). Beyond the pleasure principle. *Standard Edition*, 18:7–64. London: Hogarth Press, 1955.

—— (1923). The ego and the id. *Standard Edition*, 19:3–66. London: Hogarth Press, 1961.

Gay, P. (1988). *Freud, A Life for Our Time*. New York: Norton.

Gedo, J. E. (1979). *Beyond Interpretation*. Hillsdale, NJ: The Analytic Press, 1993.

—— (1988). *The Mind in Disorder: Psychoanalytic Models of Pathology*. Hillsdale, NJ: The Analytic Press.

—— (1994). Academicism, romanticism, and science in the psychoanalytic enterprise. *Psychoanal. Inq.*, 14:295–311.

—— & Goldberg, A. (1973). *Models of the Mind: A Psychoanalytic Theory*. Chicago: University of Chicago Press.

Gianino, A. & Tronick, E. (1985). The mutual regulation model: The infant's self and interactive regulation and coping and defensive capacities. In: *Stress and Coping*, ed. T. Field, P. McCabe, & N. Schneiderman. Hillsdale, NJ: Lawrence Erlbaum Associates, pp. 1–33.

Gill, M. (1983). The interpersonal paradigm and the degree of the therapist's involvement. *Contemp. Psychoanal.*, 19:200–237.

—— (1988). Converting psychotherapy into psychoanalysis. *Contemp. Psychoanal.*, 24:262–274.

Greenson, R. (1967). *The Technique and Practice of Psychoanalysis* (Vol. 1). New York: International Universities Press.

—— (1971). The "real" relationship between the patient and the psychoanalyst. In: *Explorations in Psychoanalysis*. New York: International Universities Press, 1978.

Heeschen, V., Schiefenhovel, W., & Eibl-Eibesfeldt, I. (1980). Requesting, giving and taking: The relationship between verbal and nonverbal behavior in the speech community of the Eipo, Irian, Java (West New Guinea). In: *The Relationship of Verbal and Non-verbal Communication,* ed. M. R. Key. The Hague: Mouton, pp. 132–148.

Isaacs, S. (1948). On the nature and function of phantasy. In: *Developments in Psychoanalysis,* ed. M. Klein, P. Heimann, S. Isaacs, & J. Riviere. London: Karnac Books, 1989.

Joseph, B. (1985). Transference: The total situation. In: *Psychic Equilibrium and Psychic Change,* ed. M. Feldman & E. B. Spillius. London: Routledge, 1989.

—— (1989). Psychic change and the psychoanalytic process. In: *Psychic Equilibrium and Psychic Change,* ed. M. Feldman & E. B. Spillius. London: Routledge, pp. 192–202.

Kendon, A. (1970). Movement coordination in social interaction: Some examples described. In: *Non-verbal Communication: Readings with Commentary,* ed. S. Weitz. New York: Oxford University Press, pp. 150–168.

—— (1972). Some relationships between body motion and speech: An analysis of an example. In: *Studies in Dyadic Communication,* ed. A. W. Seigman & B. Pope. Elmsford, NY: Pergamon Press, pp. 120–134.

Kestenberg, J. (1965). Attunement and clashing in mother-child interaction. In: *Children and Parents: Psychoanalytic Studies in Development,* ed. J. Kestenberg. New York: Aronson, 1975, pp. 157–170.

—— (1975a). *Children and Parents: Psychoanalytic Studies in Development.* New York: Aronson.

—— (1975b). Development of the child from birth through latency as expressed through bodily movement, II. In: *Children and Parents: Psychoanalytic Studies in Development,* ed. J. Kestenberg. New York: Aronson, pp. 235–266.

—— Marcus, H., Robbins, E., Berlowe, J. & Buelte, A. (1975). Development of the young child as expressed through bodily movement, I. In: *Children and Parents: Psychoanalytic Studies in Development,* ed. J. Kestenberg. New York: Aronson, pp. 195–209.

—— & Sossin, K. M. (1979). *The Role of Movement Patterns in Development.* New York: Dance Notation Bureau Press.

Kestenberg-Amighi, J., Loman, S., Lewis, P. & Sossin, K. M. (1999). *The Meaning of Movement: Development and Clinical Perspectives of the Kestenberg Movement Profile.* Amsterdam: Gordon Breach Publishers.

Klein, M. (1925). A contribution to the psychogenesis of tics. In: *Love, Guilt, and Reparation, and Other Works, 1921–1945.* London: Delacorte Press, 1975, pp. 106–127.

—— (1926). The psychological principles of early analysis. In: *Love, Guilt and Reparation and Other Works, 1921–1945.* London: Delacorte Press, 1975, pp. 128–138.

—— (1927a). Criminal tendencies in normal children. In: *Love, Guilt, and Reparation and Other Works, 1921–1945.* London: Delacorte Press, 1975, pp. 170–185.

—— (1927b). Symposium on child analysis. In: *Love, Guilt, and Reparation and Other*

Works, 1921–1945. London: Delacorte Press, 1975, pp. 139–169.

—— (1937). Love, guilt, and reparation. In: *Love, Guilt, and Reparation, and Other Works, 1931–1945*. London: Delacorte Press, 1975, pp. 306–343.

—— (1946). Notes on some schizoid mechanisms. In: *Envy and Gratitude and Other Works, 1946–1963*. London: Delacorte Press, 1975, pp. 1–24.

—— (1955). The psychoanalytic play technique: its history and significance. In: *Envy and Gratitude and Other Works, 1946–1963*. London, Delacorte Press, 1975, pp. 122–140.

—— (1957). Envy and gratitude. In: *Envy and Gratitude and Other Works, 1946–1963*. London: Delacorte Press, 1975, pp. 176–235.

Knoblauch, S. H. (1997). Beyond the word in psychoanalysis, the unspoken dialogue. *Psychoanal. Dial.*, 7:491–516.

Kohut, H. (1971). *The Analysis of the Self*. New York: International Universities Press.

—— (1977). *The Restoration of the Self*. New York: International Universities Press.

Kristeva, J. (1973). Gesture: Practice or communication. In: *The Body Reader: Social Aspects of the Human Body*, ed. T. Polhemus. New York: Pantheon Books, 1978, pp. 264–283.

Laban, R. (1950). *Mastery of Movement*. London: McDonald and Evans, 1970.

—— & Lawrence, F. C. (1947). *Effort*. London: McDonald and Evans, 1974.

La Barre, W. (1947). The cultural basis of emotions and gestures. In: *Anthropological Perspectives on Movement*, ed. M. Davis. New York: Arno Press, 1975.

Lachmann, F. M. & Beebe, B. (1997) The contribution of self- and mutual regulation to therapeutic action: A case illustration. In: *The Neurobiological and Developmental Basis for Psychotherapeutic Intervention*, ed. M. Moskowitz, C. Monk, C. Kaye & S. Ellman. Northvale, NJ: Aronson, pp. 91–122.

La France, M. (1979). Non-verbal synchrony and rapport: Analysis by the cross-lag panel technique. *Social Psychol. Quart.*, 42:66–70.

Lamb, W. (1965). *Posture and Gesture: An Introduction to the Study of Physical Behavior*. London: Duckworth.

—— & Watson, E. (1979). *Body Code: Meaning in Movement*. Princeton, NJ: Princeton Book.

Levenson, E. (1972). *The Fallacy of Understanding: An Inquiry into the Changing Structure of Psychoanalysis*. New York: Basic Books.

—— (1983). *The Ambiguity of Change*. New York: Basic Books.

Lichtenberg, J. D. (1983). *Psychoanalysis and Infant Research*. Hillsdale, NJ: The Analytic Press.

Lindon, J. (1994). Gratification and provision: Should we get rid of the rule of abstinence? *Psychoanal. Dial.*, 4:549–582.

Little, M. (1985). Winnicott working in areas where psychotic anxieties predominate. *Free Associations*, 3:9–42.

Loewald, H. (1960). On the therapeutic action of psychoanalysis. *Internat. Psychoanal.*, 58:463–472.

—— (1980). On motivation and instinct theory. In: *Papers on Psychoanalysis*. New Haven, CT: Yale University Press.

—— (1986). Transference-countertransference. *J. Amer. Psychoanal. Assn.*, 34:275–287.

Mahl, G. F. (1968). Gesture and body movement in interviews. *Research in Psychotherapy*, 3:295–346.

—— (1977). Body movement, ideation and verbalization during psychoanalysis. In: *Communication Structures and Psychic Structures*, ed. N. Freedman & S. Grand. New York: Plenum Press, pp. 291–310.

McDowell, J. (1978). Interactional synchrony. *J. Personality and Social Psych.*, 36:963–975.

McLaughlin, J. T. (1992). Nonverbal behavior in the analytic situation: The search for meaning in nonverbal cues. In: *When the Body Speaks*, ed. S. Kramer & S. Akhtar. New York: Aronson.

Mehrabian, A. (1969). Significance of posture and position in the communication of attitude and status relationships. *Psych. Bull.*, 71:359–372.

—— (1972). *Nonverbal Communication*. Chicago: Aldine-Atherton.

—— & Ferris, S. (1967). Inference of attitudes from nonverbal communication in two channels. In: *Non-verbal Communication: Readings with Commentary*, ed. S. Weitz. New York: Oxford University Press, pp. 291–297.

—— & Williams, M. (1969). Nonverbal concomitants of perceived and intended persuasiveness. *J. Personality and Social Psych.*, 13:37–58.

Miller, L., Rustin, M., Rustin, M., and Shuttleworth, J., eds. (1989). *Closely Observed Infants*. London: Duckworth.

Ogden, T. H. (1986). *The Matrix of the Mind: Object Relations and the Psychoanalytic Dialogue*. Northvale, NJ: Jason Aronson.

Oliner, M. (1988). *Cultivating Freud's Garden in France*. Northvale, NJ: Jason Aronson.

O'Sullivan, M., Ekman, P., Friesan, W. & Scherer, K. (1985). What you say and how you say it: The contribution of speech content and voice quality to judgments of others. *J. Personality and Social Psych.*, 48:54–62.

Pine, F. (1985). *Developmental Theory and Clinical Process*. New Haven, CT: Yale University Press.

Reich, W. (1949). *Character Analysis*. New York: Farrar, Straus and Giroux, 1971.

Schafer, R. (1983). *The Analytic Attitude*. New York: Basic Books.

Scheflen, A. E. (1963). Communication and regulation in psychotherapy. *Psychiatry*, 26:126–136.

—— (1964). The significance of posture in communication systems. *Psychiatry*, 27:316–331.

—— (1965). Quasi-courtship behavior in psychotherapy. In: *Non-verbal Communication: Readings with Commentary*, ed. S. Weitz. New York: Oxford University Press, pp. 182–198.

—— (1966). The natural history method in psychotherapy: Communicational research. In: *Methods of Research in Psychotherapy*, ed. L. A. Gottschalk & A. H. Auerbach. New York: Appleton-Century Crofts, pp. 201–248.

—— (1973). *Communicational Structure: Analysis of a Psychotherapy Transaction*. Bloomington: Indiana University Press.

Sossin, M. K. (1987). Reliability of the KMP. *Movement Studies*, 2:23–28.

Spence, D. P. (1982). *Narrative Truth and Historical Truth*. New York: Norton.

Spitz, R. A. (1965). *The First Year of Life: A Psychoanalytic Study of Normal and Deviant Development of Object Relations*. New York: International Universities Press, 1973.

Steiner, J. (1995). *Psychic Retreats.* London: Routledge.

Stern, D. B. (1987). Unformulated experience. *Contemp. Psychoanal.,* 19:71–99.

—— (1991). A philosophy for the embedded analyst. *Contemp. Psychoanal.,* 27:51–80.

Stern, D. N. (1977). *The First Relationship: Infant and Mother.* Cambridge, MA: Harvard University Press.

—— (1982a). Discussion of W. Condon's cultural microrhythms. In: *Interaction Rhythms: Periodicity in Communicative Behavior,* ed. M. Davis. New York: Human Sciences Press, pp. 67–77.

—— (1982b). Some interactive functions of rhythm changes between mother and child. In: *Interaction Rhythms: Periodicity in Communicative Behavior,* ed. M. Davis. New York: Human Sciences Press, pp. 101–118.

—— (1985). *The Interpersonal World of the Infant: A View from Psychoanalysis and Developmental Psychology.* New York: Basic Books.

—— (1995). *The Motherhood Constellation.* New York: Basic Books.

—— Beebe, B., Jaffe, J. & Bennett, S. (1977). The infant's stimulus world during social interaction: A study of care-giver behaviors with particular reference to repetition and timing. In: *Studies in Infant/Mother Interaction,* ed. H. R. Schaffer. New York: Academic Press, pp. 53–77.

Sullivan, H. S. (1953). *Conceptions of Modern Psychiatry.* New York: Norton.

—— (1954a). *Interpersonal Theory of Psychiatry.* New York: Norton.

—— (1954b). *The Psychiatric Interview.* New York: Norton..

Tronick, E. (1987). *On the Infant's Responses to Mother's State.* Presented to Institute for Contemporary Psychotherapy, New York City.

—— Als, H. & Adamson, L. (1979). The structure of early face-to-face communicative interactions. In: *Before Speech: The Beginning of Interpersonal Communication,* ed. M. Bullowa. London: Cambridge University Press, pp. 349–370.

Winnicott, D. W. (1949a). Birth, memory, trauma, and anxiety. In: *Through Paediatrics to Psychoanalysis.* New York: Basic Books, 1975, pp. 174–193.

—— (1949b). Mind and its relation to the psyche/soma. In: *Through Paediatrics to Psychoanalysis* New York: Basic Books, 1975, pp. 243–254.

—— (1954). Metapsychological and clinical aspects of regression within the psychoanalytic setup. In: *Through Paediatrics to Psychoanalysis.* New York: Basic Books, 1975, pp. 278–294.

—— (1955). Clinical varieties of transference. In: *Through Paediatrics to Psychoanalysis* New York: Basic Books, 1975, pp. 295–299.

—— (1956). Primary maternal preoccupation. In: *Through Paediatrics to Psychoanalysis.* New York: Basic Books, 1975, pp. 300–305.

—— (1958). The capacity to be alone. In: *The Maturational Processes and the Facilitating Environment.* New York: International Universities Press, 1979, pp. 29–36.

—— (1960a). Ego distortion in terms of true and false self. In: *The Maturational Processes and the Facilitating Environment.* New York: International Universities Press, 1979, pp. 140–152.

—— (1960b). Counter-transference. In: *The Maturational Processes and the Facilitating Environment.* New York: International Universities Press, 1979, pp. 158–165.

—— (1962). The aims of psycho-analytical treatment. In: *The Maturational Pro-*

cesses and the Facilitating Environment. New York: International Universities Press, 1979, pp. 166–170.

—— (1963a). Dependence in infant-care, in child-care and in the psycho-analytic setting. In: *The Maturational Processes and the Facilitating Environment*. New York: International Universities Press, 1979, pp. 249–260.

—— (1963b). Psychotherapy of character disorders. In: *The Maturational Processes and the Facilitating Environment*. New York: International Universities Press, 1979, pp. 203–216.

—— (1969). The mother–infant experience of mutuality. In: *Psychoanalytic Explorations*, ed. C. Winnicott, C. Bollas, M. Davis & R. Shepherd. London: Karnac Books, 1989.

—— (1971). *Playing and reality*. London: Penguin Books, 1974.

Winter, D. D. (1987). Field studies of action profiling reliability. *Movement Studies*, 2:21–22.

Index